CIVIL ENGINEERI.

Supervision and Management

CIVIL ENGINEERING:
Supervision and Management

A. C. TWORT B.Sc., F.I.C.E., F.I.W.E.

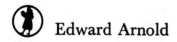 Edward Arnold

© A. C. Twort 1972

First published 1966
Second edition 1972
Reprinted 1975
Reprinted with corrections 1978
by Edward Arnold (Publishers) Ltd.,
41 Bedford Square,
London WC1B 3DP

ISBN: 0 7131 3274 4

Printed in Great Britain by
Unwin Brothers Limited
The Gresham Press, Old Woking, Surrey
A member of the Staples Printing Group

Preface to 1972 (Metric) Edition

THE continued demand for this book over a period of seventeen years since the first version of it appeared, seems to justify the original hope that it would be found useful. I would like, however, to repeat what was said in an earlier preface, namely, that whilst the book contains some things I have discovered for myself it contains much that has been generously handed to me by my chiefs, my colleagues, by contractors, foremen, gangers and workmen.

The book aims to describe, in practical detail, the measures which are necessary both in the design office and the field office, to successfully control and supervise the erection of works of civil engineering construction. The viewpoint is that of the engineer in charge and of his representative on site, the resident engineer.

To the engineer going out on site for the first time, or wishing to understand the procedures whereby drawings and contract documents are changed into real 'works', this book is intended to be of immediate assistance, indicating the common sort of problems that arise and how they may be overcome.

I have endeavoured at all times to write directly from experience so that the methods and suggestions made in the book, though not representing every possible method or policy, do represent something that has been found to work from experience. I hope the book will convey the form and manner in which things are done on site, for it is the correct approach which is important when dealing with the new problems which are always likely to arise on every new job.

The units have now been changed to conform to the metric system, and the relevant metric British Standards and other guiding codes are now referred to. In some instances both metric and Imperial units are quoted where it is thought that this will be found helpful, and a table of conversion factors has been added as an appendix. Otherwise the text of the book, save for a few corrections, remains as before.

I record my thanks to all those who have helped increase my experience of civil engineering reflected in this book, and wish every engineer going out on site an enjoyable and successful time.

A. C. TWORT

London
1972

Contents

List of Plates

Between pages 164 and 165

Between pages 196 and 197

XIII (*a*) Typical honey-combed concrete.
     (*b*) A good concrete mix for vibration, with more than the usual number of vibrators being supplied by the contractor.

XIV (*a*) A small weigh-batching plant.
     (*b*) Badly placed reinforcement, badly bent out of position.

XV (*a*) Accurately bent reinforcement of the right size can be set to exact lines. (Contractors: J. E. Jones (Contractors) Ltd.)
    (*b*) Well-placed wall reinforcement showing correct and even concrete cover to the bars. (Contractors: J. E. Jones (Contractors) Ltd.)
    (*c*) The approach to the aggregate stacks should not be a muddy area as this photograph shows; it should be clean so that mud does not get into the aggregates.

XVI Designing works to harness, or withstand, the forces exerted by water plays a great part in the civil engineer's life. Top right (*a*) is the gated spillway to the Sultan Abur Bakar Dam of the Cameron Highlands Hydro-electric Scheme, Malaysia; below (*b*) shows flood water passing over the lip of the bell-mouthed spillway to the Tryweryn Dam for Liverpool Corporation Waterworks. (Engineers: Binnie & Partners.)

CHAPTER 1

Methods of Commissioning Design and Construction

CIVIL engineering structures rank among the great material works of man. Every such work is unique in the sense that it represents a specially calculated effort to develop and place under the control some portion of the earth's natural resources at some precise location. In this effort it is needful, first, to conceive the aim of the intended works; second, to design them in practical detail; third, to construct them; and fourth, to put them into working operation. This fourfold process may last from two to a dozen years; it may use the labour of thousands of men, the accumulated knowledge of generations of experts, and the natural and manufactured products of hundreds of different trades and occupations. Until such time as the works are completed there must be a continuous resolve to pursue their construction to finality, and wealth must be provided—in the form of money, man-power, machines, and materials—to support this resolve throughout the long periods of design and construction.

It follows that civil engineering works must be commissioned, or 'ordered in advance'. They are not products that can be bought ready-made off the shelf. There must be a Promoter who resolves to undertake the works, who agrees to pay for them, and who agrees to own them when completed. The payments must be progressive throughout all the stages of development, and to do this, the promoter will have to use money from his own resources, or borrow from the resources of others, the money so expended being termed *the capital investment* in the works. Only when the works are completed can the promoter receive tangible proof that his expenditure, or the money borrowed by him, has procured for him the object he wants. Until this final stage is reached, the promoter must act in the faith that what his expert advisers say can be done, will be done; that what they say will be the cost, will in fact be the cost.

The obligations of the promoter are:

to define the functions the works must perform;
to evaluate the worth of the intended project and to be assured this satisfies his predicated requirements;
to obtain the necessary powers for the construction of the works;
to find the money to pay for it.

The promoter is the buyer and the potential owner, and he must do all that a prudent man would do to assure himself—with the aid of expert advisers of all kinds—that what he is commissioning is the right project for him, and that he has the necessary powers and finance to authorise its construction. He can be a person or a group of persons acting as a corporate body, such as a local government authority or government department, a company, corporation or joint board, or any other authority possessing adequate powers. To exercise his rights effectively he will, on the engineering side, require two key specialist advisers and executives— the Engineer who undertakes the design, and the Contractor or other engineer who undertakes the construction.

Upon the designer (or, as he is called, the engineer for the project) lies a great responsibility and trust. His primary function is to design, but this also includes the undertaking of necessary research work, the calculation of estimated costs, and the appraisal of the estimated output of the works and their economic value to the promoter. He must know and be able to give assurance that the works he proposes are practicable, can be built, and will fulfil their intended function for the price he has advised. He must know the quality of workmanship that must go into the construction of the works and must efficiently supervise their construction from the point of view of achieving fitness for purpose; and he must be able to estimate, and evaluate when completed, their efficiency and serviceableness to the promoter. In respect of all these duties and related technical matters, the engineer must exercise a realistic, thoroughly professional, and entirely independent judgment—for it is on this judgment that the promoter must almost solely rely when he makes his decision to promote and give continued support to the venture.

A civil engineering contractor is the man who normally undertakes the construction of the works. He 'tenders' (or offers) to construct them for a given sum of money, and if his tender is accepted he then 'contracts' (i.e. signs a contract with the promoter) to construct the works. To him is then entrusted the task of exercising his skill and competence in building the work in every respect as the engineer requires. He is directed by the drawings, specifications, and instructions issued to him by the engineer in accordance with rules laid down in the contract, and he acts in the faith that the works are rightly conceived and that, if he builds them as directed, he will be reimbursed in proper measure as the contract lays down, for all the expenditure he has incurred in their construction.

A civil engineering project may therefore be considered as being brought to maturity through the skilled efforts of three parties—the· promoter, the engineer, and the contractor. This implies that, for proper success, there must be a high degree of competence and integrity exercised by each of these parties, and the arrangements made between them must be such as will give adequate responsibility and support fair dealing. Together, the three parties have the task of transmuting what is but an idea into the reality and wholeness of completed works; the arrangements they make between themselves must therefore be of a kind that all unforeseeable difficulties and obstacles arising during the years of planning, design, and construction will be surmountable without endangering either the agreements entered into or the ultimate success of the venture.

Difficulties can beset any project. This the history of civil engineering most clearly shows; for the activity is of a special kind to which are always attached some unknown elements or actions that cannot be devoid of risk. From experience, therefore, there have developed over the years certain systems of agreement between promoter, engineer, and contractor that time and vicissitudes have shown to be best when venturing upon projects of a civil engineering nature.

Systems of agreement

A promoter may choose to have civil engineering works designed and built in a number of different ways. For the planning and design he may engage the services of a consulting engineer, or he may designate an engineer in his own employment to carry this out. Many local authorities and government departments employ their chief engineer and his staff to design new works required.

For the construction, the work may be let out by contract to a firm of civil engineering contractors, or the promoter may himself already employ staff capable of undertaking the construction of new works. In the latter case the promoter will expect either his chief engineer or the consultant he has engaged to take charge of the construction as well as the design.

On less frequent occasions, and in special circumstances that will later be discussed, the promoter may sometimes employ the civil engineering contractor to undertake both the design and construction of the works by contract. This is known as a 'package deal', so named because all matters—planning, design, construction, and setting to work—are all contained in the one 'package' or contract.

None of these different arrangements is unusual. Each has been used many times over in the past, is currently being used, and will so continue. However, the most frequent of them consists of the use of a consulting engineer or the promoter's own chief engineer for the design, and the employment of a contractor for the construction. These alternatives have, in general, been found the most satisfactory, but before considering them in detail we shall need to amplify the exact position the engineer holds in regard to a civil engineering project.

DESIGN

The position of the engineer

Unless the promoter uses his own chief engineer for the design of the works, he will need to engage the services of some independent engineer—a consulting engineer. He will need to enter into a contract with the consulting engineer for the design and supervision of construction of the project. In return for these services he will pay the consulting engineer a professional fee. At this stage the consulting engineer becomes designated as the engineer for the project. The promoter agrees to accept the engineer's advice on matters of engineering.

For the construction of the work by contract, the promoter will need to enter a second contract between himself and a contractor. The details of this contract—all the descriptions of the work to be done by the contractor—will be drawn up by the engineer. The promoter then becomes the employer of the contractor, and is therefore designated as the Employer. Under this contract the contractor agrees to construct the works to the designs, specifications, and detailed directions of the engineer; the employer agrees to pay the contractor such sums of money for the works as the engineer certifies are due in accordance with the contract conditions. Both the contractor and employer agree to abide by the decisions of the engineer, except where matters in dispute can be referred to an arbitrator.

If the promoter chooses to use his own chief engineer to design and supervise the construction of the works for him he will designate this chief engineer as the 'engineer for the project' in the contract for construction. This chief engineer will then hold the same powers under the contract for construction as if he were an independent consulting engineer.

Thus, we see that the engineer exercises two functions. He must first of all apply his special skill and knowledge to design the works and to drawing up the contract for construction. In so doing he must advise the promoter of the nature and extent of the works required and he must endeavour to meet the wishes of the promoter. He does not tell the promoter what the latter should or should not want; he exercises his talents to serve the promoter as best he can—advising on suitable designs, the estimated cost of various designs, and the various engineering ways the promoter's wishes can be fulfilled. But when the contract for construction is entered into by the promoter the engineer takes up a new set of duties. He has to administer the terms of that contract fairly, as between the promoter (now called the employer) and the contractor. The powers he can exercise are defined in the contract for the construction; in some matters the engineer's decisions are final; sometimes the contract may provide that 'any dispute or difference between the employer or the engineer and the contractor . . . shall be referred to an arbitrator'.

We should notice that, in the last quoted phrase, it is only disputes between the contractor and either the engineer or the employer which can be referred to arbitration. This is the usual wording contained in the recommended *Conditions of Contract for Works of Civil Engineering Construction* agreed upon by the Institution of Civil Engineers, the Association of Consulting Engineers, and the Federation of Civil Engineering Contractors. No provision is made under the contract for construction for the settlement of disputes arising between the engineer and the employer; such disputes would have to be settled in accordance with the written or implied conditions existing between the promoter and the engineer. The special relationship between the engineer and the promoter (or employer) is considered in more detail in Chapter 4, where the responsibility of the engineer for exercising impartial skilled judgment is considered.

We thus see that the engineer has two separated functions: one as designer, the other as administrator of the contract for construction. In both functions the engineer must exercise his professional skill in accordance with the ethics of his profession; but whereas, as designer, he may use all his abilities to contrive the best and most economic design for the employer, as administrator of the contract for construction he must be absolutely fair and unbiased with both employer and contractor.

It will be observed that there is no contract between the engineer and the contractor. From this fact there arises an important point, namely that the engineer has no power to accept or reject a tender or a quotation from a contractor. Only the employer can do this. This matter needs to be watched carefully, as it is sometimes rather easy for the engineer (or one of his staff) to fall into the error of 'accepting' a tender or quotation. He frequently calls upon firms to tender or quote to him for the supply of goods or erection of works. Having received such tenders and quotations, he must refer them to the employer and get the employer's authority for acceptance of them. When he writes to inform the suppliers or contractors he should then only do so in words that show that in accepting an offer he does so 'on behalf of the employer' as authorised by him. Even then, the contract may not be binding until an agreement in writing between employer and contractor or supplier has been completed. Most public bodies, local government or government departments, cannot enter into a contract except in writing and under seal.

It is therefore normally necessary for any contract for construction to be signed and sealed by the contractor and the employer before any work can commence. Nor can the engineer order anything extra on that contract without the employer's sanction. (Here the word 'extra' means anything over and above the works described in the contract for construction or reasonably to be inferred as being necessary under the contract. There is really no sharp dividing line between what is extra to a contract and what is not, and the engineer must largely rely on his common sense.) The contract for construction may include certain round sums of money called *provisional sums*. If any of these sums are for certain specific additions to the works the acceptance of a tender containing such sums by the employer will amount to an authorisation that they can be so spent, as the engineer orders, on the works described. There will also be another round sum called *provision for contingencies* included in the tender accepted by the employer. Here again the engineer has a ready sanction from the employer for ordering extra works of a 'contingent nature', i.e. arising from essential works contributing to the construction of the main works. Thus, the engineer could order deeper foundations for the building, if need be, or stronger parts of it, where he deems these essential for the right construction of the works; but he could not order, for instance, a marble staircase instead of a concrete one, or wood panelling to a room instead of distemper, without the express sanction of the employer, if these items were not envisaged in the original contract. Neither can the engineer order things he has simply forgotten to include in the original tender, if they are not to be implied from the tender; e.g. he could not order a crane for insertion inside a building as 'an extra' if he had forgotten to include the supply of the crane in the contract for construction and there was no contingency money left unspent under the contract. He must go to the employer and get his authority for rectification of the omission.

Care must always be exercised by the engineer to keep the employer informed as to what is proposed, and his prior sanction must be sought for all additions which are not an inevitable consequence of constructing the works.

The foregoing remarks are meant as a general outline of the position of the engineer; we must now go on to discuss in what ways an employer can get the engineering design work done, and what sort of contracts he can enter into for construction.

Employment of a consulting engineer

The principal advantages of the employment of a consulting engineer are that his judgment and advice are independent of all outside influences and that he is a specialist spending most of his time on the design and construction of new works. A member of the British Association of Consulting Engineers may not have any financial interest or relationship with any contractor, builder, manufacturing firm, or supplier of goods that could influence his judgment; he cannot have an investment or similar interest in the work he is advising on; he cannot charge other than professional fees for his work; and he cannot limit his liability for his own negligence by forming himself with others into a limited liability company. His main interest lies in making the project a success so as to win himself a satisfied client and enhance his reputation for good work. This, of course, is precisely the kind of service the promoter is looking for.

A consulting engineer not only has freedom to exercise his inventive abilities and incentive to drive the works onwards to proper completion, he also brings to the work specialist knowledge and past experience of similar works of construction. This is particularly useful to the promoter, who may need to promote new works perhaps only once in ten to twenty years, and whose staff are not therefore kept acquainted with new design methods by a continuous programme of new work. The consulting engineer and his staff, being engaged most of their time on new works, will be in a good position to advise what is the likely outcome of an intended project and how best it may be tackled. In civil engineering it is not enough to know theory alone, however sophisticated that knowledge of theory may be; it is essential to be tutored by years of past experience and so to have a prescient awareness at all times that even the best-laid plans may go awry, especially when the attempt entails wrestling with nature in a manner which has not been undertaken in precisely similar terms before.

Use of the promoter's own engineer

A large proportion of civil engineering work—probably the bulk of all moderately sized and small projects—is handled by the promoter's own chief engineer, or his 'new works engineer'. This engineer must have sufficient experience in the design of new works and he must be supported by an adequate staff. The system is usual and works well, because any properly qualified civil engineer is trained to put his professional duties before any personal desires to gain the favour of his employer by means other than the right practice of his profession.

The use of the employer's own engineer possesses an advantage that may sometimes be particularly useful when the design of the works is being undertaken, since he should have an intimate knowledge of the employer's requirements, and his operational experience of previously built works can often be a source of inspiration from which new ideas for design can be developed.

Design under a package-deal contract

Under the package-deal contract between a contractor and an employer, the contractor undertakes design and construction of the works, his bid covering both these services. In order to make such a bid, the contractor must make a preliminary design of his own upon which his tender is based.

Much controversy occurs at present over this type of contract, principally because promoters are increasingly inclined to favour it. Especially do promoters favour it where it is a *financed* package-deal contract, in which case the contractor not only designs and constructs the works required but he also raises the capital required to pay for it. In effect, this capital is loaned to the employer, who repays the contractor (or his financier) over a period of years. The deal is therefore a kind of hire-purchase arrangement.

In the hands of a reputable contractor the package deal can give very satisfactory service. There is nothing new about it; millions of houses are sold to satisfied owners on precisely the same basis, being designed and built by a housing contractor through whom arrangements are made for a mortgage. It would be wrong to assume that a contractor cannot design —just as wrong as it is to assume that a consulting engineer cannot undertake direct control of construction. Contractors do undertake design, and they do it well when the design is in their line of speciality. Equally, consulting engineers and local authority engineers frequently take direct control of construction and have been used to doing this for decades. But, as a general rule and over the years, there has been a tendency to specialise—the contractor to do construction, and the consulting engineer to do design.

The supporters of the package deal may well be right in pointing out that if one could bring together specialists from the two now-separated fields of design and construction these men ought to produce jointly a solution which represents an amalgamation of the best ideas for design with the best ideas for construction. On the other hand, the critics of the package deal point out this may not work out in practice. It may happen that each contractor submits a design peculiar to his own way of construction. Thus, every contractor offers something different that tends to suit his personal preferences rather than the especial needs of the project. This, the critics state, is not the same as finding the best combination of design and construction drawn from all possible methods of design and all possible methods of construction; it neither produces the cheapest combination necessarily, nor the best design, taking into account the operational and maintenance costs of the project when completed. Furthermore, it cannot be denied that if every tenderer has to produce his own design this cannot be cheap, for contractors have to build up their design staffs, and for every ten designs they submit to tender, only one may be successful.

It is also evident that if the employer places upon the contractor the onus for producing the complete project, he has no one to watch his interests and nobody to turn to for advice should he fall into a dispute with the contractor. The employer quickly finds, when he enters a package-deal contract, that his need to employ an inspection staff is just as great as under any other arrangement. To make this inspection staff effective they must have powers to reject or modify errors of workmanship and design, or their inspection is valueless. The inspection staff will thereby tend to have the final decision on what is done on site, and it is they who will have to adjudicate—as far as they are able—as between the employer and the contractor. Should unforeseen major difficulties arise, the employer will find himself even more in want of an independent engineer adviser.

It would be more important to pursue these arguments if package deals were widespread; but they are not. Many so-called package deals are nothing of the kind when heavy civil engineering work is being carried out. For any work below ground the package deal invariably includes a schedule of priced rates against provisional quantities, or a schedule of unit rates only. In this respect, therefore, the bid is by no means a fixed offer. The amount the employer will actually have to pay may vary substantially from what was included as an estimated amount in the package bid, and the amount paid will be a good deal higher than expected if trouble is encountered. As Little says in his book *Foundations*, 'The engineer's troubles begin when he descends below the ground surface'; so likewise may the employer's. Even if a contractor were called upon to shoulder the large risks always attendant upon construction below ground surface by quoting a lump sum for this kind of work, he would be bound to quote a much higher all-in risk rate than he would do if paid by the measure of the work he does. Thus, in the construction of tunnels, deep foundations, cofferdams, earth moving and placing, the package deal tends to be less of a reality.

Above ground, the package deal is more realistic, especially where it involves the construction of 'repeat structures', such as factory buildings, which can be made suitable with minor amendments to the needs of more than one promoter. A package deal can also be appropriate where the contract is primarily for the supply and erection of specialist equipment or machinery and the civil engineering content is incidental or of a simple nature.

Hence the package deal has its uses, but these are less concerned with civil engineering construction than is ordinarily supposed. The financed package deal has come to stay, but it possesses a number of unusual aspects which usually make it possible for the employer to have an independent engineer to advise him. Although the employer finds himself financially bound to the contractor (or his backers), this does not prevent them both from agreeing that the design and construction shall be to the requirements of an independent engineer, neither does anything stand in the way of having the work paid on measure.

CONSTRUCTION BY FIXED-PRICE CONTRACTS

Bills-of-quantities contracts (see also p. 131)

The total sum tendered under a bill-of-quantities contract is the sum of the individual items as priced in the bill, including any prime costs, lump sums, and provisional sums. The quantities placed against the items showing the amount of work to be done are, for the purposes of tendering, quantities measured from the contract drawings. The quantities are not approximate; *they are exact*, being measured as accurately as possible from the drawings. When the work is constructed the quantities are replaced by the measurement of the actual quantity of work the contractor carries out under each item. Again this is an accurate calculation.

The superiorities of this method over any other are that:

(i) it results in payment to the contractor according to the amount of work he does;

(ii) nevertheless, it limits the price to be paid and if the work to be done is happily the same as shown on the contract drawings, then the employer pays exactly the tendered sum;

(iii) the method gives freedom to alter the work of construction and yet remains the basis of fair payment between employer and contractor;

(iv) all tenderers price on exactly the same basis, and their tenders may therefore be closely compared with one another;

(v) the bill itself gives every tenderer a very clear conception of the amount, the kind, and the detail of the work to be carried out.

Properly drawn up, a contract based on a bill of quantities is the most equitable type of agreement for both contractor and employer, it invites the most competitive prices from contractors, and it leaves the way open for the engineer to exercise his responsibilities properly by allowing him to alter the amount of work undertaken so that it best suits all the revealed conditions on the site. It is the most widely used type of contract and is, without any doubt, the best type of contract for civil engineering work.

It comes in the class of fixed-price contracts because the unit rates tendered by the contractor for the individual items in the bill are fixed. It does not give a fixed total sum, because the actual quantities of work measured in the field may be different from the quantities measured from the design drawings; but if the construction closely follows the design the total price paid by the employer will not be far different from the total sum tendered.

Schedule-of-rates contracts

There are some civil engineering operations where it is not possible to put into the bill of quantities, measurements of quantities based on the contract drawings. A typical instance of this is a contract for the sinking of a borehole for a water supply. It is frequently not possible to state in advance how deep the borehole must be in order that it shall produce a given quantity of water. There are other occasions when it is needful to commence the work of construction before the design and contract drawings are ready, i.e. before measurement of quantities can be made from such drawings. In these instances the contract can be based on a *schedule of rates*. The schedule of rates is similar to, but not the same as, a bill of quantities. The differences are:

(i)   quantities against the individual items are either not inserted, or they are entered in estimated amounts or in round-figure provisional quantities;

(ii) more items are scheduled for temporary work than usually appear in a bill of quantities (e.g. items such as for setting up plant, etc.), because the amount of temporary work that the contractor will have to undertake is uncertain;

(iii) the remainder of the scheduled items tend to describe operations by the contractor rather than outputs, and the number of items is less than in a bill of quantities;

(iv) there is no implied guarantee given that all or any of the work scheduled will in fact be carried out.

It is important that the schedule is clearly headed 'Schedule of Rates' so that the contractor is forewarned that all the items must be considered as provisional. The unit prices he quotes against each item must therefore be such that if twice the amount of work estimated were done, or if none of the work in the item were done, the contractor does not incur a loss of money.

This is different from a bill-of-quantities contract, where there is an implied condition that the total work undertaken will not be so substantially different from what is delineated in the contract that a contractor could maintain he had been misled as to the size of the contract. In a bill-of-quantities contract the setting up and overhead costs to the contractor will be spread over the bill items (excepting the provisional items) as the contractor chooses, in the knowledge that the great majority of these items will be carried out. In a schedule-of-prices contract there is no guarantee that all or any given proportion of the items will be carried out; therefore each item must carry its own overheads, and bring the contractor adequate reward if undertaken in large or small quantity, irrespective of the amount of work done under other items.

The schedule-of-rates contract, when properly drawn up, is an extremely useful contract to have where the full extent of the work to be done cannot be foreseen. It can be made quite fair to the contractor, but it does not, of course, give the same assurance in regard to total cost to the employer as does a bill-of-quantities contract.

Lump-sum contracts

The third type of fixed-price contract consists of a single lump sum tendered and accepted as the fixed price. Naturally, the works to be built must be entirely specified and dimensioned before the contractor can offer a lump sum, and this type of contract is therefore far more suited to above-ground structures than below-ground structures. To avoid later trouble, the specification and drawings need to be complete in every detail before a lump-sum offer is called for. A bill of quantities may even be provided, not for unit pricing, but to list out for the convenience of the tenderer every operation he must do, thus assisting him to calculate his total offer.

Lump-sum contracts work quite well provided:

  (i)   the job is not very large;
  (ii) the work required can be precisely described in all its details;
  (iii) there is no great risk attached to its construction;
  (iv) no large or numerous alterations are called for during construction.

Typically, houses, garages, depots, factory sheds, or other buildings of modest size and traditional design can be built under this type of contract; or the method may be used for the supply and building-in of equipment of different kinds. Quite often, a large bill-of-quantities contract may contain within it single items which are in effect lump-sum contracts for portions of the work within the overall contract.

The advantages offered by lump-sum contracts are that they avoid a lot of detailed accounting and measuring work, they give the employer assurance of a fixed total price, and they give the contractor a clear straightforward job to do. The disadvantage is that they run into trouble immediately the employer or the engineer wants an alteration of design, or some additions during construction, or if the job itself runs into unforeseen troubles. Nevertheless, if the site conditions are right, and if the employer and engineer feel quite satisfied that the drawings and specification are final and see no liklihood of wanting to alter them, there is much to be said for this type of contract.

Lump-sum contracts are sometimes used in conjunction with a schedule of rates which are to be applied to the pricing of variations. This practice is particularly used in America, where the bill-of-quantities contract is not favoured. The advantage appears to be that the engineer is saved the trouble of producing a bill of quantities and need only measure quantities which vary from the intentions as shown on the drawings. In Britain this method is more often resorted to for contracts for the supply and installation of mechanical or electrical equipment.

CONSTRUCTION BY CONTRACTS NOT FOR A FIXED PRICE

Cost-plus percentage contracts

These give no assurance of limitation to the total cost. The contractor is paid the actual expenditure he incurs in the purchase of materials and employment of labour and plant, and he is paid a percentage over and above this to reimburse him his overhead expenses and profit. This type of contract is justifiably unpopular. The employer dislikes it because he sees no incentive in it to make the contractor efficient; indeed, the less efficient the contractor is, the more the cost of the works and the more his profit. The engineer does not like it because, for the sake of efficiency, he must control even the day-to-day methods of the contractor, and in fact finds himself virtually dictator of everything that happens on site. The contractor does not like it, because he can do practically nothing without the sanction of the engineer and, even when matters are so sanctioned, every invoice, pay sheet, plant record, materials sheet, etc., will probably have to go before the employer's auditors before it can finally be authorised for payment.

Enough has been said to show that this is not a worthy sort of arrangement; it does not give enough freedom, it sows seeds of mistrust from the beginning, it saddles all parties with a great deal of paper work, and it is seldom efficient. It is suitable for use only in an emergency, for a limited period, before there has been time to draw up some other form of contract.

Cost-plus fixed-fee contracts

These also require that the contractor is paid his actual costs, but the fee which is intended to cover his overheads and profit is fixed, so the chief objection to the cost-plus percentage contract is removed. This fixed fee may be tendered in competition with other contractors, or it may be negotiated between employer and contractor. This type of contract is acceptable and useful, provided the contractor is efficient. There is no doubt that, in a world of greater perfection, this type of contract would be the right way to tackle difficult civil engineering projects. It puts the engineer and contractor together, so that they can act jointly to produce the highest quality of workmanship possible at the most economic cost. It also gives great freedom to adopt different methods of construction or to tackle unusual problems or get out of unforeseen troubles. But individuals are not perfect, and before embarking on this sort of contract the employer and engineer must assure themselves that the contractor will undertake the work with an acceptable degree of efficiency.

Target contracts

These are much like the cost-plus fixed-fee contracts, but the 'fee' (or profit) to the contractor increases if the final cost of the work is less than the estimate, decreases if the final cost is more. It seems a good principle to give the contractor an incentive in being economical, but in practice there are many reports that it does not work. The primary reason is simple. If all the operations on a job can be specified, drawn out, and quantified in advance there is no reason to have a cost-plus contract at all. The bill-of-quantities contract can be used, giving good competition of prices, reasonable assurance of ultimate cost, and reasonable freedom to alter the design at reasonable extra cost if unforeseen conditions arise. If therefore the cost-plus contract is deemed to be of value when all the operations cannot be foreseen, when the extent of the work required cannot be measured in advance, or when risks attached to the work are large and may or may not materialise—then precisely because of this it is practically impossible to set 'the target'. A target contract is a kind of contradiction. The moment a risk materialises which is other than a risk for which due allowance has been made in the target, or the moment an operation or an amount of work has to be done which was not included in the target, the target must be deemed wrong and unfair to the contractor. Hence such contracts mostly end in extensive modifications to the target as the work proceeds, and these modifications are a source of friction and dispute.

A target is even more a contradiction if mistakenly attached to any contract under which payment is made according to unit prices. The extent of the work to be done is at the direction of the engineer and not under the control of the contractor; therefore to attach a cost target to a contract paid on measure is a mistake.

Bonuses and penalties

A bonus or penalty can be included in any sort of civil engineering contract if it relates to completion of the whole or part of the work within a given time, provided a practicable time target is set. However, it is not usual to offer a bonus unless there are definite engineering or financial reasons for wanting completion by a given date, and a penalty clause is normally included only where the employer would be put to financial loss or would not comply with other obligations he has undertaken if the works were completed late. 'Performance' bonuses, i.e. bonuses or penalties related to the output or efficiency of the finished works, are seldom applicable in civil engineering contracts; they mostly apply to mechanical engineering contracts.

CONSTRUCTION BY DIRECT LABOUR

A promoter does not have to employ a civil engineering contractor to construct civil engineering works if he already employs sufficient staff and workmen and has sufficient machines to tackle the work himself. A large amount of modestly sized engineering work is undertaken by direct labour—particularly remedial or maintenance work. All local authorities have an engineering staff and a labour force in permanent employment, and they may, from time to time, be seconded from their routine work of maintenance to construct capital works where this is convenient. It is always possible to increase the man-power and plant available by temporarily hiring extra men and plant from outside sources.

In so far as direct-labour construction permits an employer to keep his own labour force properly employed on a full-time basis, this method of construction is advantageous. It helps the employer to retain a good body of skilled workmen of various trades whom he can use to meet emergency repair conditions. Thus, a waterworks always maintains a good nucleous of skilled pipe-layers and jointers to meet any emergency water-main repairs required. During the rest of the time these gangs can be used on the capital work of extending the mains system of the undertaking.

But for the construction of large capital works where extra engineering staff, tradesmen, labourers, and plant of all kinds would have to be hired, experience shows that direct-labour construction tends to be more expensive than construction by contract. The reason is that contract construction is highly competitive; the contractor's staff and workmen are attuned to working at top pressure; the contractor's directing personnel are forceful, energetic men used to driving a job onwards at maximum speed. Such men must frequently act on their own initiative; they will brook no delay, they do not take kindly to directives received from more than one master; they expect verbal sanctions to be adequate for what they do; they work by end-results achieved and do not expect to have to account—by means of a lot of paper work—for every penny spent. The competitive character of the work makes it needful that such men be in control and that such methods be adopted. But the staff who serve the employer—especially if the employer is a localg overnment or government authority—must necessarily be of a different sort. Their job is not so simple as a contractor's. They serve committees and boards, they have to liaise with other chief officers of their employer, they have to comply with internal administrative regulations designed largely to check and hold them back from any rash decisions. They have to gain the end-results they foresee as being necessary by means of persuasion and argument, and therefore have to exercise tact, patience, and tolerance, virtues which a contractor can only permit himself to indulge in to a very limited extent on a construction site. Seldom have such men powers to summarily hire and fire, reject or accept bids over the telephone, bargain and threaten as a contractor can, even if they wished. A contractor can fire an ineffectual workman or engineer in a day if he so wishes, and can find a substitute for him the following day by any means at his disposal. In local government it may take more than a month to do the same thing; or it may even be impossible to do it at all. For these and similar reasons, although direct labour can in theory be as cheap as contract work, it seldom is—but it does give advantages to the promoter in the special circumstances outlined earlier.

References

Civil Engineering Procedure. I.C.E. Publication (1963). (Essential reading.)
The Placing and Management of Contracts for Building and Civil Engineering Work (1964) H.M.S.O.
Charter, By-Laws, Regulations and Rules, I.C.E. Publication.

CHAPTER 2

The Contract for Construction

Documents of the contract

The contract for the construction of the works binds the contractor to construct them and the employer to pay for them. It describes comprehensively what the works are, and how payment is to be made. The works are often complex, involving the contractor in thousands of different operations and requiring him to buy hundreds of different manufactured items and materials and to employ a wide variety of men and machinery. Hence the contract itself comprises a number of documents as follows:

(a) the *contract drawings*, which pictorially show the works to be built, their dimensions, levels, etc.;

(b) the *specification*, which describes in words the works to be built, the quality of materials and workmanship to be used, and methods of testing etc.;

(c) the *bill of quantities*, which sets out the expected measure of each operation of construction as calculated from the drawings, classified according to trade or location within the proposed works;

(d) the *general conditions of contract*, which define the liabilities, responsibilities, and powers of the employer, contractor, and engineer, and covers such matters as methods of payment, insurance, liability of parties to the contract, etc.;

(e) the *tender*, which is the signed financial offer of the contractor to construct the works in accordance with (a), (b), (c), (d) above;

(f) any *letters of explanation*, which are agreed between the parties to the contract as elucidating or amplfying their intentions with regard to the foregoing matters;

(g) the *legal agreement*, which is signed by both parties, confirming their respective intention to have a contract between them as defined by all the foregoing documents.

For a contract to exist between the employer and contractor the latter · must have made an offer (the tender) which the employer accepts without amendment. If the employer accepts subject to an amendment of the offer there is no contract unless the contractor amends his offer as required, or until both employer and contractor agree upon some other amendment.

The contract documents for large projects which are put out to international bidding are bulky affairs which may run into several printed volumes each containing two hundred or more pages. These are now the classic 'bibles of construction', especially made for each particular project, representing the final co-ordinated design output of several teams of design and specialist civil engineers for a period of maybe two, three, or four years. One wonders sometimes how bidding contractors manage to digest, analyse, and understand them.

A typical three-volume contract of this kind may be seen to contain the following matters:

(i)   *Instructions to tenderers* (20 pages)—telling the contractor how to prepare the tender, when and where to send it in; requiring him to fill in various schedules; informing him of sources of major materials; guarantees and bond required; tax and import position, etc.

(ii) *Appendices to instructions* (10 pages)—listing prohibited imports; terms and abbreviations used; bond required.

(iii) *Tender bond and schedules for completion* (12 pages)—the schedules dealing with tenderer's estimated division of his expenditure in local and foreign currency, for labour and for materials, and the phasing thereof and rates of exchange taken.

(iv) *General conditions of contract* (70 pages)—generally taking the usual form, but expanded to cover the special conditions (and laws) which exist in the country of construction, and the special duties, risks, and liabilities attached to the particular construction.

(v) *The specification* (200–300 pages)—normally starting with an amplified description of the intended project, and informing the tenderer of local geography, communications, climate, and so on. It may then present a great deal of data which is relevant to the contractor's working—such as rainfall, river flows, general geology, the employer's relationship with other contractors, and his aims and requirements generally. The specification itself will have its items grouped under several sections as the job demands. This grouping may be by trades, or in order as item by item of the bill of quantities, by units of construction according to location or entity, or according to the speciality of work required keeping sub-contract work, and temporary works (such as living camps, cofferdams, etc.) separate.

(vi) *The bill of quantities* (length varies)—for convenience is usually a separate volume. A former tendency to display a bill having several thousand separate items is now being replaced by a tendency to reduce the bill to no more than a hundred items (if possible), where, for instance, one such item may read 'Concrete in all major structures as Spec. 33–64', and the next items read 'Concrete in all minor structures as Spec. 65–96' and 'Concrete in piles Spec. 97–107'—thus getting through concrete with less items than are found in some bills for a few manholes!

(vii) *Bill schedules* (some 20 pages)—follow the bill of quantities; these schedules may require the contractor to set out unit rates for certain operations, or to supply different types of labour or materials; also the schedules contain lists of proposed sub-contractors, detailed technical data concerning parts of the offer, the proposed programme, and the phasing of labour intended.

(viii) *contract drawings* (a complete volume)—are usually reduced from the normal double-elephant size for ease of handling and forwarding to all parts of the world. There may be well over a hundred such drawings, which show not only the precise details of construction, but also give extensive geological, hydrological, and soil mechanics information, including results of testing of materials proposed to be used in the construction.

On small and medium jobs all the above contract documents may be bound in one volume. The instructions to tenderers will probably occupy no more than a page. The General Conditions will not be printed in full, but will be stipulated in some form of words such as, 'The General Conditions of Contract shall be those published jointly by the Institution of Civil Engineers, the Association of Consulting Engineers, and the Federation of Civil Engineering Contractors, the Fifth Edition thereof as amended in June 1973. . . . etc. with the following insertions and amendments'. Then will follow a list of the alterations required to the printed General Conditions. The bill of quantities may well be printed as a separate document, for convenience, so that several priced copies can be made available for all those on both the contractor's side and on the engineer's side, who have to work on the contract. The original tender, signed by the contractor, together with copies of all correspondence relating to negotiations about the tender, a set of contract drawings and the general conditions, will then be fixed to the legal agreement which is signed by both parties and which then forms 'the contract' between the parties.

Tender considerations

Calling for tenders. An employer may publicly advertise (by way of notices in the Press) that he is open to receive tenders. It is usual for the engineer to draft this notice so that it contains a brief but adequate description of the proposed works and their location, so that contractors can judge whether they are interested in tendering. It is also usual to state that no expenses incurred in tendering will be reimbursed, and that the employer does not bind himself to accept the lowest, or any tender.

Contractors are normally required to make a deposit of £5 or £10, or perhaps higher for large contracts, before they are sent a set of tender documents; the deposit being returnable only when 'a bona-fide tender' has been received. This is to discourage frivolous enquiries and ensure the return of the documents. Sometimes a contractor returns the documents, saying he finds he does not wish to tender for some reason or other. The engineer should normally advise the employer to return any deposit in response to a reasonable excuse. Contractors often have to tender for several different jobs at the same time in the hope that one or two may be successful. Occasions may therefore arise where a contractor is more successful than he has expected, and he may have to withdraw offers not yet accepted, lest he overstretch his resources. It is not always possible, either, for a contractor to judge whether he can rightly undertake a job until the whole tender documents are in his hands. Therefore deposits should always be returned once the documents have been sent back, unless the engineer has evidence that the enquiry was frivolously intended.

An alternative procedure to public advertisement of tenders is to invite certain contractors only to submit tenders. Probably the best way to do this is to advertise that contractors may, if they send in their qualifications and experience, apply to be placed on a list of 'selected tenderers'. This method is called pre-qualification, and it saves time for both contractors and the engineer and employer. Thus, for the construction of a bridge, a public advertisement might be issued inviting contractors experienced in bridge building to apply to be placed on the list of selected tenderers. Applicants would be asked to provide details of their past experience, present labour force, plant, and equipment, and to give the names of previous employers they have worked for. The engineer will then follow these matters up and, if it appears to him that certain contractors are not suitably qualified, their applications would be rejected, so that no waste of time occurs from their submitting tenders.

Sometimes the engineer may himself draw up a list of selected tenderers in consultation with the employer, without resorting to public advertisement. This may not be fair to certain contractors, who may be excluded from the list simply because the engineer does not happen to know of their existence or their capacity. In special cases a contract may be negotiated with one selected firm only—but this would occur only when the work required is specialised and suited for placing with one firm rather than any other; or where the employer (not being a public authority, but perhaps a private individual or company) wishes the work to go to a certain contractor in preference to any other. Many companies, having once found themselves a good contractor, like to continue to place work with one firm only, thereby obtaining prompt and favourable service in return for the continued commissioning of work.

Comparing tenders. It is the engineer's job to recommend to the employer which contractor's offer should be accepted. It should be noticed that the engineer does not accept the offer, nor does he make the final decision. The engineer recommends; the employer decides and acts.

The first criterion is, of course, the sum total offer made by each contractor—but it is important to see whether each contractor is, in fact, offering the same thing. Some tenders may be submitted with certain reservations or provisos, which are contrary or additional to the conditions laid down in the tender documents. Some tenders may contain arith-metical mistakes, or mistakes of interpretation of the documents; in yet other cases there may be certain portions of the tender where the tenderer is left to propose his own specifications of materials or methods to be used in the construction, or he may be asked to give guarantees of some kind or another. There is also the time of completion offered by tenderers to consider. All these matters must be listed side by side and, where necessary, adjustments made to the total sums offered to take into account additions or subtractions in individual offers as compared with a suitable standard offer. Only then is it possible, having put all tenders on a par, to make a fair comparison between them.

From this comparison, the lowest three or four tenders are then meticulously examined. If the tenders are based on bills of quantities the detailed prices submitted by different contractors for the same portions of work are compared. This will reveal relatively high or low unit prices for certain types of work, so that the engineer can decide whether any particularly low prices are acceptable, or whether they foreshadow impending trouble with certain parts of the work. While a contractor is entitled to price the bill of quantities so that he will make a loss on some items and a high profit on others, the engineer will not wish to see this carried to extremes, so that he feels there is a danger of the underpriced work being shoddy, or the cost of the high-priced items being exorbitant if the measured quantities exceed the estimated quantities in the bill.

As an instance, the prices quoted by one tenderer for excavation may be exceptionally high, and his rates for concreting low. Perhaps, since excavation normally precedes concreting, the contractor hopes by this method to get himself a high cash reward in the early part of the contract so as to finance himself. Within reason, such an action may be justified, since a contractor must always initially lay out a great deal of money to get the job started; but if the variation of pricing is excessive the engineer may be led to doubt the contractor's financial situation if he appears too much in need of ready cash. Furthermore, if any difficulty is experienced with the excavation and the contractor does not make the early cash profit he is hoping for, his situation could deteriorate as he undertakes the rest of the work, which is relatively underpriced and gives him small, if any, profit.

Even without such apprehensions, the engineer will know from past experience that underpriced items of work—irrespective of profits gained elsewhere—will tend to receive less attention from the contractor than work which is well priced. Hence the engineer must examine the offer to see that vital operations where quality of work is most desirable, or where difficulty must surely be encountered, have been properly priced, because he will want evidence to show that the contractor has understood the obligations the contract imposes. Of course, here and there in every priced bill of quantities will be found single items or small groups of items of no outstanding total value which appear to be oddly priced either high or low. These minor variations are of little importance; they may express a contractor's personal prejudice or, not infrequently, his ignorance. With a thousand or so items to price, perhaps more than one or two have to be guessed on the part of the contractor. The important parts of a bill of quantities, both to a contractor and the engineer, are those few items—probably no more than 10 per cent of the items in the bill—which represent some 70, 80, or 90 per cent of the total cost. These items are the ones that must be scrutinised most carefully.

The unit price quoted for items to which provisional quantities have been attached require special attention. If the provisional quantity entered is small the unit price can be quoted very high with little effect on the total sum tendered. But if it should be necessary to undertake more of this kind of work than has been estimated, then the total price paid may be excessive. Prices for provisional quantities for rock excavation are typical.

Choosing a tender.   With the completion of the close scrutiny and comparison, the engineer may now have to invite one or two of the lowest tenderers to his office, to discuss certain points of their offers with him. Principally, he may wish to be provided with further evidence from a tenderer as to the latter's proposed methods of construction, and his projected programme. The engineer will not, of course, reveal to any contractor the prices offered by others; but it will be obvious to the contractor who attends such a discussion that he is 'in the running'. The engineer must therefore be on his guard against accepting assurances too glibly given, or offers to make reduction of prices. This discussion is not for bargaining; the technical questions the engineer needs to pose to the contractor must be met by answers of pith and substance, which are technically reasonable and competent; they must not be just the hopes of an optimist. Meantime the engineer will have made private contact with the referees named by the contractor, and in respect of these it must not be forgotten than any reference—good or bad—is somewhat shaky evidence. Alleged faults of a contractor can relate to a passing phase, a period of difficulty, or an unlucky job; virtues likewise may come and go according to circumstances. It is best to classify references as either satisfactory, or without doubt unsatisfactory; setting aside others as of doubtful value one way or the other.

The decision must now be made as to which tender should be recommended for acceptance. Once the tenders have been compared on the same uniform basis, and each has been shown to be in conformity with the requirements of the documents, and all misunderstandings and queries have been cleared, the engineer must ask himself whether there is any cogent reason why he should not recommend acceptance of the lowest tender. If he does wish to recommend other than the lowest tender he should think over most carefully his reasons for this. They must be real reasons, the truth of which it would be difficult to deny. Thus, if the engineer has definite information (such as a banker's reference) that a contractor is on the verge of bankruptcy this would be a 'real' reason for rejecting his tender. If a contractor has not had the experience that the engineer deems essential, or if the tenderer has disclosed that he intends to sub-let most, or the most important part of the work, these, too, might be real reasons for rejection. On the other hand, it is scarcely possible to reject a tender just because the tenderer has received an unfavourable report from one of his referees, or because he is involved in a dispute with some other employer. Other information has to be coupled with such information, evidence of a like nature from other referees, or evidence from the tender itself, or from questioning the contractor. Nor can a low price, *of itself*, be regarded as sufficient ground for rejecting the lowest tender, unless it can be regarded as unreasonably low, because there can be occasions when a contractor may wish to obtain work for little or no profit, simply to keep his men in employment, or with an eye to obtaining more favourable contracts in the same area later. Possibly the most serious danger involved in recommending a tender other than the lowest is that the engineer may thereby feel some guarantee that the one he does recommend will result in a trouble-free job. Alas, if the job runs into unforeseen trouble this may be far from the truth, and the employer will question why he was recommended this particular contractor, and not the one who had at least the merit of being cheapest.

In his report to the employer the engineer will therefore be particularly careful not to overstate a case, either for or against any tenderer, and he should stick to the old journalistic rule of 'keeping facts separate from opinions'—presenting the facts first, then his deductions, and then his resulting recommendations. The engineer cannot do more than present his honest opinion, resulting from his own knowledge and experience.

If tenderers have been selected by means of some pre-qualification test, it becomes more difficult to justify any other course than acceptance of the lowest priced offer, since each firm is prior approved. This point should be borne in mind when selecting tenderers.

Risks and unforeseeable conditions

Normal risks. On the subject of risks, the belief is sometimes held that the contractor can be 'made to pay for them'. This is not so. A contractor will certainly shoulder risks, but he will charge higher prices accordingly, so that, in effect, the employer is forced to pay a premium against the risks included in his contract. If the risks do not materialise the employer will have paid more than he need have done for his works; but if the cost of meeting the risks exceeds the premium paid the resulting deficit will be carried forward by the contractor to be offset by better profits made on other jobs. There is no other solution to the problem if the contractor is to remain in business.

For 'normal' risks—such as delays due to bad weather—the system averages out. In the British climate an average allowance of about 10 per cent of the wages cost would be usual for meeting the cost of delays due to inclement weather. On some jobs, of course, the incidence of bad weather costs 15 per cent, on others 5 per cent. On the whole, this is fair to employers, who each pays an average price for the cost of wet weather.

But when risks are abnormal the system can work out rather unfairly. Sometimes a contractor sustains a very heavy loss on a single job, perhaps £200 000, because of great difficulties encountered. If the employer in this particular case does not pay to the contractor the extra £200 000 spent on meeting risks which have become larger than expected, then it is clear that—if the contractor is to remain in business—he must get the money from extra profits made elsewhere on other jobs. The only alternative is for the contractor to go bankrupt and make his creditors go short of some or all of the missing £200 000.

If the loss of money arises from the contractor's own inefficiency or lack of competence, then this merely illustrates that in a fiercely competitive world the inefficient and the incompetent are driven out of business. But not infrequently these very large losses stem from the imposition of excessive risks upon a contractor with no possible means of escape.

Unsuitable risks. As an instance of an unsuitable risk, one may take the case where the engineer suspects, but does not actually know, that running sand may be encountered in parts of an excavation. He therefore calls upon the contractor to tender an excavation price to cover 'excavation in all materials whether hard or soft, whether in chalk, clay, loam, marl, peat, rock, running sand or sand . . . etc.'. This specification may be all right so long as the variations encountered in the excavation come within the range of variations reasonably to be inferred from the specification. The contractor is forewarned that he may meet materials of any of these kinds within the excavation. But if the whole excavation should turn out to be in running sand and in none of the other materials the contractor might maintain this was not reasonably to be inferred from the description given. If a *range* of materials is described, a range of materials is reasonably to be inferred. If one material only is described, then only one is inferred. There is no escape from this interpretation, because the subject of the contract is not the literal meaning of the words taken one by one, but the intention meant to be conveyed by the use of those words taken as a whole in their context.

The proper course is to call for 'extra-over' prices for operations of a more expensive kind—such as excavating in rock or running sand. Then these more costly operations can be justly paid for if and when they occur, but not otherwise. This is fairer to both employer and contractor.

Another type of unsuitable risk to impose on a contractor is to make him in some way responsible for part of the permanent design of the works. A simple instance is where a contractor is asked to leave the side batter to an excavation 'to a suitable permanent gradient'. For an engineer to act thus is unprofessional, since he is responsible for the permanent design, and he may not delegate the responsibility to anyone else. But even if there is no engineer, the employer is ill-advised to put the responsibility for permanent design features on the contractor if he has not specifically employed the contractor on a design-and-build basis. Under normal contractual arrangements it is of no concern to the contractor if, the day after he has completed the maintenance period satisfactorily, the works fall down through ill design. If he is employed purely as a contractor to undertake the construction of the works, his responsibilities cease as soon as he has constructed the works as specified. If he is also to be employed as designer, wider safeguards must be called for, and naturally his prices will be increased accordingly.

A third type of unsuitable risk illustrates the futility of trying to make a contract cover too much. This arises when the onus of locating suitable natural materials—such as gravel, earth-fill, or rock-fill of a specified kind—is placed upon the contractor. This would put tenderers at the time of tendering in an almost impossible position. They cannot all go round with boring and augering equipment prospecting for these materials, especially in Britain. No landowner would permit tenderers to riddle his land with boreholes. Neither would he quote firm prices for the sale of his land to a succession of tenderers, each demanding a figure on which to base firm prices in a tender. Even if the tenderer successfully wrested a price from a landowner on which to base his tender, he may later find the price has been raised, or perhaps the landowner may have changed his mind altogether.

A better way to deal with this situation is for the employer to purchase the land or source of materials in advance of letting the contract. If he cannot do that, then tenderers should be asked to base their tenders on an estimated price for the supply of materials, which price can later be varied according to the price actually paid.

Summary in regard to risks. The root difficulty with regard to imposing excessive or indefinable risks upon a contractor is that there cannot be a valid contract between two parties to do something which cannot be defined. There are three essential parts to a valid contract: the intentions in the mind of the employer as expressed in the contract documents; the interpretation in the mind of the contractor as evidenced by his tender; and the object of their mutual agreement.

Therefore, if a risk materialises of such magnitude that it is out of all proportion to what the parties could conceivably have had in mind when they respectively wrote or read the words written in the contract, then this materialised risk is of such a nature that it is not covered by the contract. No contractor can be deemed to have contracted to do things which are beyond the possibility of his conceiving (as a practical civil engineering contractor) when he read the wording of the contract. Thus, every risk mentioned in the contract has implied outer limits, and it is not possible to safeguard the employer's position beyond those limits.

The best policy in regard to risks included in a contract is to disclose as much information as possible and not to attempt to hide them away. If the engineer wants the contractor to shoulder unusual risks it is best to itemise the risk separately and try to put some measure to it—even if rough—which the contractor can price. By this means, the payment made can at least be roughly apportioned to the amount of extra work the contractor is put to when the risk materialises.

Covering unforeseeable conditions. The above remarks concerning risks have even more point when one considers Clause 12 (1) of the *Conditions of Contract for Civil Engineering Work* agreed by the Institution of Civil Engineers, the Association of Consulting Engineers, and the Federation of Civil Engineering Contractors. This Clause reads:

> 12 (1) If during the execution of the Works the Contractor shall encounter physical conditions (other than weather conditions or conditions due to weather conditions) or artificial obstructions which conditions or obstructions he considers could not reasonably have been foreseen by an experienced contractor and the Contractor is of the opinion that additional cost will be incurred . . . he shall if he intends to make any claim for additional payment give notice to the Engineer . . . etc.

Subsequent parts of the Clause indicate that such a claim, if properly presented, will be payable by the employer.

The effect of this Clause is that, irrespective of what the rest of the contract says, unless it specifically deletes the application of Clause 12 (1) to a particular risk, when that risk materialises as an 'unforeseeable event', then the employer will have to pay the cost of meeting it. It is no use, therefore, writing in the contract documents—'the contractor shall include in his prices for excavation in all materials whatsoever, including running sand, etc.'—unless either Clause 12 (1) is deleted with reference to this particular operation, or the amount of running sand, etc., that will be met can be measured from the drawings or can be reasonably foreseen. To delete the application of Clause 12 (1) in reference to risks of any importance would bring immediate objection from the Federation of Civil Engineering Contractors on behalf of tenderers, unless the contract made special provision elsewhere for the shouldering of the risk under a separate sum. Hence, so long as Clause 12 (1) stands, the engineer cannot, without special wording in the contract, get a contractor to shoulder risks (other than weather) which the engineer cannot himself foresee or fore-estimate.

It follows that in a clause such as this—

> The contractor shall be deemed to have satisfied himself as regards existing roads, railways, or other means of communication with and access to the site, the contours thereof, the risk of injury or damage to property adjacent to the site or to the occupiers of such property, the

nature of the materials (whether natural or otherwise) to be excavated, the conditions under which the works will have to be carried out, the supply of and conditions affecting labour, the facilities for obtaining the materials or articles referred to in the specifications and bills of quantities and generally to have obtained his own information on all matters affecting the execution of the works and the prices tendered therefor.

No claim by the contractor for additional payment will be allowed on the ground of any misunderstanding or misapprehension in respect of any such matter or otherwise or on the ground of any allegation or fact that incorrect information was given to him by any person whether in the employ of the authority or not or of the failure of his part to obtain correct information, nor shall the contractor be relieved from any risks or obligations imposed on or undertaken by him under the contract on any such ground or on the ground that he did not or could not foresee any matter which may in fact affect or have affected the execution of the works.

—which used to be found in some well-known documents, is meaningless if Clause 12 (1) is allowed to remain in the General Conditions. One cannot make a contractor responsible for incorrect information given to him, or for things he cannot foresee. A contract is based on the declared intentions of the two parties to it, and it is this which dominates the contract.

Providing information for tenderers

There is seldom time for a contractor to appraise all the risks attached to a job in the few weeks he is allowed for tendering. It is therefore in the interests of the job as a whole that, during the time allowed for tendering, the engineer should put all the information he has at the disposal of tenderers for their examination. He must be careful about:

(i)   guaranteeing that such information is correct;
(ii) implying that such information as he gives is, by itself, a sufficient basis on which to tender;
(iii) interpreting the information or making deductions therefrom which could sway the contractor's opinion.

The information presented should be factual and include all relevant matters that the engineer knows about. Tenderers should always be instructed to visit the site of the works before preparing a tender, and the engineer might well make private arrangements so that he is able to know which contractors do visit the site and which do not.

Even so, there is a practical limit to what contractors can be expected to do during the time allowed for tendering. Consider a contract for the laying of a 20-mile pipeline. Even if the engineer provides all the information he has in regard to the geology of the area and the results of test pits along the proposed route, these are not likely to permit more than a rough appraisal of the ground conditions. The contractor might conceivably take some borings along the route, but he does not have unlimited money and time at his disposal to do this, and in many instances the landowners concerned would limit such operations. At the stage of tendering the employer may only have obtained permission from landowners to walk across the lands to be affected, since there is no need to pay landowners compensation for loss of crops and grazing rights in any particular field until the construction actually enters it. Inevitably, it is not possible for a contractor to get complete information before he tenders, nor is this really necessary. So long as the contract is worded fairly and separate items for excavation in different sorts of ground are put to the contractor for pricing, the price paid for the work will amount to much the same as it would have done, had all been known beforehand.

Time allowed for tendering

Considerable pressure is often brought to bear upon engineers and contractors to persuade them to quote their minimum times for design and construction. This pressure ought to be resisted. The truth is that the demand for more speed comes because it now takes longer than ever for an employer to get the necessary powers for construction. What with planning consents, awaiting for government and local government permissions, publishing notices, hearing objections, arguing about land acquisitions, going to arbitration about land prices, considerable alternative proposals, quelling the fears of the local Press, notifying and getting the views of every conceivable public or private institution even remotely connected with the proposed scheme—engineers would be well advised to draw the attention of employers more frequently to the fact that although it takes only four years to design and build a major works, it often takes at least four more years to get the necessary permissions to do it.

Four weeks should be regarded as the absolute minimum time for tendering for even the smallest jobs; six weeks should normally be regarded as the least time to allow and, for large-scale projects or projects overseas, three months or more may be necessary.

On the question of time for design and construction, the author has, on several occasions, cause to regret being over-persuaded that speed is foremost. A job can get into an inconceivable mess—both physically and financially—if everyone gets so overwrought as to be persuaded that 'emergency temporary measures' must be taken, and mixed up with permanent constructional measures. The completion date stands a high risk of being no earlier than it would have been had the job been tackled with due speed in the right order, and the cost of all the unforeseeable extras come high. It has wisely been said, that once the job is completed, the employer will forget that it took six months longer to build; but if he is given a poor job he will never forget.

Opening tenders

Some employers have tenders opened at a public meeting, and this is an admirable procedure where, as in international tendering, there is great interest in the project. The public opening, which the tenderers can attend, makes 'backroom juggling' with offers impossible, lets contractors know what their hopes can be as soon as possible, and in general is an open-handed, straightforward method. It does not, of course, guarantee that the lowest-priced tender will be accepted. The most frequent practice in Britain is, however, for tenders to be opened all at the same time by the Chairman or Managing Director acting for the employer, in the presence of other officials. The tenders, once opened, are then handed to the engineer for his report, and it is during this report stage and consideration by the employer that contractors will try to find out from the engineer how they are positioned. The engineer should certainly not disclose this information without the consent of the employer, and even if he does receive that consent he should not make the disclosure prematurely. But if the enquiry comes from a contractor whose price is among the highest, early disclosure of this fact will do no harm, provided the employer consents. When the employer has reached his decision there is no reason why all the prices submitted (but not necessarily the names of tenderers) should not be made available to all tenderers as soon as possible.

'Cover prices'

An engineer may occasionally be telephoned by a prospective tenderer during the tendering period and asked what a 'good cover price' would be. This action arises because a contractor may fear that, having taken the tender documents and paid a deposit for the same, he will not recover his deposit except by submission of some kind of tender, even though he finds on inspection, that he does not want the job or cannot undertake it. Furthermore, the contractor may fear that if he does not submit a price, the engineer or employer may not consider asking him to tender for other jobs, or may give his later tenders scant consideration. Therefore the contractor seeks a 'cover price'—a figure low enough to look a reasonable offer, but which is high enough to make certain he will not get the job.

This procedure is a complete waste of everyone's time, and it should be stopped. The contractor should be permitted to return the tender documents and receive his deposit back so long as his original enquiry was not frivolously intended. He should also receive an assurance that his withdrawal will not debar his later tenders for other jobs receiving full and fair consideration.

Mistakes in tenders

Mistakes in tenders can arise innocently, and they should be the earliest matters cleared up by the engineer before he starts comparing tenders. Preferably he should write to the tenderer in whose tender the mistake appears asking for a correction rather than interview him; alternatively, it is quite usual for the engineer to lay down rules in advance concerning the correction of mistakes. Typical rules are that the unit price quoted against an item takes precedence over any miscalculation of the total sum against that item; that where an item is not priced at all, nil charge for that item will be assumed; that any page or summary totals will be corrected for arithmetical errors so that they represent the true total of items on that page or for that summary. These rules may be necessary to prevent 'juggling' with prices by contractors after tenders are in; but it is also necessary to apply common sense to such errors, lest a manifest injustice be done to a contractor simply because of a genuine clerical mistake.

If the engineer finds a mistake in the documents he should circulate a correction notice to all tenderers and request an acknowledgment in each case that the correction has been noted and the effect on the tender taken into account. It is best to keep such correction notices to a minimum, because they can result in confusion and error. Where corrections apply to quantities of no great importance, there is no point in issuing such corrections at the tender stage, since all tenders are on the same basis, and the alteration can be made to the adopted tender only.

Qualification of a tenderer's offer

When a tender is received it may be accompanied by a covering letter which sets out some qualification of the tenderer's offer, or some interpretation of the contract documents upon which his tender is based. This may reveal to the engineer something in the contract documents which has not been made clear.

Since the proportion of successful tenders is under 10 per cent, a contractor is rarely able to give all the time he would like to every tender, and it is a great advantage to him to be able to give further study to one which he knows is in the running. The engineer must be on his guard, therefore, against entering into a bargaining session with tenderers after their tenders are in. If it is vital to have a doubtful matter cleared up, it is probably best for the engineer to issue his own interpretation of the matter to tenderers and let them send in their objections if they have any; or else he may set aside a qualified tender as not in line with the others.

Many contract documents contain a clause to the effect that qualification of tenders will not be considered; but it is hardly possible to reject a good tender out of hand because it contains a qualification. It is also wrong to assume that a contractor may not qualify his tender; he is perfectly entitled to do so, because, as we have seen above, a valid contract is based on the intentions of the two parties to it—and if one party is not clear what the other party means he must get the issue clarified before he can make an acceptable offer. The 'qualified offer' is not therefore an offer on the basis of the employer's contract documents, it is a counter-offer of a different kind which does not bind the contractor unless either the employer accepts the qualification or the contractor withdraws or cancels the qualification.

Offer and acceptance

A private individual could enter a binding agreement with a contractor simply by writing him a letter which says 'I accept your offer'. But a simple acceptance of this kind may not be valid if:

(i) the tender documents say the acceptance is to be 'subject to contract'; or

(ii) if the acceptance is undertaken by any body of persons acting as a Company, Joint Board, Local Government Authority, Government Department, or similar. Such bodies often have standing regulations which must be complied with before they can be committed to a contract.

In the vast majority of cases civil engineering contracts are entered into by local or governmental authorities, or by other statutory authorities who require that contracts shall be by deed to which their seal is affixed. The engineer takes no part in these proceedings other than to act as a channel of communication with the contractor and to provide the original tender documents which form the basis of the contract.

After the engineer has reported upon tenders to the employer and has been notified of the employer's decision he may write to the selected contractor as follows:

Dear Sir,

Contract No. 64.

I am pleased to inform you that at their last meeting the North Western Water Board resolved to accept your tender amounting to £15 330.50 for the above contract, subject to the Board receiving Ministry consent and to a formal legal Agreement being drawn up between yourselves and the Board.

The basis of the Agreement will be (i) your tender offer and covering letter of 23rd January, (ii) our letter to you of 15th February and (iii) your letter to us of 18th February together with all the tender documents and drawings.

Yours faithfully,

This letter does not constitute an acceptance of the contractor's offer; it merely advises him that the board will accept it:

(a) as modified by certain correspondence which passed between the contractor and the engineer;

(b) provided the ministry give permission to the Water Board to accept it; and

(c) when a formal legal agreement is prepared and presented to both parties for signature.

After this letter has been sent the engineer will send the original tender offer, the tender drawings, specification, and priced bill of quantities, the original contractor's letters, and the carbon copies of his own letters referred to, back to the clerk or solicitor to the board, asking him to prepare the formal contract for signature. He will keep copies of these documents for his own use, and when ministry consent has been received and he has checked with the clerk that it is in order to proceed he may call upon the contractor to start work.

There are occasions when the whole of this formality is not required, and the reader must not be confused by such exceptions. Firstly, there may be no 'tender documents' in the usual sense—there may be only a 'quotation' from a supplier. Thus, an engineer may, on behalf of the employer, call for quotations for the supply of pipes or valves. He does this by a letter. In due course the employer may resolve to accept one of the several quotations received. In this case the engineer may then write a letter to the supplier which says:

Dear Sirs,

Contract No. 65.

With reference to your quotation JW/5345 under the above contract, dated 12th January, I am pleased to inform you that the Board have resolved to accept it.

A copy of our letter to you of 5th January together with your original quotation is being forwarded to the Clerk to the Board and, in due course, the Clerk will draw up the necessary Agreement for your signature.

In the meantime I am authorised by the Board to instruct you to proceed with manufacture of the items listed in your quotation so that there may be no delay to your quoted delivery time.

Yours faithfully,

If the quotation is for a relatively small amount it may be that the standing orders of the employer permit an official of the employer to authorise the expenditure, in which case the engineer may send an even simpler version of the above letter to the contractor, which reads:

Dear Sirs,

Quotation No. JW/5345.

With reference to your quotation JW/5345 dated 12th January I am pleased to inform you that this has been found acceptable.

An official order covering the work will therefore be sent to you by the Board in a day or so and, in the meantime, I am authorised by the Board to instruct you to proceed with the work.

Yours faithfully,

The Standing Orders of a local authority, joint board, or company usually fix an upper limit to the amount of expenditure which may be authorised by an official, acting on any single occasion on their behalf, by the issue of an 'official order'. But even when the amount exceeds such upper limit, the clerk may often advise that a contract can be quite satisfactorily based on 'an exchange of letters' where the contract is for the supply of materials. When such a contract is entered into, the general conditions of it are, in effect, the terms laid down in the engineer's original letter calling for quotations and the contractor's conditions of sale, usually printed on the back of the accepted quotation. The engineer must naturally examine these printed conditions carefully and, if he wants them modified, copies of the correspondence arranging for the modification must also be bound up with the contract.

Bond

On contracts for the construction of work it is usual to stipulate that the contractor shall obtain a security bond. This means that he has to find another party (usually a bank) who is willing to guarantee to meet any damages up to a certain amount sustained by the employer as a result of default by the contractor. Normally a contractor can get such bond from a bank only by lodging securities of equal amount with the bank, which he may not sell, encash, or otherwise dispose of without the bank's consent. If the bond is for 10 per cent of the contract value (which it often is), then for a £1 million contract the contractor would have to keep £100 000 of securities lodged with the bank.

There is criticism of this stipulation that it is too onerous, and that the employer has plenty of other 'holds' on the contractor. For instance, 10 per cent of the payments due to a contractor are withheld up to the time of substantial completion of the works; the plant that the contractor brings on to the site for construction can also be legally taken into the possession of the employer; and it is seldom the case that payment does not lag at least a month or two behind the actual work done by the contractor. As a result, bond is not always called for—particularly where pre-qualification of tenderers has been adopted or where a negotiated contract has been entered into. It is not necessary in contracts for the supply of goods where payment is made upon delivery and not before. Nevertheless, in open tendering, calling for bond has its uses, for if a contractor fails to obtain bond this will almost certainly be an indication that his financial situation is not satisfactory. For this reason an engineer should not authorise a contractor to start work until he is informed that the contractor has obtained bond when required.

Starting the contract

It is necessary to be reasonable in appointing a starting date for the contract. Under the usual General Conditions of Contract a contractor must commence the works within fourteen days of the starting date, and this requirement does seem a little unreasonable. A contractor may be left in doubt for as long as three months wondering whether his tender will be accepted or not, then suddenly be asked to commence the works within fourteen days. He may have to pull key men off other jobs in progress. It is hardly practical to advertise for more staff and get them employed and out on the works in fourteen days. In practice, the contractor usually complies with the 'letter of the law' by sending a couple of men and a shed to the site within fourteen days of the starting date, and it may be several weeks later before he actually moves in properly. This is a proper practice, as long as the contractor appears capable of conforming with the agreed programme of construction

It would also be extremely helpful to contractors if the contract documents were to state when a decision will be made upon the tenders and when the work can be expected to start. The engineer usually has a good idea of these dates once the date for advertising for tenders has been fixed. In Britain the seasons have an important influence on civil engineering work; cheaper prices would be quoted for six- to twenty-four-month contracts if the starting date for them could be guaranteed to be in March or April. Quite often, however, a contract is advertised in January or February, thus raising the hopes of tenderers that it will start in the early summer, only to be delayed subsequently.

The engineer should do his best to arrange for the contractor as fair a start on the job as might reasonably be inferred from the time of advertising for tenders, and he should seek to impress on administrators the need to avoid a winter start.

References

Conditions of Contract for Works of Civil Engineering Construction. I.C.E. (or Federation of Civil Engineering Contractors, or Association of Consulting Engineers).
Engineering Law and the I.C.E. Contracts, M. W. Abrahamson (1965). C. R. Books Ltd.
Hudson's Building & Engineering Contracts, I. N. Duncan Wallace (10th Edition). Sweet & Maxwell. (The classic work of law on this subject, first published in 1891, now brought up to date. A lucid account of engineering contract law.)
International Conditions of Contract, 1969, I.C.E.
Overseas Conditions of Contract, 1956. I.C.E.

CHAPTER 3

The Contractor's Site Organisation

IT is helpful to first consider the contractor's site organisation before going on to deal with the main topic of this book—the engineer's site staff and their supervisory duties.

Key site personnel for contractor

The key personnel employed on site by a contractor to take charge of the construction are shown in Fig. 1 for a job of magnitude £1 million

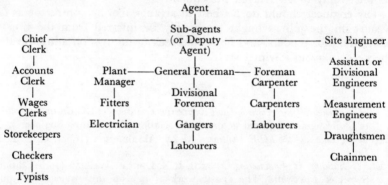

Fig. 1. The contractor's site control staff for a medium-sized job.

to £2 million. The same principles of organisation apply to larger or smaller jobs, and the numbers of persons employed depend not only on the size but also on the complexity of the job and its physical extent. The five key persons are:

the agent, who is in charge
a site engineer
an office manager
a general foreman
a plant manager

On small jobs, the duties of engineer and agent may be combined, and the general foreman may also be the plant foreman. On large jobs, a contracts manager may be appointed over the agent, his job being managerial rather than one of technical and executive control; the agent may be served by a deputy agent and several sub-agents; the site engineer may be served by a team of assistant engineers. If the work of a large job can be sectionalised it may be split up into a number of sections, each under the control of an engineer assisted by a section foreman. The provision of common services, such as labour, plant, and transport, may then be under the control of a sub-agent and general foreman (or works supervisor). Whatever the actual division of responsibility and the designation of the personnel, it is always possible to distinguish the main activities of the five key persons listed above.

A good contractor always tries to keep his site staff to a minimum to aid in swift, economic construction. In order to achieve this, the right type of men must be used, and they must be given freedom and responsibility to act on their own initiative. They must have quick communication with one another, and their areas of action must be clearly defined. Hence, the less complex the organisation is, the better will it function. The contractor cannot afford to tolerate ineffectiveness in any of these responsible positions. In the early stages of a job changes of personnel occur which may possibly seem swift and ruthless to the outsider. However, this must be so, because the key men have to work together as a team, and it is better for a man not to hold a position where he becomes open to criticism for failing to match up to his responsibilities.

The agent

The agent is responsible for directing and controlling the whole of the construction work on site, and he will have wide powers to enable him to employ men, hire machinery and equipment, purchase materials, and employ sub-contractors. His powers to do these things without reference to his firm's head office will depend on the size of the job, its nature and distance from head office, the policy adopted by his firm, and, of course, his standing within his firm.

An agent must display a considerable number of talents. He must not only be knowledgeable in the civil engineering arts of construction; he must be able to command men and be a good organiser and administrator. Furthermore, he needs sound business sense, because his job is not only to get the works built properly to the satisfaction of the engineer but also to make a profit for the contractor. He is therefore tough, practical, experienced, fair-minded, and energetic. In some cases his training will have consisted only of experience gained through many years of life on site, but nowadays the younger agent will more than likely have some academic engineering qualifications. Any agent will still need the talents listed above if he is to become successful.

A good agent is probably the most secure guarantee an employer can have that his works will be built well; if he is a poor agent, then not even the combined pressure of the engineer and his resident engineer and staff can guarantee to make every detail of the job as good as it ought to be.

Some firms give their most experienced agents virtually complete charge of the job, both financial and engineering. Sometimes, however, he may have a contracts manager over him, and to some extent, the business functions of the agent are then taken over by the contracts manager. The latter is more usually appointed when a contract is very large and is split under the control of two or more agents, or where, as on a large building contract, many sub-contractors are employed to carry out the major portion of the work. For the traditional type of heavy civil engineering job there should be little need for the appointment of a contracts manager over the agent. But whatever authority the agent is given, there will usually also be appointed, at the head office of the contractors, a project engineer to help the agent with design assistance and advice, and one of the contractor's managing directors seconded to take final responsibility at topmost level for what is done. The project engineer and managing director will usually expect to act as counsellors to the agent, supporting him in his decisions, guiding him, and helping him when difficulties involving major decisions arise. Seldom will they actually instruct the agent as to what he should do. The managing director naturally has the final decision where alternative courses of action pose especially difficult problems.

In his daily work the agent will give the great majority of his instructions verbally. He will have frequent contact with the general foreman, the sub-agents, and engineers as he goes about the job; only occasionally will he call a joint meeting of several key personnel in order to work out a programme of attack on any particular part of the job. This decision having been arrived at, the agent will issue any needful instructions through his office manager, his general foreman, or through his sub-agents. When things go wrong with an intended plan—and this is an almost daily occurrence—the agent must be informed immediately, because upon him centralises all information, and from him must come the decision to alter the proposed course of action. He may have to act quickly to make the necessary change, and here his capacity for making right decisions in times of emergency are put to the test. As he considers what to do in some newly developed situation he may have to take into account many interrelated factors, and he may have to make a judgment as to which of these factors have the most important bearing upon the situation. Principally his decisions will be influenced by the need to keep the job moving; he cannot afford to let men and machines stand idle. But he also has to bear in mind the capacities of the people who work for him. Once the agent has made up his mind, it is the office manager and sub-agent's job to see that the necessary instructions get through to the right persons without delay.

The deputy agent and sub-agents

On large contracts there is frequently a deputy agent who takes over for the agent over the whole contract, and sub-agents who have responsibilities for particular parts of the job or particular services.

Frequently the agent will delegate most of his office work and the ordering of materials to his deputy or to his senior sub-agent. Sometimes the whole responsibility for measurement is placed upon one sub-agent, who collates the measurements from the section engineers and quantity surveyors, and supervises the production of the monthly claim. On jobs which naturally divide up into separate parts the agent may put one of his sub-agents in charge of a remote part, making him responsible for the whole of that part. Thus, sub-agents' jobs vary, being sometimes administrative rather than engineering, sometimes for complete parts of the work and at other times for special aspects of it only.

The site engineer

Upon the site engineer and his staff rests the main responsibility for seeing that the works are constructed to the right lines and levels. Their work will also include advising the agent on all design and engineering matters. These duties will be varied, and will include taking site levels, lining in and levelling constructional work, planning temporary access roads and bridges, dealing with power supply, water supply, drainage, concrete batching plant foundations, and so on. An important aspect of their work will be the keeping of progress and quality records. Each engineer will, in addition, normally have a section of the work to look after, measuring up the work in his section weekly or monthly and making returns to the central organisation. Some firms expect their engineers to take an active part in the executive control of the work so that they may be regarded as in training to become agents. On small sites, the site engineer may virtually act as sub-agent as well, the two jobs merging into one when the job is not large enough to justify having both a sub-agent and an engineer.

The plant engineer

The position of plant engineer is normally always separately designated from that of general foreman, even on small jobs; although, depending on his status, he is either called plant engineer or plant foreman. His job is to maintain and service the plant and to have it available as required by the constructional programme laid down by the agent. He will be kept advised of long-term planning by the agent, and of day-to-day planning by the general foreman or a sub-agent. Under his control come the fitters and welders, and it will often be his job to maintain power supplies to site—i.e. to run the site generators. His job is rather a difficult one, in that he is responsible for the care of the plant, and he frequently finds himself at loggerheads with the agent and foremen, who usually want to get on with the job at all costs. He often has to persuade his fitters to work overtime to get the plant in readiness for the next day's work, or to cope with breakdowns. There is a growing opinion that the plant foreman's status ought to be equal with that of a sub-agent; that he ought to be designated as plant engineer so that he is in a position of greater strength to resist the unsuitable use of the plant and to demand its withdrawal from site for proper maintenance. Properly maintained and operated plant can have double the life of plant which is not looked after carefully.

The office manager

Within the site office, the agent's principal administrator is the office manager, upon whom lies the responsibility for carrying out most of the paper work—correspondence, issuing of orders for materials, receiving and checking accounts, making up pay sheets, etc. He will usually have working under him a pay clerk, order clerk, correspondence secretary, and accounts clerk, who in turn control other staff, such as invoice checkers, storekeepers, messengers, tea boys, staff car drivers, and night watchmen. The office manager must be efficient, because upon him rests the responsibility for seeing that materials flow on to the site as required and that all invoices and accounts are properly dealt with. There may be a thousand or more accounts to deal with per month. Unless there is a separate site cashier, the office manager will also have to handle the workmen's pay. Large amounts of cash may pass under his control, and he must therefore be a man of integrity, sharply sensitive to any mishandling of the cash. His work of this nature will naturally be subjected to auditing checks carried out from time to time by accountants from the head office of the contractor.

The general foreman

The general foreman is the agent's right-hand man for the execution of the work in the field. His explicit duty is to keep the work moving ahead daily as the agent has planned it. On a large contract, much of his daily work is concerned with issuing detailed instructions to the foremen and co-ordinating their work. He has to be a man of wide practical knowledge and long experience, so that he can, if need be, demonstrate personally how things should be done. He should spend a lot of his time outside, visiting all parts of the work under his control at least once a day. He needs to keep the sub-agent advised of his wants for materials and equipment, the plant engineer about machines needed, and he constantly calls upon the engineering staff to set out lines, levels, and sight rails.

General foremen have much authority on site and any junior engineer who fails to get on with a foreman of standing may find days on site will be numbered by the patience that foreman is willing to exercise. The agent must support a foreman who is keeping the job going at the right speed and in the right manner, irrespective of minor errors of decision. General foremen may sometimes have strange prejudices and inexplicable attitudes, but are often astonishingly capable men. Frequently it is the general foreman who contributes most to changing the job from a set of plans into a finished structure. The foreman must be able to read engineers' drawings—a feat made no easier by the way some engineers draw them. He has to have an extensive practical knowledge of a wide variety of crafts, coupled with a feeling for natural materials, especially for the behaviour of soils and rock. He has to have a knowledge of what machines can do, the basic principles of levelling and surveying. In all this he must have a thoroughly practical turn of mind. But he has also to be boss of the gangers and their men; not just in title, but in an actual all-persuasive way to get the best out of the men by the force of his own personality and example. This, by itself, is a rare capacity. He must finally possess foresight and planning ability, and at least a modest clerical ability sufficient to shuffle up time sheets and get them in some semblance of order. Good general foremen often do not get the honour they deserve from the profession.

The skilled tradesmen and gangers

The skilled men include carpenters, bricklayers, pipe jointers, steel fixers, crane and machine drivers, fitters, miners, and similar specialists. They are usually recruited locally for the job, the contractor having relatively few such men permanently in his employment. On a site employing perhaps a hundred workmen, probably no more than a dozen are in the permanent employment of the contractor, though many will either have worked for that same contractor on some previous site elsewhere or in the same area for other contractors. A contractor who deals in a number of small contracts in a limited area finds it much easier to keep key men in permanent employment, but his livelihood is then dependent upon finding enough work in the area of his choice.

The system unfortunately frustrates any proper growth of loyalty between a contracting firm and the bulk of the men normally in its employment. Inevitably the men are concerned first and last with the pay they can get; they are not much concerned with working conditions, because these are only temporary; and they see little point in going out of their way to act diligently on the contractor's behalf, because the contractor is in no position to reward such loyalty by offering a guarantee of further employment. As a result, pay is often very high; the actual cost of labour to the contractor (and therefore to the employer) being frequently double the nominal hourly rate paid because of the bonus, overtime, lodging allowances, and other inducements which have to be added to the basic rates. The working conditions are often poor—far below that which would be tolerated by other groups of workers; the workmanship is frequently poor, and is seldom better than adequate. The system achieves not much more than getting the numbers of men required; it can seldom produce a selected team of good workers unless the job extends over a number of years. More often than not an element of irresponsibility among the men makes site life unattractive for the older and wiser man, so that his conscientious approach to the work is lost when he takes up other employment in better conditions and in more congenial company elsewhere. Something will eventually have to be done about this system, or standards of skill and workmanship, already low, will decline still further, and there will be little possibility of applying on site new techno- logical skills to improve methods and outputs, save those which directly replace labour with machines.

General labourers

As to the workmen, they work—and they are much the same the world over. But before they will work they expect two things from the job—the right pay to the last rightful penny, and clear instructions as to what to do. They do not expect, and a surprisingly large number do not even want to know, what is the plan for tomorrow or next week. But they have a sixth sense for knowing if there is not a plan, or if the job is floundering through lack of proper direction from above. The moment this happens they lose respect for the personnel directing them. They do not mind the agent being strict and tough; what they ask is to be fairly treated in regard to pay and to have someone to work for who 'knows what he is doing'. Under the latter circumstances they will give unstinted loyal service, even in the most arduous of conditions, or in positions of personal danger, so long as they respect and have faith in the man who is their boss. It is an educational experience to work alongside men on a construction site. It will then be learned that, though a man works primarily because of the pay offered him, he is not without a pride in his work however simple that is. His reputation among his workmates and with the agent will not relate to what he does but whether, at his level, he is a 'good worker'. A man will therefore resent criticism on the grounds of his intel- ligence because this is unjust. He cannot help his limitations. What he offers is his loyalty to do what he can do—if he is properly paid—and he knows, as every engineer should know, that civil engineering would be impossible without his help.

On many sites, small groups of men arrange themselves naturally in teams under an acknowledged leader, and an intelligent foreman is quick to recognise this, for they will form a stable and trusty team of workers. More than likely they will have worked together elsewhere, and to sack one may frequently bring about the resignation of the whole team; but, on the obverse side, to appoint one may well bring in a whole gang for the good of the job. Such groups are formed for mutual protec- tion on the basis of confidence in the leader and amiable tolerance for the weaker members of the gang, who, whatever they might lack in mental capacity, are known to be capable of pulling their weight. The loyalty within such groups is strong, and the ability of the leader to get effective and willing work from otherwise unpromising men is an instructive lesson in the art of management.

Safety precautions and regulations

The main legislation covering safety precautions to be taken on civil engineering construction sites is contained in four sets of Regulations issued by the Minister of Labour under the Factories Act, 1961. These are:

the Construction (General Provisions) Regulations 1961
the Construction (Lifting Operations) Regulations 1961
the Construction (Working Places) Regulations 1966
the Construction (Health and Welfare) Regulations 1966

There are other acts and regulations in force relating to certain aspects of civil engineering work—e.g. the Mines and Quarries Act 1954; Work in Compressed Air Special Regulations 1958; Diving Operations Special Regulations 1960; together with older regulations and acts applying to electrical supplies, petroleum storage, and woodworking machinery.

Under the Construction Regulations, the contractor is made responsible for the safety of his own employees, and he is also responsible in certain circumstances for the safety of other people—such as when he undertakes blasting operations, or in the use of machinery. The employee, on his part, must co-operate in observing all safety precautions the employer lays down. The full Regulations are extensive, and the resident engineer should possess a copy of them on site. Only the salient points can be mentioned here.

Any contractor having more than twenty men in his employment is obliged to appoint at least one experienced person to act as a safety officer, charged with general supervision of the safety requirements of the Regulations and with promoting the safe conduct of work generally. He need not be fully employed on safety work, but must be given sufficient time to discharge his duties with reasonable efficiency. His name must be entered on the copy of the Regulations (or an abstract thereof) which is required to be exhibited on sites.

Before the contractor's men are allowed to work in excavations, tunnels, cofferdams, or caissons there must have been conducted a *thorough examination* of all parts of such excavation, tunnel, etc., by a competent person within the previous seven days. A thorough examination of all parts is also required before the men commence work after some unexpected fall of material, or damage to supports, or possibility of damage from the use of explosives. Reports of such thorough examinations have to be made in the prescribed form on the same day as the examination has taken place, except where the work will be completed within six weeks.

In addition, daily *inspection* of that part of an excavation in which men are to be employed is required; and an inspection must be made at the commencement of every shift of the face of every tunnel, the working end of every trench more than 2 m deep, and the base or crown of every shaft. These daily inspections do not have to be recorded.

With regard to lifting appliances, the Regulations call for a number of *inspections*, *thorough examinations*, and *tests* at different intervals of time according to the type of apparatus being inspected or tested. Weekly inspections of lifting appliances by the driver, if competent to carry this out (if not, by some other competent person), are called for, together with weekly inspections of safe-load indicators on cranes. Most other apparatus has to be tested and/or thoroughly examined after erection or alteration and before it is put to use. Cranes, crabs, and winches must have been tested and thoroughly examined within the previous four years; lifting appliances thoroughly examined within the previous fourteen months; and hoists thoroughly examined within the previous six months—and all must be re-examined or re-tested after undergoing any substantial alteration or, in the case of hoists, tested and thoroughly examined after erection or heightening. Certificates of test and thorough examination must be issued on the prescribed form before any apparatus is put into use.

Other provisions of the Regulations cover such matters as—the fencing of excavations or drops, a guard rail or barrier being required (where practicable) wherever a person might fall more than 2 m; scaffolding; use of explosives; ventilation of excavations; safeguarding men working over or adjacent to water; precautions in the use of locomotives and other vehicles; demolition precautions; provision of safety nets and belts; precautions when raising or lowering loads, and the inspection of timbering and various forms of lifting devices.

Both a legal and a moral obligation lies upon the contractor to comply with these Regulations because of the great need to reduce accidents in the civil engineering industry. The Federation of Civil Engineering Contractors point out that, on present statistics, the chances are that one man out of every fifty now working on civil engineering sites will meet his death from an accident on site.

Accounting methods

While the agent may have very wide authority on the site, the large sums of money he must necessarily commit his firm to spending mean that some form of auditing and control over expenditure is desirable, and this is best exercised by his head office.

A normal procedure is to require the agent to make all his purchases, which are not from local suppliers nor extremely urgent, through head office. This system can only work, of course, if both head office and the site are in the same country and not too great a distance apart. Under this method the agent decides what materials he wants and from whom he wishes to obtain them and at what price, but the actual order to the supplier is issued from the head office of the firm in response to a 'requisition' from the agent stating all the details. In this manner the agent is relieved of a considerable proportion of accounting work and most of the paying. When the materials ordered are delivered the materials clerk fills in a delivery sheet. In due course the supplier's account comes to the agent; it is checked against the original order and the 'materials received' sheets. All being in order, it is then signed and forwarded to head office for payment. Alternatively, invoices are sent to head office after they have been checked against 'materials received' notes from site before payment.

Thus, the agent does not have to handle cash other than that necessary to meet wages (sent to him weekly or credited to a local bank account) and the amount necessary to meet relatively small local expenditure. Meantime, since head office are receiving requisitions and accounts regularly, they are in a position to keep a running total of the expenditure on the job and can carry out any necessary costing. From time to time the head office accountant, or his representative, will visit the site to examine the local accounts, pay sheets, and so on, thus relieving the agent to some extent of the need for local auditing.

The method is also useful in that it permits bulk purchasing by a central purchasing department at the contractor's head office. The experience of this department is also available to the agent, who may not know who are the suppliers for certain types of specialised materials. In such a case all the agent has to do (in good time of course) is to send a requisition to his head office describing what he wants, and the central purchasing department will tell him what is available and at what price. It is always advantageous to an agent to use head office as much as possible in order to keep the site staff numbers down. The more site staff an agent has, the less effective time he will have for his real work, which is to keep the job progressing in the most economical way. On the other hand, if he does call upon head office for assistance the system must be such that he gets swift assistance which is not fettered by a large amount of paper work.

Providing plant

Another matter on which the agent cannot have complete control is the provision of plant. A large portion of a contractor's capital is tied up in plant, and an agent cannot buy additional plant, as this means committing the contractor to laying out more capital. Obviously the total amount of money that a contractor can permit to have tied up in plant is a decision that lies with him, and it cannot be simply the summation of what all his agents require on their different jobs at different times.

It is usual therefore for the contractor to set up a head office plant depot as a separate organisation. He permits plant to be purchased up to a given total capital expenditure, and the plant organisation loans the plant out to the various agents at certain fixed rates. The rates are calculated to give enough return to the plant organisation to enable it to maintain plant in good condition, undertake major overhauls, and to purchase renewals when old plant is worn out. The rates are set high enough for a 'profit' to be shown on the capital outlay—this profit, of course, going back to the contractor. There is no actual cash transfer, but when an agent orders a piece of plant from the plant organisation he knows that the head office accounts for his job will be debited with a weekly amount which represents the cost of that plant. Since the agent's task is to make a profit on his job for the contractor, in which profit he may hope to share, he will be economical in ordering plant from his head office, and that which he does order he will try to use with maximum efficiency. Also charged to his job will be the cost of transporting the plant to the site and away from it. These transport costs can be heavy, so the agent will not willingly change around the type and numbers of plant he is using. All this is conducive to good usage of plant if the rates of charge to jobs are fair.

In a typical arrangement the cost of plant to a job would be debited weekly in accordance with a weekly return from the agent showing the plant he has on site and the amount it has been worked. If the plant is idle on the site the rate per hour may be two-thirds or one-half of the rate charged when the plant is working; if the plant is broken down there should be no charge until repairs are effected. The site fitters are expected to carry out all normal maintenance, the plant foreman having to order all spare parts required, which are then charged to the job. Major over-hauls, i.e. stripping down plant completely, would be undertaken at the plant depot or at the maker's works and not charged to the agent's job. The plant idle charges would be effective in preventing the agent holding on to plant on the site, simply because he thinks he might need it. Either the idle rate continues or the agent must declare the plant no longer required by him, in which case it can be removed from the job and sent to another, immediately the need arises.

An agent is normally permitted to hire further plant from outside plant-hire firms where specialist plant is required, or where the contractor feels it is not economic to lay out more capital on plant. The internal hire rates may be so fixed that there is a small advantage to the agent in hiring from his own firm, so as to encourage maximum usage of the firm's plant; but not so great a difference as between outside and inside hire rates as to cause an agent to complain he is hardly done by in having to use more outside hired plant than another of the contractor's agents.

The cost of working repairs to contractor's plant is very high, representing some 25 per cent or more of the normal outside hire rate. The frequency of repairs is particularly high for mobile plant, where tracks and tyres may need renewal every few months at substantial cost. Wire ropes for cranes and cable controls for scrapers need constant renewal, and it is necessary to hold a stock of such ropes.

References
Construction (General Provisions) Regulations 1961. H.M.S.O. (SI 1580).
Construction (Lifting Operations) Regulations 1961. H.M.S.O. (SI 1581).
Construction (Working Places) Regulations 1966. H.M.S.O. (SI 94).
Construction (Health and Welfare) Regulations 1966. H.M.S.O. (SI 95).
Guide to the Construction Regulations 1961.
Supervisor's Safety Booklet
    (Both above from Federation of Civil Engineering Contractors.)
Working Rule Agreement—Civil Engineering Construction Conciliation Board for
    Great Britain. Romney House, Tufton Street, London S.W.1.
Safety on the Site. B. A. C. Whyte. United Trade Press 1970.

CHAPTER 4

The Engineer's Site Organisation

The resident engineer

The engineer's representative and chief responsible person on site is known as the *resident engineer*.* He is the opposite number to the agent, being the chief executive on site for the engineer. His job is primarily one of seeing that the works are built as the engineer has designed and instructed they shall be built, and that the contractor carries out all his obligations under the contract for the construction.

The resident engineer is therefore responsible only to the engineer even if, as happens occasionally, he is actually paid by the employer or is a member of the employer's staff seconded to act as a resident engineer on the construction of some new works. In whatever circumstances he finds himself, every resident engineer's loyalty must be to the engineer who designed the works and who is responsible for administering the contract of construction entered into between employer and contractor. It follows that the resident engineer must always remember that his actions may have consequential effects on the responsibilities and obligations of the engineer, and therefore in all cases of doubt as to correctness of his attitude or procedure he should first report to the engineer. He may make suggestions to the engineer; he may point out difficulties and advise on their overcoming; he is the engineer on the spot, able by his close connection with the work to anticipate site conditions and see when trouble is coming and report to and forewarn the engineer accordingly. His job is a technical one, acting as a 'scout' for the engineer on engineering matters; but it is not his job to take upon himself responsibilities and decisions which properly lie with the engineer.

The engineer cannot pass on to anyone else the final responsibility he alone holds for the design and supervision of construction of the works. He may employ others, or use others, to do part of the actual work required in the processes of design and supervision of construction, but he cannot rid himself of his responsibility for their actions, since his contract with the employer is a personal one, by which he undertakes to use his own skill and judgment. He is therefore negligent if his supervision is so lax that his agents or servants can make errors amounting to negligence which he does not notice.

Further, it follows that an engineer cannot rely on the employer to

---

* Care should be taken to distinguish this term from the 'site engineer', who is the contractor's engineer serving the contractor's agent.

say whether work is satisfactory or not (from an engineering standpoint), nor can he throw upon the employer the responsibility for making a proper examination of foundations, levels, etc. If he uses the employer to obtain this information for him the engineer is liable for any negligence of the employer. A little thought will show the justice of this, for if an employer uses an engineer to design and supervise the erection of a building he employs the engineer for just that special skill which he, the employer, does not himself possess. The engineer is employed for the specific purpose of saying whether or not foundations are satisfactory, whether or not the site surveys are adequate, and whether or not the work is satisfactory.

The resident engineer needs to bear these matters in his mind, so that he is absolutely clear to whom he is responsible and to whom he must refer matters. He must be careful himself not to call in the employer or to rely on the *engineering* opinions of the employer when he should in fact be obtaining the opinions of the engineer.

Duties of the resident engineer

The resident engineer may be expected to carry out some, or perhaps all, of the following activities as may be requested of him by the engineer, but without relieving the contractor of his obligations:—

> to co-ordinate the work of various contractors; to agree detailed programmes of work; to check that all necessary instructions have been given to contractors and authorisations obtained.
>
> to check that all materials are ordered in good time and all necessary permits for them are obtained;
>
> to see that the requirements of specifications in regard to materials and workmanship are complied with by contractors;
>
> to watch for faulty workmanship or material incorporated in the works and to issue instructions for remedying such faults;
>
> to check the line and level and layout of the structure while it is being erected to see that it conforms with the drawings and intentions of the contract;
>
> to issue such further instructions and clarifications of detail as are necessary;
>
> to measure the amount of work done for the purposes of payment and to calculate such payments;
>
> to keep a record of all measurements and tests and to bring plans into conformity with the work as actually executed;
>
> to act as a channel for all claims and disputes and to provide the facts which are relevant;
>
> to see that the finished works are free from defects, tested, and set properly functioning;
>
> to ascertain the final value of the work done under the various contracts;
>
> to report regularly to the engineer on all the above matters.

The list above does not necessarily include all the duties the resident engineer may have delegated to him by the engineer. At the start of any contract the engineer should make clear, by means of a formal letter to the contractor, what powers he is delegating to his representative on site* so that the contractor is fully aware of this and so that no misunderstanding occurs. Thus, it should be noted that the resident engineer will not normally have powers delegated to him to order extra work, since this must be by written Variation Order signed by the engineer. The letter is therefore important, for, if omitted, the contractor has no proper guide as to the validity of instructions issued by the resident engineer—he could, in extreme, either repudiate them all as not coming from 'the engineer' designated in the contract; or he could accept them all under the assumption (which is not far from the truth in the event of no letter of authorisation being issued) that the engineer must be bound by all actions of his representatives.

A resident engineer will be wise to make sure for himself that in the first stages of the work no delay will be caused by the employer in such matters as allowing access to the site or getting the necessary permits to build. All such permits and agreements with landowners should have been obtained before the contract has been let, but in some cases this may not have been possible, and the resident engineer must ascertain whether there are any restrictions on the use of the land and advise the engineer accordingly.

It is normally required that all orders for materials placed by the contractor are to be approved, and this duty will commence early in the contract. In like manner, at a later stage in the contract the resident engineer must see that all sub-contractors who are appointed are to the approval of the engineer.

The resident engineer's chief duty is to watch and check the workmanship and materials used. He acts in this manner as an agent for the engineer, and therefore in all major matters he must refer to his superiors, particularly in the case of disputes. He should always bear in mind that the engineer is responsible for the actions of the resident engineer and that, in addition, if the engineer is a consulting engineer his responsibility is unlimited in law. That is to say, if a resident engineer acts carelessly for instance, in founding a building on doubtful ground without sufficient precautions, and the building collapses as a result, then the consulting engineer (whose agent the resident engineer is) will be held to be responsible, and the employer may sue the consulting engineer for the loss of the building and all incidental damage. Any passers-by injured may also claim compensation, and if the consulting engineer is proved to have acted negligently or carelessly, then all his wealth and possessions may be distrained upon, if necessary, in payment of compensation. Where the engineer is in the employ of the employer, then the latter is, of course, responsible for all the actions of his agents and servants.

* As required by Clauses 1(1) (d) and 2 of the General Conditions of Contract.

Responsibility for impartial skilled judgments

It is also frequently said that the engineer (and thus his resident engineer) acts as an arbitrator between the employer and the contractor. This, however, is only so far as the contract conditions do not permit any dispute to be referred to an independent arbitrator. It will, or should, be obvious that the resident engineer must act impartially. That is to say he may not take the opinions of the contractor or the employer as being the basis of his own opinions. Exactly like the engineer, the resident engineer has been appointed for his special engineering skill and knowledge, which he is bound to apply to matters put before him, and his decisions must be based on that skill and knowledge.

This does not mean that the resident engineer refuses to listen to the opinions of the contractor or employer—indeed, he must do so, as he must listen to the opinions of any other interested party, but it is his duty to base his resulting advice to the engineer on his *own* opinions, and the decision eventually arrived at by the engineer, if given honestly and in the absence of provisions to go to arbitration, is final, even if later shown to be wrong.

The last statement may at first sight appear surprising, and needs some explanation. The position arises as follows. An employer, wishing to have a structure erected, but not being knowledgeable in the art of building, employs an engineer (either a firm of consulting engineers, or an engineer from his own staff) whose skilled profession it is to design and supervise the erection of buildings. This engineer does not represent himself as having more than the normal skill of members of his profession, though he may have certain specialist knowledge of certain techniques. The employer appoints this engineer in charge of his proposed works, and, having made his choice as to which engineer he shall employ, the employer must thereafter abide by decisions made by the engineer of his choice.

So long as the engineer (and his resident engineer) acts honestly, use at least the ordinary skill and knowledge of a member of his profession, has no concealed relationship with the contractor or does not receive any secret commissions, payments, or gifts from the contractor, and, finally, acts within the terms of the contract between himself and the employer, then the employer is bound by the actions of the engineer, and must pay to the contractor such sums of money as the engineer certifies as being due.

The exercise of 'ordinary skill and knowledge of a member of his profession' includes the duty to refrain from negligence. Negligence has been defined as 'being under the duty to use care and not doing that which a prudent man would do, or doing that which a prudent man would not do, and thereby causing damage'. Hence if an engineer possesses normal skill and knowledge, exercises these attributes in his decisions, gives such decisions with care, and honestly holds them to be his own, then—even if he has made a mistake—this decision is valid and the contractor must be paid by the employer for what he has been told to do.

In short, and put colloquially, if an employer 'buys himself an engineer' to see a building go up for him, then so long as this engineer acts honestly and with normal competence and care, then the employer must accept the decisions this engineer makes for him.

As mentioned in Chapter 1, there is no contract between the contractor and the engineer, and so long as the contractor has to carry out his work 'to the satisfaction of the engineer' he must fulfil this obligation unless he can prove that the engineer has acted fraudulently, or deceitfully or in collusion with the employer or beyond the terms of his warranted authority.

It is as well to remember that fraud has been held to be proved when 'a false representation has been made (1) knowingly; or (2) without belief in its truth; or (3) recklessly, careless whether it is true or false . . .'.

In all his dealings with both employer and contractor in approving materials and workmanship, in measuring up and issuing certificates, in issuing extra-works orders and variation orders, in preparing subsidiary estimates, in issuing further engineering drawings and designs, the resident engineer must exercise the same virtues as the engineer. Finally, he must act within the terms of the agreement between the employer and the engineer.

A resident engineer must therefore particularly note the requirements of the employer, especially where this employer is a local authority or other statutory body, so that the engineer may be guided to conform with the standing rules of such authority. He must be careful not to accept any favours from the contractor, and he must be careful not to let important matters slip through his hands without checking them for himself.

Miscellaneous points to watch

Where a penalty clause exists, the resident engineer must remind the engineer to take this into account (if necessary) in the production of the final certificate. An issue of a final certificate without reference to any penalties written into the contract might be taken as an act of negligence by the engineer if he should have deducted penalty money from the certificate but did not.

The resident engineer should not accept lower grade materials or workmanship at prices lower than the prices tendered in the bill of quantities unless the engineer agrees that the inferior material or work is still satisfactory for the purpose of the structure. It is the duty of the engineer to present a completed contract to the employer, not an incomplete or unsatisfactorily executed contract, however much the price may have been adjusted.

The resident engineer should, whenever an alteration is proposed by the contractor, automatically reply, 'How much more is it going to cost?' This question will prevent misunderstandings arising later about whether or not the contractor was expecting extra payment for the alteration.

He must give *prompt* notice to the contractor on defects arising. Otherwise the contractor is entitled to assume that the work is satisfactory.

If part of the works are taken over by the employer before a completion certificate is given, the resident engineer must be watchful over the work taken over so that he is in a position to advise the engineer as to what subsequent deterioration in the condition of the work is due to its premature use, and what due to inherent defects in it. The contractor is not responsible for deterioration due to wear and tear.

If the resident engineer gives to the employer estimates for additional work, either direct or through the engineer, he must be careful in such estimates, because the engineer can be held responsible for want of care in making such estimates.

Where a problem in the construction calls for the exercise of special skill which the engineer himself possesses, or which specialist engineers possess who have already been employed in the design stages of the work in addition to the engineer, the resident engineer should not exercise his own judgment, but should refer the matter to the engineer.

The legal position of the resident engineer

The legal or contractual standing of the resident engineer is, on the surface, somewhat weak and ineffectual when compared with the responsibilities and duties he is asked to undertake in connection with a contract for construction. He is, in law, only the agent for the engineer, who is responsible for the supervision of the construction of the work, and all the resident engineer's rights and duties are as a servant to the engineer. He is not legally an arbitrator; he may have no power to order extras; he has no power to instruct the contractor to deviate from the contract drawings; he cannot certify any payments to be made to the contractor; in many cases he is not even the final judge of what is and what is not good workmanship: in fact, so far as he acts he can only do so with the express sanction of the engineer, and his signature on any document is only of significance to that engineer.

Yet, in practice, he is frequently called upon to act as if he had these powers for himself. By his competent judgment, by his engineering skill, by his tact and successful negotiating qualities, and by his co-ordinating and organising abilities he can be, and often is in practice, the key man and the chief responsible person for the successful carrying out of construction works. His legal standing may be almost worthless, his existence but casually mentioned in the General Conditions of Contract, and yet he is without a doubt one of the most important persons on a contract.

At first sight, therefore, the position of the resident engineer would appear to be most unfavourable: he has a job with duties and responsibilities so ill-defined that it would seem to be a post which had more frustration in it than compensations, more kicks than rewards. And yet the reverse is the case. Probably no job is more dear to the heart of a true engineer; on no other type of work is the engineer so happy, so free to take his own decisions, so fully compensated by the nature of the work he puts into it. Every engineer who has been 'out on works' looks back on those days with unalloyed pleasure, and his conversation and his thoughts are ever afterwards coloured by his experiences during those exciting and hectic years. Why is this?

There are many reasons, but perhaps the most powerful is that in a job of this nature the engineer at last begins to create. His working output consists of solving the multitude of problems that need to be tackled successfully to create a structure. His judgment, though perhaps legally invalid, is in fact decisive. Everything he does is to the one end of creating a real and working structure that was once but a collection of ideas on paper; he derives from this a satisfaction which defies proper description.

Furthermore the detailed nature of the work is so varied that there can be few men who are not keenly absorbed in some aspect of it. Each day brings fresh engineering problems, demanding skill and ingenuity to solve, and a solution must often be found without delay or hesitation. If an engineer cannot rally to the need for quick thinking and clear, responsible judgment he is not made in the likeness of a true engineer at all.

Likewise, there are problems of organisation, the need to plan into the future, the need to direct multitudinous and often complicated operations into one organised whole. Here the organising abilities of the engineer come into full play, and many men find great satisfaction in this aspect of the work.

There is the need to exercise a human understanding also. The engineer must learn to judge the capabilities of his band of technicians, their reactions to emergencies and certain types of work. He needs care in his personal approach, and must know when to cajole or explain, when to ask for guidance, or to sympathise, and, at times, when to stand upon his rights (such as he has) and insist with courtesy on certain lines of action. He stands or falls by his abilities in this respect.

The resident engineer's staff

Even on a small job it will be necessary for the resident engineer to be assisted by an inspector and a typist or other office worker. On the large jobs he will need a team of engineers and other technical specialists to assist him, together with several inspectors, a secretary, accounts clerk, and other administrative workers. A resident engineer with two assistant engineers, two inspectors, a typist, and a clerk should, however, be able to control a substantial amount of work unless twenty-four-hour working is being adopted by the contractor or the work is very widely spread. On major projects costing several millions of pounds, the staff will be very much larger, as shown in Fig. 2, and will include a number of experts.

There is a school of thought which believes that the whole responsibility of the resident engineer and his staff ends with the obligation to see that the works are constructed precisely in accordance with the requirements laid down by the specification and drawings. Laudable though this conception is, it is wrong.

The resident engineer and his staff should regard themselves as engineers capable not only of supervising the construction of the works as laid down in the contract documents but capable also of contributing towards the superiority of those works over what has been done before. There can hardly be a project which has not been bettered by suggestions or advice coming from the site staff. Thus, while all contractual matters must be expeditiously attended to, all proper records kept, all required tests and measurements made, all instructions properly channelled, sufficient time must be allowed for surveying the project as a whole, to ensure that the methods and designs being pursued are at all times best suited to the revealed site conditions and the intended function of the project.

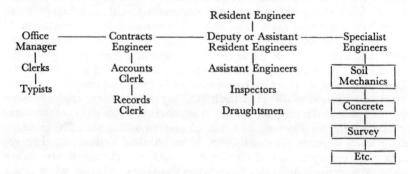

Fig. 2. The engineer's site control staff for a medium-sized job. The specialist engineers will vary in number according to the nature of the work. Assistant resident engineers may each take a different section of the work if it is a large job, in which case there is likely to be a chief resident engineer with two or more resident engineers under him.

Engineering assistants. In general, a wise resident engineer will ensure that his engineering assistants are kept continuously informed about the progress of the job as a whole, and he will from time to time rearrange their duties so that in due course each engineer becomes familiar with all parts of the job and has an opportunity to take part in all the aspects of engineering that the job offers. The time an engineer spends on site is one of the most instructive periods of his career, and it is a duty laid upon professionally qualified civil engineers to see that their younger colleagues have the fullest opportunity to learn as much as they can while on site.

Tolerance must be extended to a young engineer's mistakes. An accident-prone man can quickly compile a legion of troubles. He can, for example, set a building out the wrong way round, or lay a drain with a rise instead of a fall. The junior engineer on site may mistake a busybody for a foreman or order the employer off the site as an intruder; he may park his car on the spot reserved for the agent, or do many other things which bring a despairing gasp from his elders and a whistle of amazement from his colleagues. Provided he does not intend to be a genius at this sort of thing and is simply a victim of ordinary human error, he will survive, and live the wiser. But he must not make the same error twice, for the sake of his record sheet, and should he fail to learn by experience, there must result a swift withdrawal of his services from site.

Inspectors. The inspectors on the resident engineer's staff have the task of continuously inspecting the work. Theirs is primarily an outside job, but they must also book down detailed accounts of the progress of the work and all relevant conditions of working. They are usually skilled tradesmen having special practical experience in one or more trades, so that, if need be, they can advise the resident engineer whether the contractor is complying with standard trade practices and what are the practical implications of the requirements of the specification. They must be able to judge quality, workmanship, and finish of work; and if there is something wrong they must be able to advise why it is wrong and what is the right method that should be adopted.

Inspectors naturally tend to be older men, but this need be no handicap, because they must be tough in character in order to exert their influence properly on the job. The trouble is that adequately experienced inspectors are scarce, because a good tradesman can find employment as a tradesman up to a late age. The young inspector, on the other hand, may be too enthusiastic; he may lack tact, and may try to get things altered, but not have sufficient experience to be able to do this tactfully. His youthful energy may lead him into discontent with his job as inspector because he may quickly perceive better ways of doing things, and not find himself successful in getting them done his way. Thus, the handling of inspectors by the resident engineer often calls for understanding. Good inspectors are rare; they deserve good payment, because they can be of immense benefit to the job—preserving the contractor from errors, and taking off the shoulders of the resident engineer much responsibility for seeing that the quality of work is maintained. In return the resident engineer must back them up in any dispute with the contractor. They have a very difficult task to undertake, and to have any of their instructions counter-manded by the resident engineer rapidly destroys their authority over the contractor.

The bad, or ineffective, inspector must be mentioned, because he does exist, and the resident engineer will then have a most difficult problem on his hands. Such a man can upset the relation between the resident engineer and agent, acting as a continual bone of contention between them. The resident engineer must not let this situation continue; he may have to do what everyone hates doing—sack a man because his capacities do not fit to the job. But before doing this, opportunities should be given several times over to see how the inspector fits in other sections of the work or in other duties. More consideration of the training of inspectors is needed; they are expected to be available on the labour market, yet no one has hitherto had any responsibility for training and producing them.

Office staff. On very small jobs the resident engineer may have to do his own typing. On larger jobs he will need a typist and probably an accounts clerk. On the largest jobs he will need a full administrative and clerical staff. Whatever the size of the staff, the chainman-cum-teaboy must not be forgotten, for his presence on even the smallest project can make the life of the staff a good deal more comfortable. When site conditions are miserable and engineers come back from outside work wet and cold it is a great help if the chainman is ready to serve up a warming drink and help get wet clothes dried, run errands for the engineers, and generally get them back in working condition again. The good resident engineer will see that his staff get this service; it helps the work a lot. The chainman is usually provided by the contractor under the contract, and woe betide the drafter of contract documents who does not include in the bill of quantities some item or other which provides for this service.

Relationship between resident engineer and agent

The resident engineer must not be surprised to find that on a new contract he is at first treated with a great deal of circumspection by the agent. He has to be, because one of the unknown factors the contractor has yet to discover, which is of considerable importance to him, is what kind of resident engineer will be in charge. The agent will need to go carefully at first so that he 'can get the measure' of the man who can daily interfere with contractual work, so that he can understand what are the special matters in which the resident engineer is interested, the methods of working he will want adopted, and whether he will be generally easy or difficult to get on with. In like manner, the resident engineer will be waiting to observe how competent the agent is, and what degree of trust can be placed upon him, so as to find out what amount of control will have to be exercised.

So far as the agent is concerned, he will want the resident engineer to be fair, reasonable, and understanding. He will want clear decisive instructions from the resident engineer, and he will want prompt answers to his requests for information. An agent must be given proper information and instructions *before* he does the work; *not after*, or when he is part way through. It is a frequent complaint by agents that the resident engineer fails to give this service or is indecisive in his instructions.

Another sort of nuisance to the contractor's agent is the resident engineer who is too keen on interfering in matters that should properly be handled (at least at first) by the contractor. Such a resident engineer may get into touch with sub-contractors, or let such sub-contractors approach him, without telling the agent what he is doing. Similarly, the over-keen resident engineer may be tempted to discuss the job with the foreman or gangers, a practice which is not permissible for the resident engineer or his staff without the agent's permission.

If the resident engineer has any complaints the agent will wish to be told about them personally, and he will want the complaints made *before* they are passed to anyone else. An especial nuisance to the agent is the resident engineer who is too meticulous and rigid in his views—who thinks he has been appointed to measure up every cubic yard to the third decimal place; or that every word written in the specification must be exactly and rigidly complied with by the contractor, irrespective of the practical consequences to the job or need to apply such conditions.

To be able to rely upon one's own judgment and to have that judgment considered right and fair, both by contractor and engineer, should be the principle aim of every resident engineer. This judgment must be founded on engineering skill and knowledge, and a proper perception of the intentions laid down in the specifications and drawings—tempered with a sense of justice and what is reasonable in the circumstances, and motivated by a desire to get the best end results.

Handling troubles

There will, of course, be times when troubles arise naturally. When bad workmanship comes to light, or when quite unsuitable methods are being used, it is the resident engineer's duty to have the work rectified or the unsuitable methods stopped. This is easy to say, but not so easy to carry out in practice. Suppose, to take an example, it comes to the resident engineer's notice that a partly built wall is being built to a very inferior standard—the bricks are chipped, the joints are irregular, and the face is not uniformly plane. Now the first essential in such matters is that the bad workmanship ought to be discovered at an early stage. It is no use letting it carry on; nor is it of use to find the defects out when the structure is complete or nearly complete—or all the troubles and difficulties of trying to get things right will be magnified.

The second essential is common sense; this is to keep one's temper, to refrain from accusing the contractor of fraud or incompetence, or from saying to the workmen, 'That has got to come down for a start.' Any one of these methods can be guaranteed to start things off with a row, which is not in the least helpful to anyone.

Instead, the resident engineer ought to ask the agent to come and look at the wall with him, indicating that he is unhappy about it. When they meet at the wall the wise resident engineer will say nothing, but will allow the agent to examine the wall for himself. One of two things will now happen—either the agent will make some admission of fault or he will say, 'What's wrong with it, then?' If the agent is ready to admit some fault there is no doubt that with careful handling all will be made well. If, on the other hand, the agent asks what is wrong, the resident engineer must tell him clearly, saying not only what is wrong but what would be right in the circumstances—confining his remarks to the work itself. A discussion will then have to take place as to the possible remedies to be adopted and, in discussing remedies, the resident engineer will have to be flexible. His main aim must be to get the matter put right, but he must be prepared at the same time to accept any reasonable alternative for achieving this purpose. For instance, instead of pulling the wall down and rebuilding it, the agent might offer instead to plaster the wall, at his own expense, to a presentable appearance. If, however, no solution appears possible which the agent will accept it is best to leave the matter over for the time being, either for another discussion after both parties have had more time to think about the problem or for reference to the engineer for his decision.

There will be occasions for the resident engineer when he is not at all sure what he should do. Even the opinions of experts may differ, and it may sometimes be very difficult for the resident engineer to decide whether or not he will accept some method proposed by the contractor's agent. The agent has to think up ways and means of doing things that are easiest and cheapest for him, which use the men and machines he has got, rather than men and machines he would otherwise have to bring on site. Naturally, he is quite likely to propose methods which come as a surprise to the resident engineer, who has been schooled to think in terms of using the 'right' machines and 'right' methods for each particular job. He will therefore find himself in considerable doubt as to whether some novel method, or some short-cut, proposed by the agent will bring about the end result required, or whether it will result in some eventual harm to the quality or durability of the permanent works.

The reasonable resident engineer will not wish to deprive the agent of opportunities for benefiting from his own skill; on the other hand, he must not allow chances to be taken which might eventuate in damage to the works. It is the quality of the work which is his main duty to safeguard. If, therefore, he permits the agent to proceed on his proposed method he would be quite within his rights to forewarn the agent that if any harm does result, then the contractor must make this harm good at his own expense. In coming to his decision, and in the event of his not being able to discuss the matter in time with the engineer, he will be wise if he discusses the problem with his own inspectors and engineering staff, for on these difficult matters it is always useful and encouraging to have a consensus of opinion on one's side.

More difficult cases

In the preceding examples it is presupposed that the agent knows what good workmanship is, and that he and the resident engineer intend to work out their differences. There are, of course, more difficult cases where matters cannot be settled on site and have to be brought to the attention of the engineer. It should be remembered that the main preoccupation of both engineer and contractor is to see the work done properly and in good time. If they feel that the resident engineer and agent are becoming too disputatious over matters not of primary importance it may be that they will conclude—as a matter of expediency rather than justice—that one or the other of the two men ought to be moved elsewhere.

Hence a word or two about the matters which are most commonly the cause of friction, and how to deal with them, might not be out of place.

One of the most difficult things for the resident engineer to tolerate is to stand by and see the agent make a mess of things. He sees the contractor's money and time being wasted, yet his suggestions for improvement are not accepted; he gets to hear, perhaps in a roundabout way, of complaints about how the job is being run; he fears that all this is stacking up trouble for the future and does not know quite what to do about it. In the first instance the resident engineer must convey his opinions to the agent. But he really cannot do more than this until either the speed or quality of the work is manifestly suffering. He must bear in mind that some people are less efficient than others, that the way one man goes about a job is not necessarily the only way, and that probably all contractors have periods when they do not give a job their best attention. He must therefore wait for a while and see what happens. When eventually he considers that there is the basis for real complaint he must place the facts before the engineer, and the latter will make the necessary decision. The engineer may take the complaint up officially with the contractor. If this action brings no remedy the situation begins to be serious and must be all the more carefully handled. It is true that the engineer has the right to require the withdrawal of an agent from site, but this is an extreme step, not to be taken unless all else fails. It can only be done if there is positive proof that the job is being mismanaged by the agent, not because the agent is a difficult character, or is eccentric, or because he has odd ways of going about things.

Hence, if a job is running badly, by far the most persuasive information likely to lead the contractor to make a necessary change is to inform him of any excessive amount of work that has had to be rejected as unsatisfactory, and to tell him of the probable loss on the job to date. This information must, of course, pass to the contractor via the engineer. It is not difficult to estimate a contractor's costs to a given date and to compare these with the payments due, and if this calculation shows a loss to the contractor and a probable continuation of it if the job flounders on under the same leadership, then the resident engineer may be gratified to see how quickly a contractor can act when convinced of the need in real terms.

The agent's side of the picture must not be forgotten. First and foremost, he will regard lack of appreciation of his difficulties as unreasonable. Secondly, the most certain way to lose an agent's respect and co-operation is to be continually 'reading the Specification at him' as if it were a holy writ, non-compliance with which is unthinkable. When the agent faces difficulties and is in dire need of help it is up to the resident engineer to relax conditions that are not essential, to permit other ways round to the end result desired. An agent will never resent a call from the resident engineer for especial care in some operation, or for strict compliance with the specification in matters of importance, or for a top-class finish for those parts of the job which will remain prominently in view; but in return for these extra services he will expect there will be other occasions where the strict letter of the specification is not appropriate and will not be called for by the resident engineer where compliance presents real difficulty.

Temptations

At Christmas—or some other festive occasion—cheerful visitors may appear in the doorway of the resident engineer's office, wishing him and his staff the season's greetings and perhaps extending refreshment. Politely but firmly, and without giving any offence, the good wishes may be accepted, but the gifts not. No doubt the gift is innocently intended; a nominated sub-contractor may be well pleased at the work sub-let to him and the fair dealing he has received, and wants to express his gratitude in tangible form. The engineer and every member of his staff stand in a very special position. They occupy a position of trust from whence the employer expects to receive truly independent professional judgment and the contractor expects to receive just interpretation of the conditions of contract. To accept a gift from a contractor destroys the engineer's claim to be acting impartially. Hence the acceptance of gifts, free services, cut-price materials, and matters of like nature from any contractor or sub-contractor is unprofessional and dangerous. Neither the resident engineer nor any member of his staff should receive them.

The question of acceptance of hospitality is a different matter. It is uncivil to refuse all invitations of this kind; courtesy demands that on the right occasions hospitality will be accepted and enjoyed in the spirit that it is given. The engineer's common sense will tell him whether it is right to accept any particular invitation. There are plenty of occasions when it is right—when a triumph on the job is to be celebrated, when personnel depart from the job, when troubles on the site need an 'off-the-job' atmosphere for settlement, when simply one man desires the company of another for a drink and a talk. As long as the giving and receiving of hospitality is conducted reasonably, these actions do much to promote friendly and willing co-operation on the site for the benefit of the job.

CHAPTER 5

Starting the Construction Work

The contractor's work

The contractor's agent will probably come to site with a small nucleus of permanent employees, and his main aim will be to get started on the actual work of construction as soon as possible. He will already have discussed with his head office a proposed layout for the site so that he will know where the temporary offices are to be sited, and the first of these he will have erected as soon as possible. He will have to visit the local labour exchange to make arrangements for taking men on at the site, and the work of choosing and appointing labourers he will probably delegate to the general foreman. From the very first moment on the job, the agent will find it necessary to have some clerical assistance; for preference his office manager will accompany him to site. This manager must immediately get to site a wide variety of equipment, machinery, and materials. Some of this will be sent out from the plant and equipment yard of the contractor's head office, but a large amount of supplementary equipment will be required from local sources. A visit to the local bank manager is necessary to make arrangements for withdrawing money for the payment of the men and, high up among the urgent tasks, will be a visit to the local G.P.O. manager to arrange for delivery of post to site and for the installation of a telephone line.

At first it may be necessary to adopt a number of temporary measures to get the job started. Concrete for hut foundations and other incidental work may have to be 'ready-mix' delivered to site; some small excavating plant may have to be hired, particularly for the work of excavating trenches for water supply and drainage, and a dozer may have to be hired for site clearance. A gang of labourers may first of all have to be set fencing off the site area, another gang on digging hut foundations and carrying out drainage work, a third gang assisting in the off-loading of materials and equipment; a carpenter will be necessary to take charge of hut erection; a site engineer will quickly be necessary for the setting out of levels and for producing quick sketches so as to direct the foremen and gangers what to do. It should not be much over a week before the agent, office manager, and general foreman have some kind of hut in which to work and before some kind of a start has been made on the permanent construction.

In the purchase of materials or the hire of machinery and equipment the agent will not commit himself overmuch. At first he may have to use sources of supply most readily at hand, but as soon as he can begin to estimate his long-term wants he will probably begin to 'shop around' to find out whether he is, in fact, using the cheapest sources. Once he is able to quote to possible suppliers his likely steady wants in the future, he will call for quotations on a comparable basis from several different suppliers, will have discussions with them to see that they can give both the quality and quantity he requires, and he may then place commencing orders with those most likely to give him the service he wants at the best price. Even so, a contractor seldom enters into formal contracts for the supply of goods; he makes arrangements for supplies to be delivered according to daily advice by telephone, covering the supply of such goods by a written order usually issued immediately the telephone call has been made. This gives him freedom to change to other suppliers, to alter, reduce, or increase orders just as he pleases. This may seem an unusual, indeed a risky arrangement to any local authority engineer, especially when the value of the orders to be placed (for such materials as concrete aggregates and so on) may be expected to run into tens of thousands of pounds. A local authority would normally invite tenders for the full expected amount of the order and then, by written contract, would enter into a binding agreement fixing supply and payment, the latter probably at fixed rates. Not so the contractor, who will seldom do more than order as he wants from week to week, giving at most only a verbal assurance that if the quantity, quality, and price of materials supplied continues acceptable he will continue to place his orders with the same supplier. Where a monopoly of supply exists—as in the case of cement—the contractor's agent will be forced to make the best bargain he can and, especially with regard to quantity and rate of supply, he may well call upon the resident engineer to back him up in his request to the supplier. The resident engineer should then give every assistance he can. It too often requires the combined efforts of the agent and resident engineer to get satisfactory prompt service in such matters as the installation of telephones, power lines, sewer connections, water supply, and in the supply of materials such as bricks, pipes, and cement, for the resident engineer to leave this all to the agent.

The resident engineer's work

The engineer who finds himself newly appointed to take up the position of resident engineer and who has previously had but little experience outside may well feel somewhat alarmed at the prospect before him. He has no doubt been told by well-wishers that he 'will manage all right', but this seems small comfort as he thinks of all the things he doesn't know about the job and all the unknown questions that are likely to arise requiring an answer right away. He may also feel a little uneasy at the prospect of having to tell everyone what to do (instead of deciding action *with* them) and may wonder how he is likely to match up to the contractor's agent who appears to be a tough and forceful character.

However, the resident engineer is not expected to be able to solve every problem by himself, nor is it likely that problems of any engineering magnitude will be immediately encountered, for there are a whole host of organisational details to settle first.

Work before going to site. The resident engineer should have spent some time before he goes to site examining the contract drawings and specifications, and there should have been an opportunity for him to have conversations with the designers. He should get to know how the job has been designed, so that he is able to make intelligent suggestions if the conditions revealed during the course of construction differ from those expected. He should make a file of all information which is basic to the job: soil test data on which the design has been based; levels; rainfall and run-off data; geological information; lists of sub-contractors who might already have been sent a preliminary enquiry; copies of quotations for special materials or equipment to be incorporated in the job; lists and addresses of authorities and personnel who have been written to about the job, such as the local planning authority, the district road engineer, the local building surveyor, the employer and his directors or councillors and staff; a brief history of how the job came about and the dates and references of major decisions.

The compilation of this file acts as a check on the situation to date so that the resident engineer can advise the engineer of any matters still outstanding that have to be settled. Once the resident engineer is appointed, everyone previously connected with the job will expect him to take a large part of the responsibility for seeing that all matters are done in due time and in the right order. Thus, the tentative programme of construction proposed by the engineer will be one of the documents most carefully studied by the resident engineer so that he is ready to understand and check what the contractor proposes as soon as the work starts.

The site office. Upon arrival on the site, one of the first things the resident engineer will have to decide is where he will have his office placed and what size and layout it shall have. If there is any choice in the matter the office should be placed so that from it the main traffic in and out of the site can be observed. It is a mistake to choose a situation which overlooks the job but which does not have a view of the main entrance. Little worthwhile can be seen of the normal civil engineering job from a distance, whereas even a distant view of the entrance to it will enable the resident engineer to notice a number of happenings—the delivery of materials, plant going off the site, when callers are about to descend, and so forth.

The office itself can range from a simple hut to a veritable barracks, according to the size of the job. On the moderate-sized job where the resident engineer has two or three engineers to assist him he will need his own room, a drawing office, and a typing and filing room. In addition, he will want a washroom, a small kitchen area where hot drinks can be made, and, separately, a room where wet clothes can be stripped off and hung up to dry. A small store-room is invaluable for the storage of surveying instruments and for storing away special equipment to be incorporated in the job which is of too delicate a nature for the rough handling it might get if delivered to the contractor's main stores.

On most civil engineering jobs a soils and materials testing laboratory is necessary, and this is more conveniently placed near the resident engineer's offices than elsewhere. Outside every entry to offices an essential item of equipment is a boot scraper, to prevent an excessive amount of mud finding its way into the offices, and a small outside area of concrete provided with a hose-pipe water supply and drain will be of much help in the cleaning of gumboots.

Early matters to discuss with the contractor

The question of an office and its siting having been settled with the contractor's agent, the next items to be discussed will almost certainly concern the laying on of services to the job—telephone, water supply, electric power, and drainage. Almost before anything else, the telephone will be wanted, although it will not always be obtained as soon as required. The agent may well seek the help of the resident engineer in pressing the local telephone manager for a service as quickly as possible, and he may need the engineer's sanction for the routing of the line over the employer's land. Water supply will also be required; the agent will want the resident engineer's consent for the source of supply used, and he may ask the resident engineer to check the design of the pipeline and to help him approach the local water authority. The resident engineer should go out of his way to help in these matters, not only because upon them depends the effective start of the work but also because everything he can do to help the agent at this stage will assist in building up a good relationship later.

The question of drainage and sanitation may prove difficult to solve. The resident engineer has to watch that what was promised to be a small 'sewage treatment works' does not get whittled down to no more than a tank and a soakaway, or a tank and overflow to a near-by ditch or river. This is the time to make sure that any sewage works proposed are of the right sort and are large enough to treat all the sewage from the maximum number of men who will be employed on the site. If these sewage works are later found inadequate, it may prove easy to get promises for their enlargement from the contractor, but considerably more difficult to get effective action if the agent feels that, given a few more weeks, the numbers of men on the job will decline and the problem will solve itself. The question of waste oil disposal from plant is a thorny one, and should be brought to the agent's notice. Discharge of used lubricating oil or waste diesel oil to public sewers may be forbidden; to discharge it through the site sewage works may ruin their proper functioning; and the discharge of even small quantities to a river will almost certainly be detected by the River Authority, who will demand immediate rectification. Any large discharge may lead to the contractor being sued for damages.

The waste oil should be led to a pit and disposed of by tanker as the local sewerage authority advises.

The resident engineer will next need to know what part of the job the agent intends to tackle first, and from this may follow an immediate visit to that part of the site and a discussion as to the extent of the work required there and the necessary setting out that must precede it. The agent will need to know what are the local benchmarks which have been used for the original survey of the area and, if these are some distance away, they may both agree that their staff should jointly arrange for a convenient benchmark and base line to be set out on the job.

When the immediate proposals for working have been sanctioned by the resident engineer the next topic is the programme as a whole, and this is the first of many such discussions that will occur. Sometimes the agent wants more information from the resident engineer so that he can continue with making his detailed plans, or he may have perceived some thorny problem ahead which he thinks might be avoided if the engineer would sanction some action not exactly in line with the contract requirements. The resident engineer had best give only a guarded opinion if this is his first acquaintance with such a proposition.

In the early stages of a job the resident engineer should also be wary in discussing matters of design with a contractor, or alterations in contract requirements. It is better to point out that the design of the works and the terms of the contract are the engineer's responsibility and must be followed. The resident engineer may well find later that there are very good reasons, which he did not at first appreciate, for the design being as shown on the drawings or for the requirements being as set out in the specification. Thus can too early a desire to agree with the contractor lead to later trouble. It is better not to make unnecessary promises for the future, which may later have to be broken because of increased understanding of the job.

Some early tasks for the resident engineer

At the end of the first day the resident engineer will no doubt find that he already has a number of tasks that will take up all his time during the next few days. It is likely that excavation for foundations will have commenced, or will commence immediately, on a large scale. It will thus be imperative for the resident engineer to take levels of the natural ground over the site where the excavation is to take place, if these levels are not already available in sufficient detail. This is urgent work, for there will be no chance later of finding what the natural ground levels were, and the calculations for quantities of excavation will be largely intelligent guesswork, or agreement will have to be sought on bill quantities—figures which may well differ from the true value. Indeed, if the contractor has had his own levels taken over the site and the resident engineer has let pass the opportunity of checking them he will be in no position to argue against the contractors' claim for excavation, even if this comes to substantially more than that shown in the bill of quantities. It is not sufficiently reliable to assume the ground levels shown on the contract drawings are accurate, because frequently they have been based on Ordnance Survey maps many years old, and alterations may subsequently have taken place, or they may not be accurate enough for measuring quantities.

The question of the disposal of excavated material will have to be considered. The resident engineer must see that the top-soil is being stripped off and stacked separately for re-use if necessary. The removal and disposal of existing materials on the site or the pulling down of existing structures will have to be discussed.

The next task the resident engineer may well be called upon to do, if he has not done it already, will be to check the ordering of materials necessary for the first stage of the work. The type of materials to be considered will be such things as the reinforcing bars required for concrete foundations and any pipes, particularly cast-iron or steel pipes, which it may be necessary to have for building in during the early stages of construction. Though the ordering of reinforcing bars is, of course, the responsibility of the contractor, it is not a helpful attitude on the part of the resident engineer to decline to be prepared to check the contractor's orders when asked to do so. Where materials to be incorporated in foundation work have been ordered under separate contracts from the main contract, such as pipes and valves, it will be urgently necessary for the resident engineer to check these contracts to see that every item that will be required has been placed on order. He will have to write to the suppliers under these direct contracts notifying them of the commencement of work on the site, giving instructions about the addressing of invoices and advice notes and the delivery of materials. He will ask for the speedy delivery of materials which may yet be outstanding and which are required in the early stages of the work. This is a particularly necessary task when important items are to be supplied under separate contracts which do not come under the control of the main contractor, because if not delivered in time, the contractor may claim for delays.

Meeting the employer

On the first opportunity after arrival, the resident engineer will see if the employer for whom the works are being built wishes to see him, and will set aside a morning or afternoon for going over the site and discussing plans with him. It frequently happens that the employer does wish to see the resident engineer and does many times thereafter chat with the resident engineer about the work. These talks should be noted down, and anything requiring a decision or an opinion should be sent through to the engineer so that he may give the necessary directions. From this discussion a great number of points may arise, and frequently there may be a number of problems left for the resident engineer to solve or to send back to the engineer. In the first place the employer may have definite views or needs in relation to the programme of work. He may have decided that he requires certain sections of the work to be completed before others are commenced; on the other hand, he may want certain small or large items of the contract left entirely untouched for the time being, as he may be considering some alternative propositions. He may have opinions about the access roads to be used by all vehicles coming on to the site. All these requirements the resident engineer will refer to the engineer and later transmit the relevant decisions to the contractor, and should arguments arise he must do his best to settle them amicably.

Many of the questions, both technical and procedural, he can answer by a judicial appraisal of the needs of the contractor and the wishes of the employer. He will become engaged on necessary site design work, i.e. revised design of certain small parts of the work in the light of new information to hand or changed circumstances. These designs he should discuss with contractor and employer and then forward to the engineer for comment and approval.

To the resident engineer the first week will seem to pass quickly, and looking back over it, if he is new to this work, he will wonder why he should ever have worried about what he would be required to do. Now he will find his chief worry will be to get all the urgent things done before it is too late to do them.

Setting up the clerical work

It will be necessary to set up a clerical system for the handling of correspondence, filing, measurement of quantities and checking of contractor's claims, and for log sheets of all technical data. The resident engineer will find that a typewriter is an essential part of his equipment, even if he has to get down to 'one-finger' typing himself. Files, a filing cabinet, box files, diaries for everyone and a large site diary, level books, notebooks, graph paper, drawing paper—the usual drawing-office paraphernalia will be required. If the chance of an adding machine comes the resident engineer's way he should grasp it immediately, since the contractor always tends to put in his monthly claim at the last possible minute and wants it checked and sent off the same day. Petty cash must not be forgotten, and the correct recipe is—'enough but no more'. Petty cash never seems to balance (whatever accountants may say) when the sum total of what is and has been is compounded of a miscellaneous assortment of stamps, a variety of small change, some crumpled notes, a bunch of folded receipts, and a list of expenditure in practically everybody's handwriting. If, when checking, a 'surplus' is found, leave it there—someone is sure to remember he 'booked it down but hadn't got any change at the time'. If a deficit is found, leave that too, in the hope it will be self-healing; but if deficits continue and there is no criminal reason for it save human forgetfulness, the wise resident engineer will make it up out of his own pocket, perhaps taking steps to 'improve the system' and thus better safeguard his financial future.

CHAPTER 6

Site Surveys, Investigations, and Layout

Site surveys

A detailed plan of existing ground levels on site is essential if excavation or filling quantities are to be accurately measured. The most convenient method for surveying and levelling small sites is to use spot levelling on a 20 m grid, and picking up any abrupt changes of grade between these intervals. An instrument man and two chainmen are needed to carry out the work. Ranging poles, two linen tapes, and a number of pegs are required to set out the sight lines at 20 m intervals at right angles from a given base line. Plotting work is easy, and contours may be readily interpolated between the 20 m interval readings.

Tacheometric work can be faster in the field, but only if a special reading staff is used and the surveyor and chainman are both experienced. If tacheometry is tried with a normal staff held vertical (or at right angles to the sight line of the instrument) a good deal of instrument and calculation work is necessary and—unless the booking down is very clear—plotting work is difficult. Tacheometry may seem temptingly easy; in practice, it is not so simple or expeditious as spot levelling over a grid.

Aerial surveys may give ground levels up to 2 m error, because the camera tends to record the level of the top of vegetation and not the actual ground level.

Responsibility for site surveys. The contract drawings will normally include a plan of site levels, but this may not be sufficiently detailed for the calculation of excavation or earthwork quantities. Either the contractor's staff or the resident engineer's staff will take the necessary levels; but preferably the work will be jointly undertaken because it is necessary that the original ground levels shall be agreed by both parties as a basis for the calculation of quantities. If the resident engineer does not check the site levels before excavation commences he will have no valid reason for disputing levels as measured by the contractor.

Responsibility for setting out. Responsibility for setting out the works lies with the contractor. He is entitled to call upon the resident engineer to check that his setting out is correct—although this does not absolve the contractor from holding responsibility for all errors which, even so, escape the notice of the resident engineer and his staff. This is the usual contract position. But whatever the contract may say, the resident engineer acts churlishly—indeed, unprofessionally—if he does not give such reasonable checks as the job demands and his staff can reasonably be expected to undertake; or if he does not immediately inform the contractor on finding an error. The contractor's staff are often hard pressed to set out all necessary levels, sight rails, etc., when work is going at full speed, and if the resident engineer is willing to answer a call for help in checking work or in 'giving a level to the foreman', good relationships will be fostered between contractor's and resident engineer's staffs.

Setting out buildings

An accuracy of about 2 mm in 30 m is desirable; errors of over 5 mm in 30 m should be rectified. The setting out is done from a given base line by use of the theodolite and a steel tape. All distances must be measured horizontally and a plumb bob used to transfer horizontal distances down vertically. The appropriate time for precise work is when the blinding concrete to foundations has been placed. At this stage centre lines of columns, centre lines and outside or inside lines of walls and their footings must be precisely fixed. The main centre, or reference line, for the building should already have been fixed by pegs sited well away from the work, and it is usual to work from co-ordinates along this line and right-angle distances off them.

The main base line, or some other line parallel to it, may have to be transferred down into the foundations by theodolite sighting and by careful steel-tape and plumb-bob work. When the theodolite is set over any given co-ordinate great care must be taken to set it precisely over the given point to an accuracy of 1 mm or less. If this is not done errors will be magnified. It is possible to set a theodolite in line with two points, between them, by siting first on one point and transitting to sight on the other, shifting the theodolite until it transits accurately to each point. Sighting points for theodolite work should be nails with their heads filed to a point. For the assistance of bricklayers and shuttering carpenters, sight boards can be provided, with the top of the cross arm fixed a given amount above formation level and a saw cut made exactly on the precise line of sight. A string can then be fastened through such a saw cut.

Setting out larger sites. Triangulation from a measured base line is the usual method adopted; the triangles being as well proportioned as possible. This method is usually better than a lengthy closed traverse when the weather is changeable, since a closed traverse represents more work to be done at one time and may be interrupted by bad weather. If survey of a closed traverse has to be interrupted there is always a danger that one or the other of the last two traverse pegs will be disturbed by plant. Even if the pegs have not been disturbed, a large closing error may cause the surveyor to think this has happened, and he will feel it necessary to do the whole job over again.

It is worth going to some trouble to find a suitable base line which, for preference, should be level. A level tarmac road is ideal; if this is not available it is worthwhile cutting the grass and removing any humps from another piece of level ground so that the tape may be laid flat and given the standard pull required by means of a spring balance. A new tested steel tape should be used, the maker's corrections being known and allowed for. A thermometer is also necessary. The temperature should be fairly steady, e.g. the work should not be undertaken if there is intermittent hot sunshine between periods of cold. A quiet, still, and cloudy day is best. Accurate measurement of angles with a theodolite is easier than accurate measurement of distances by tape, so it is worth finding a good base line at the expense, possibly, of not having the best angled triangles for setting out the other points. Preliminary calculations before deciding on the base line will indicate whether a satisfactory degree of accuracy will be obtained.

In accurate surveying it is best not to resort to more than the standard checks with the instrument (face right, face left, etc.). It is often tempting, seeing another previously set-out point, to range that in the observations 'just as a check'. This is likely to lead the engineer into a puzzling conundrum of calculations when he gets back into the office in trying to relate one lot of setting-out calculations to another. The trouble is that such 'check observations' are likely to be done more hurriedly, and therefore less accurately, than the principal setting out. Attention should preferably be paid to taking the main observations as accurately as possible.

Measurement of other distances is usually undertaken by using the linen tape. When measuring distances on steep slopes it is a good deal easier to use a 3 m piece of timber than to try to pull the tape out horizontally. A 3 m interval is accurately marked on the timber, a plumb bob being suspended from one end-mark. Work proceeds downhill, the timber being kept horizontal by means of a small builder's level. Pegs are put in at the 2 m intervals, the exact 2 m distance—as shown by the point of the plumb bob—being marked off on each new peg.

Levelling

A carpenter's spirit level should not be used for setting out the level of anything more than incidental work. It is not sufficient in conjunction with a straight edge, for instance, for getting a floor screed level. It is difficult to get concrete floors uniformly level to an accuracy less than 5 mm, and a contractor should always be warned when greater accuracy than this must be obtained with concrete. Usually discrepancies of this magnitude are taken up in the floor finish, which is either ground down to the desired smooth finish (as with terrazzo) or is placed with especial care, as in floor tiling. To get tiling accurately laid, small pieces of tile are mortared on to the floor base at intervals across it, their level being fixed precisely to the correct finished level by use of the instrument level. A straight edge is then used to keep the finished tiling at the right level between the set levels, the pieces of tile being chipped off as the finished tiled area approaches.

PLATE I

(a) Bamboo scaffolding to bell-mouth spillway and draw-off tower, Lower Shing Mun Dam, Hong Kong.

(b) There are other ways of handling glass sheet—but the methods used depend on what men and machines a contractor happens to have available at any given time.

b)

(a)

PLATE II

(a) Fixing the reinforcing steel on the spillway of the Dibbis Dam, Iraq.

(b) A mechanical tunnel digger—the Robins Mole—used at Mangla Dam, Pakistan.

Photos on this page John Howard & Co. Ltd.—Contractors.

PLATE III

(a) Underpinning techniques used by a contractor for taking down a deep excavation for the Severn Bridge.

(b) A contractor's temporary works—a cofferdam of precast beams anchored by post tensioning to the rock formation below, for a bridge pier at the Severn Bridge.

(c) An off-shore drilling and piling crib for the construction of an oil terminus jetty.

(a)

PLATE IV

(a) Mud can be really troublesome.

(b) Hillside slips of this nature can be an incidental matter or indicative of something very serious.

(b)

Site investigations

Major site investigations will normally be completed before the resident engineer goes to site and construction work commences. These site investigations will have been carried out either by direct labour or by contract and will have been conducted under the close supervision of the engineer and his expert soil mechanics advisers. The resident engineer should always receive a copy of the report on such investigations before he goes to site, and he should know the precise location of all previous borings and tests.

Notwithstanding such early work, more detailed investigations may be required during the course of the construction—either to amplify or confirm previous knowledge, or to investigate new areas. The British Standard Code of Practice (CP 2001) 'Site Investigations' acts as a general guide to the approach when conducting further site tests, but this needs to be supplemented by information contained in other publications as suggested at the end of this chapter. The resident engineer will be expected to have an understanding of the major principles and practices of soil mechanics so that he can direct the work intelligently, though he will not be expected to have a full acquaintance with soil mechanics theories and design methods.

The usual means whereby information of conditions below ground is obtained are by trial pits, borings, trenchings, and augering.

Trial pits

Hand-dug trial pits are always expensive (in Britain), take time to excavate, and are not always as informative as expected. When more than $1\frac{1}{2}$ to 2 m deep, the muck must be hauled up by skip, or shovelled up on stages. This slows the work, and timbering slows it still further. The worst defect of a trial pit is that, once it has been commenced a given size, this size limits the depth to which it can be sunk. If a trial pit is to be taken to a depth of 5 m for instance, it will have to be started between 3 and $3\frac{1}{2}$ m square, because the timber supports will have to be 'brought in' twice, and the reduced area at the bottom of the pit must still be sufficient for a small pump, the crane skip, and two men working. At labouring rates of £0.45 per hour, such a pit can cost anything from £250 to £500.

Hence, before starting a trial pit it is necessary to consider whether:

(a) worthwhile results will be obtained;
(b) the expenditure to get the results is justified; and
(c) whether the time period available is sufficient.

It may take up to six weeks to get the required information—the best part of two weeks sinking the pit, another period for taking the samples and getting them sent off, then another long delay as the samples are tested and the report on them got through to the engineer. If some important part of the contractor's programme of work is held up for this length of time it can sometimes happen that it is best to carry on with the construction, assuming the worst, until such time as the actual foundation conditions will be revealed through the natural course of the excavation.

Another important point to consider is—what is the trial pit supposed to show? Is it to find evidence of rock or evidence of a soft clay band, or is it to take undisturbed samples? If a pit is simply required to find rock level, then a boring could prove cheaper and quicker. If the pit is to pass through rock the same applies. If one is looking for clay, silt, or soft material a most important matter the resident engineer should ask is whether the pit is expected to pass right through the soft material or just go into it. The former is much the most difficult and costly.

If undisturbed samples are to be taken one needs to know whether they are to be taken horizontally from the sides of the trench or vertically from the bottom. The former will require more room than the latter, and will be more difficult to take. Pushing a U4 sampling tube horizontally into clay will involve the use of jacks, and digging the sample tube out again is no easy matter. It may take as long as a day to take two samples. Further possibility must be borne in mind that water, rock, or very soft material may prevent the pit from being taken down to the intended depth. The resident engineer must also bear in mind the likelihood that, when the full depth has been reached, the soils engineer may ask for excavation of a further $\frac{1}{2}$ m or so to find out the nature of the stuff in the bottom. The helpful resident engineer will normally make the trial pit slightly larger than first conditions appear to dictate.

The question of timbering and safety is the agent's responsibility, and he must be given a free hand to do what he thinks is necessary.

Trial borings

Trial borings can generally be classified into three kinds:

(i)   cored holes in rock, rotary drilled by diamond drill;
(ii) uncored holes in rock or in soft and hard ground, drilled by percussion bits;
(iii) lined holes in soft ground, sunk by shell and auger or by clay-cutter.

It is, of course, necessary to have an idea as to the sort of ground to be penetrated before the right type of boring can be chosen; one also needs to know the kind of information required. Herein lies the major difficulty with trial borings and the major cause of delay.

Cored holes in rock can be drilled only by the rotary method using a diamond drill bit. The standard sizes in use are listed on page 71. The most usual sizes adopted are BX and NX so as to give good-sized cores less liable to be fractured during the cutting process. It is important that cores are inspected immediately on withdrawal in order to note whether fractures are fresh and caused by the drilling, or whether they are natural to the rock. The cores must be labelled 'top' and 'bottom', the depth must be marked on them, and they must be placed for safe keeping and later inspection in properly made sample boxes.

If, in any length of boring, it is not deemed necessary to take cored samples the drilling may be changed to percussion drilling using a cruciform-shaped chisel-edged drill bit of the right diameter. This is faster and cheaper drilling than diamond drilling.

Size	Drill Bit O.D. mm	Hole Diam. mm	Core Diam. mm
EX	37·3	38·1	20·6
AX	47·6	49·2	30·2
BX	59·6	60·3	41·3
NX	75·3	76·2	54·0

If gravel or soft ground is encountered below rock, difficulties are immediately increased, and a wide variety of boring methods may have to be used on a trial-and-error basis until the material is penetrated.

Uncored holes are drilled by percussion, the drill bit being of chisel or cruciform shape and being bumped up and down in the hole. The rock fragments are blown out by compressed air or are washed out by the drilling water supplied down a waterway inside the drilling rods to the bit face. This wash water must therefore pass to a small stank or tank where the rock fragments settle out and can be examined. This examination must be at regular intervals. Percussion drilling is fast, but because the rock is fragmented it is not very informative. However, it is a useful means of finding the depth of rock or the depth to rock foundation, since modern small percussion drills of the 50–75 mm size can penetrate something like 6 m of rock per hour. It is easy and cheap with such drills to prospect ahead of excavations and so quickly get extensive information of the depth to which an excavation must be taken to find a rock bottom.

If soft ground is encountered it may be necessary to stop drilling and insert a lining tube in the ground. In consequence, the drilling thereafter must be to a smaller diameter. Gravel is troublesome to get through, though it is surprising what can be done with care and gentle handling of the drill. If the gravel repeatedly falls into the hole pre-grouting before redrilling may be necessary.

Lined holes in soft ground are usually of considerably larger diameter than other types of holes, being often 6 in. diameter, or perhaps even larger diameter at the start, if much depth must be penetrated. The hole is excavated principally by bumping the 'shell' into the hole. This shell is simply a cylindrical heavy tube, provided with a cutting edge at the bottom and some form of non-return valve inside. Material entering the shell is held in place and withdrawn with the shell, which is removed after every ½ m or so of boring. This method is primarily used for the penetration of soft strata and, since it is soft strata which primarily needs investigation for civil engineering works, very many trial borings are taken down in this manner. The equipment used (apart from the lining for the hole) is cheap and easily transportable. The work of boring may be interrupted at any time so that, after the hole is cleaned out, a sampling tube may be lowered into it and an 'undisturbed' sample of the ground below the base of the hole may be taken. Sampling tubes take various forms, the most usual tube being 100 mm diameter to take a 'U4 sample'.

If rock should be encountered, the drilling proceeds by percussion methods using a chisel bit bumped up and down. Because this chisel must clear the inside of the lining, it is impossible to push the lining any farther down to meet more soft ground below the rock. Hence a smaller-diameter lining must be inserted for soft ground below, and a smaller shell for the boring. Herein lies a prolific cause of delays, because a hole cannot be reduced in diameter without all the necessary new-diameter tubes and boring equipment being available on site for the reduced size. There is, in any event, a practical limit to the number of reductions in diameter that can be adopted. A further cause of delay is that penetration of rock by percussion methods at the relatively large diameter of 150 mm or over is very slow work indeed.

Hence the moment boulders or rock are encountered, when using shell-boring equipment for soft ground, delays are likely to mount up, both by reason of having to wait for delivery of new sizes of lining and equipment and because the boring in hard ground is slow and laborious. It may take only a day or two to get through 10 m of clay, but three to six weeks before a further 2 m of rock or boulder is penetrated if the right equipment is not to hand. The resident engineer has to sum up the position and query whether the expense of meeting the changed conditions and the cost of the delay is going to be worthwhile in terms of information to be gained from that particular hole. Sometimes a 150 mm or 200 mm hole may be laboriously chopped down at great expense in an effort to get 'undisturbed' samples of clay strata, only to find that nowhere is there any clay strata of sufficient thickness in which to take a U4 sample. It can save money and time if, suspecting this may happen, the resident engineer first tries a small percussion boring which can rapidly penetrate rock and boulders cheaply and which, if intelligently handled, can reveal the depth and thickness of soft strata in between the hard.

Trenching

Trenching by dragline is too often neglected as a means of revealing the nature and extent of shallow overburden material on site. An hydraulic hoe can excavate a trench up to 5m deep in soft or friable rocks at a fast and cheap rate, and the substantial cross-section of material so revealed can be much more informative than a few samples from a few borings. Furthermore, the act of trenching will itself have revealed in practical terms what difficulties may attend proposed excavation methods; the trench can probably be left open for tenderers to see, and the soils engineer can pick and choose where he will have undisturbed samples of the material taken.

Augering

The auger may be used in conjunction with the shell for taking down lined borings in soft material. In such a case the auger is of fairly large diameter and needs two men to turn it, working on hand dogs fitted to square-section boring rods. This method is not often used, as it is very slow, and the shell gives better results. The *hand-auger* is a simple little hand boring tool for penetrating shallow depths of soft material. About 300 mm of material are penetrated at a time before the tool is withdrawn and the material taken out of it and examined. Two men are usually used to twist the auger, the hole being watered from time to time in order to reduce friction. Penetration is usually of the order of $1\frac{1}{2}$–$2\frac{1}{2}$ m, to get a hole deeper than 3 m the ground has to be very soft. Gravel or cobbles cannot be penetrated. The tool is useful for locating the extent and depth of shallow, very soft areas of ground.

Judging the safe bearing value of a foundation

The safe bearing pressure that may be applied to a foundation material is not a matter for the resident engineer to decide. This is a technical design matter for the engineer to decide, as advised by his experts. It will be the resident engineer's task to ensure that the contractor places the foundations upon material of the required strength and quality that the engineer has designated. To help the resident engineer arrive at a proper appraisal of the foundation conditions, a simple soils mechanics laboratory may be set up on site, where continuous tests are taken of the foundation materials and the results regularly forwarded to the engineer. If any occasion arises where the tests fail to comply with the engineer's advised requirements the resident engineer will naturally draw the engineer's attention to this, and ask for instructions.

Testing apparatus for a site soils laboratory

The usual apparatus suitable for a small soils laboratory to be run by the resident engineer's staff without the full-time guidance of a properly qualified soils engineer is set out below.

For moisture content determinations

1. Beam balance weighing by 0·01-gramme divisions. (The type of balance used in schools.)
2. Drying oven, thermostatically controlled. (Not absolutely essential. For rough measurement of moisture contents and quick site control determinations the sample can be dried on a flat tray over a stove.)
3. Six drying trays.

For grading analyses of soils

4. Set of B.S. sieves (woven wire) with lid and pan for each different diameter of sieve

300 mm diam.—38 mm, 25 mm, 19 mm, 13 mm, 10 mm.

(These are also used for testing concrete aggregate gradings.)

200 mm diam. 7 mm, 5 mm, 3 mm, and Nos. 7, 14, 25, 52, 72, 100, and 200.

5. Balance weighing to 25 kilogrammes.

6. .Balance capable of weighing up to 7 kilogrammes by 1-gramme divisions.

For in-situ density tests (sand replacement method)

There are several possible tests—15(A), 15(B), . . . 15(F)—contained in B.S. 1377, of which 15(B) and 15(C) are of widest use. In the latter two tests a round hole 8 in. diameter by 8 in. deep is dug in level formation; the volume of the hole being measured by pouring sand into it—in test 12(B) by using a special pouring cylinder, in test 15(C) by putting the sand in with a small scoop.

Apparatus required for both tests:

Items 1, 2, 3, 6 of above.

7. Small tools for excavating hole.

8. A metal tray at least 450 mm square with an 200 mm diameter hole cut in it. (This tray must be rigid.)

9. Dried, clean sand all passing No. 25 sieve but retained on No. 52 and suitable air-tight containers for holding it. (About 20 kg or 0·01 m³ of this sand will be required initially; more being obtained as sand is lost with use.)

10. A calibrating container 200 mm diameter by 200 mm (as B.S. 1377, Fig. 26).

11. Air-tight containers for the excavated soil.

For test 15(B), additional apparatus:

12. A pouring cylinder (as B.S. 1377, Fig. 28).

For test 15(C), additional apparatus:

13. A small scoop for placing the measuring sand.

14. A steel straight edge 300 mm long by 3 mm thick with one bevelled edge (for striking off surplus sand poured into hole).

Test 15(D) uses a core cutter (B.S. 1377, Fig. 30), but its use is limited to soft, fine-grained, stone-free soils which do not compress when the cutter is pushed in.

For gravelly soils a conical hole of larger than 200 mm diameter may be cut into the formation using a bigger tray than Item 8 above. The sand is poured in layers into the hole from a watering can with a top spout. To prevent the sand impacting into the hole from a height, a length of rubber tube is pivot-hung on to the spout. At the bottom end of this tube a small conical tin shield is wired so that the fall of the sand is broken as it passes out through the annular space between the tube and the shield The hole is 'watered' with this so that the sand has only a standard short distance of free fall.

For standard (Proctor) compaction tests:

Items 1, 2, 3, 6, 14 above.
15. Standard compaction mould (B.S. 1377, Fig. 20).
16. Standard 2·5 kg metal rammer and guide (B.S. 1377, Fig. 21).
17. Palette knife.
18. Glass sheet or metal tray (for mixing in added moisture to sample).
19. 19 mm sieve (from Item 4 above).
20. A 1000 cm³ glass measuring cylinder (for measuring volume of surface-wet material over 19 mm size).

Other apparatus. A small unconfined compression testing apparatus for testing the shear strength of 38 mm-diameter undisturbed clay samples is a useful addition to the laboratory in certain circumstances. This machine is cheap, easy to operate, and gives useful indication of variations of clay strength (as in road making). The results given by it are not, however, adequate for design purposes. The triaxial compression testing machine would be used for testing soils for design purposes; but this is a sophisticated piece of apparatus, not suitable for site-control purposes unless a full-scale soils laboratory has been set up on site under the direction of a properly qualified soils engineer.

To complete the list of apparatus which the non-specialist engineer can use successfully the liquid limit testing apparatus might be added (B.S. 1377, Figs. 5 and 6).

With this amount of apparatus the site engineers should be able to carry out all the usual tests asked for by the soil mechanics engineers which do not require a specialist knowledge of soil mechanics theories and techniques.* The only important site test which cannot be carried out with the above apparatus is the estimation of the particle-size distribution of the silt and clay fractions of a sample. Most of the other tests that might be required—e.g. consolidation, permeability, and triaxial compression tests—must be regarded primarily as laboratory tests to be conducted under skilled supervision rather than as routine site tests.

If samples have to be taken for laboratory testing off site much delay will be prevented if an initial stock of sampling tubes for cored samples (U4s) is purchased instead of waiting for the laboratory to send out a fresh set of sampling tubes every time such samples are called for.

Site layout considerations

Factors influencing layout

Means of access to the site will usually be described in the contract for the construction. It is the contractor's task to plan his choice of layout

* T. W. N. Akroyd's book *Laboratory Testing in Soil Engineering* is a comprehensive guide to the subject.

for his temporary works and buildings, subject to obtaining the sanction of the engineer and complying with any specific restrictions or directions. Key factors influencing the choice of layout are set out below.

(i) *Haulage roads*, for taking excavated material off the site (to tip) and for bringing in filling, must be planned for greatest economy and efficiency. The decision is related to the kind of equipment used for haulage. Scrapers can pass over hard or soft ground and will not seriously disrupt the surface; tracked vehicles, having grips to their tracks, can pass over hard or soft ground, but they cannot pass continuously over water-bound, bitumen sprayed or tarmac roads without breaking them up and destroying their water-shedding properties; flat-tracked heavy vehicles, such as diggers, cannot pass over soft ground; ordinary haulage trucks apply high wheel loads and cannot run over soft ground, they are also sometimes slow on steep gradients both uphill and downhill.

Usually there needs to be a distinct division on site between areas to be served by 'metalled' or water-bound roads, and areas reached by rough access roads. The former roads are designed to take all on–off traffic to the site; the latter are designed to cater for the main internal site movement of larger excavating and other plant. Careful planning is required where these two areas overlap, such as where haulage lorries must place their filling brought in from off site, the roads in this area being tracked both by these lorries and also by dozers and other heavy tracked vehicles. Constant maintenance of roads in such areas is necessary to prevent break-up of the road and destruction of haunches and ditches by tracked vehicles, to prevent potholes from damaging wheeled transport, and to prevent mud being taken off the site to cause a nuisance on public roads.

(ii) *Lifting and excavating positions.* Cranes and excavators must be so positioned that complete coverage of the job is obtained with the minimum amount of repositioning of plant. Certain types of cranes, e.g. derricks, tower cranes, cableways, etc., should not have to be moved at all. Excavators should 'work as they go', and not have to change around their positions. The lifting equipment over any deep excavation should be so placed that it is not necessary to move it until a late stage in the work.

(iii) *Concreting plant* must be placed so as to give minimum delivery distance to the parts of the structure requiring the bulk of the concrete output. At the same time the adjacent aggregate stockyards and cement hoppers must be so placed as to give easy access for aggregate delivery lorries coming on site. Delivery lorries should preferably not have to follow the same routes as muck-shifting plant, or they will pick up mud and track it into the aggregate bays. Aggregate bays must have a good drainage and be capable of being washed down when empty. It is seldom found economical to shift a concrete batching plant once it has been set up, so its initial position is usually permanent, different methods of conveyance of concrete out from the plant being adopted for various distances and locations. This implies that the mixers must be so positioned that they can feed alternatively to concrete pumps, dumpers, skips on lorries, and to jubilee or mono-rail wagons as may be required from time to time.

(iv) *Compressors and power-generating units* are usually mobile, but where much compressed air is being used (as in tunnelling) a central compressor station may need to be set up near the tunnel mouth, or near to access shafts leading to it. The airlines need to be as short as possible to reduce leakage losses. The diesel fuel-oil tank must be housed near by at the right elevation to give gravity feed to the compressors or generators, and good access must be provided for the fuel delivery vehicles.

(v) *The contractor's main offices* and stores need to be near the main entrance to the site. Most materials being delivered on or off site must be booked in at the central checker's office, and it is convenient to have this office within a step or two of the agent's clerical and accountancy sections, and also adjacent to the main store huts for site equipment. It follows that the resident engineer's offices should also be near, so that easy communication is maintained at all staff levels and there is economy in providing such services as telephone, heating, lighting, cleaning, etc.

Temporary works

Temporary works are designed and constructed by the contractor, but the contract usually gives the engineer power to approve or disapprove the design and siting of these works. On an ordinary job the temporary works consist of no more than the construction of access roads, small bridges, drains, and the erection of huts, concreting plant, service bays, etc. On a large job the temporary works may be extensive and costly, involving the contractor in substantial engineering design and construction works—as, for instance, in the design and construction of caissons, sheet-piled structures, earth stanks and cofferdams, bridges, or even small dams. The engineer's site staff should be prepared to give advice and assistance whenever this is requested by the contractor, as the latter is new to site conditions whereas the engineer's staff should be more familiar with such conditions from their perusal of, or participation in, the design of the permanent works.

The diversion of services often requires joint action by agent and resident engineer. The latter should have, or obtain, information showing where such services are located. If need be, the resident engineer must arrange for meetings with the district engineers of various interested bodies on site so that practical arrangements can be made for diverting sewers, drains, gas and water mains, electrical power lines, G.P.O. lines, telephone lines, etc., to the satisfaction of all concerned. In these matters the resident engineer must ensure that the reasonable requests of statutory authorities are met by the contractor and that the diversions are properly undertaken by exercise of careful workmanship; on the other hand, he should see that unreasonable requests are not put upon the contractor, and he may have to negotiate payment rates to cover extra or unforseeable work.

Many statutory authorities prefer to undertake diversion of their own services themselves, and this is advantageous, as no quarrels then arise regarding unsatisfactory workmanship. In some cases—as in the diversion of telephone lines, power cables, gas and water mains—the contractor would neither be permitted nor would expect to undertake the skilled work required. Many local authorities also prefer that they should effect the permanent reinstatement of excavation of public roads. This, too saves a lot of argument as to quality of workmanship. Accounts for diversion work will be paid by the contractor, who recovers their cost under appropriate items in the bill; the resident engineer should check such accounts to see that they are reasonable and contain no errors.

The Public Utilities Street Works Act 1950 provides a uniform code of procedure which must be followed when work is to take place in any 'street' or 'controlled land' or where any work is likely to interfere with roads, bridges, or gas, water or electricity mains. A 'street' means any length of highway, road, lane, footway, etc., and 'controlled land' is any land adjoining a street which is controlled by the highway authority. Before commencing any works which come within the provisions of the Act, notice of intention (with plans) must be given in the prescribed form to the highway authority and to all statutory authorities having apparatus or rights in the street or controlled land. The work must comply with the directions of the highway authority, which may cover such matters as agreed location, nature of work, fencing, watching and lighting, traffic control, and length and width of openings made. Reinstatement must be carried out as the highway authority directs, and must be maintained for six months. Services which have to be diverted must be to the reasonable requirements of the authority owning the service, the cost of the diversion being paid for by the person (or contractor) needing the diversion made.

Before any such work is undertaken, the resident engineer or contractor should approach the local highway authority and other statutory authorities whose services are likely to be affected so that informal discussions can bring about agreement on the best procedure. It is also advisable for the resident engineer to obtain a copy of the local authority's byelaws, together with any byelaws or official directions of traffic-control authorities (the police) or other statutory bodies.

Site drainage is of some importance. Difficulty often occurs in draining a site on which large-scale earth moving is taking place. The process of excavation disturbs the natural drainage of the land, and large quantities of mud may be discharged to local watercourse during wet weather. Complaints may then arise from riparian owners and water abstractors downstream, who will object to the contamination of the water. The local river authority may also lodge a complaint and demand that the nuisance cease. The problem is often difficult to solve. On the first occasion it arises, the resident engineer should visit the persons objecting and try to arrange a meeting between them and the contractor. A reasonable objector will frequently reduce his complaints on realising the difficulties involved—more particularly, he is likely to be accommodating once it is explained that the contamination is of a temporary nature. Nevertheless, if the objection is not withdrawn, or if the contamination is doing real harm, the contractor is bound to take steps to reduce it, and may have to pay compensation for damage done.

It is the contractor's job to dewater the site, and this includes the obligation to do so without causing harm or damage to others. 'Dewatering' can range from simple diversion or piping of ditches and drains to full-scale twenty-four-hour pumping or ground-water lowering.

It is usual to cut a perimeter drain around all excavations towards which the ground slopes. This work may appear at first sight to be a waste of time, the ditch being perfectly dry for months on end. But there may come a day of excessively heavy rainfall following a wet period when such a ditch prevents disaster and delay. Even in the temperate climate of the British Isles, once the ground is saturated, a further sudden rain-storm can bring about surface run-off of staggering proportions. If no protection exists for these occasions extensive damage can be caused to the works.

Dewatering of an excavation is the rule rather than the exception. Once dewatered, an excavation should be kept dewatered. Continuous pumping is required, therefore, even when work is not proceeding on site. It can be dangerous to let an excavation fill up repeatedly overnight and to pump it out in the daytime. The ground may be caused to move by the frequent rise and fall of the water level, and the timbering to the excavation may shift in consequence and become unsafe. The need for twenty-four-hour continuous pumping should be insisted upon by the resident engineer if any damage or danger is likely to result from intermittent pumping. The electric self-priming centrifugal pump is the most reliable pump to use for continuous pumping, provided there is a reliable electricity supply to keep it going. Failing this, a diesel- or petrol-driven 'vacuum' self-priming pump would be the next choice. These pumps are 'lift-and-force' types. They are reliable, but suffer from the disadvantage of being heavy and bulky.

Ground-water lowering is, of course, a continuous process. Pointed and screened suction pipes are jetted into the ground at intervals around the proposed excavation site and are connected to a common header suction pump leading to a vacuum pump. When the process works well its effect is near magical. It permits excavation to proceed with such ease and facility as far outweighs the labour and cost of installing the system. However, it is difficult to get the well points jetted down into ground containing cobbles and boulders, and in clays—unless the well points are protected by carefully graded filters—withdrawal of water may eventually diminish and be defeated by the sealing of the well points by clay.

The drainage of clay presents much practical difficulty in site construction. The chief trouble is not so much that it cannot be done, but that it takes a long time, perhaps weeks or months. Sand drains, i.e. bored holes filled with fine sand, are often proposed as a means of draining a clay area. As a permanent measure, or as part of the permanent design of the work, they are effective; but they are of no use to the contractor faced with the problem of getting out very soft clays over which no excavating plant can move. Such a problem needs to be considered very carefully in advance. The obvious solution of 'getting stuck into it' with the digger (or dragline) may prove disastrously true, the digger getting in so far and then finding itself thoroughly bogged down. The act of excavation in an already soft area may make that area even softer as overburden is removed; springs and streams, otherwise held back by the overburden weight, are released to change the area to liquid mud. The moment this is noticed the resident engineer should advise the contractor to stop working and reappraise the situation.

Sewerage and sanitation arrangements on site ought to be made initially for the maximum number of men to be employed. The disposal of the effluent may present difficulty unless a proper small-scale sewage treatment plant is installed. It is of no use just to construct a holding tank for the sewage, unless proper arrangements are made for regular emptying by cesspool-emptying vehicles. If this is not regularly done the tank will inevitably fill up and discharge neat sewage to the near-by watercourse, causing a serious nuisance downstream. It is wise to call in the local public health authority or drainage authority before any sewage treatment works are constructed, so that their co-operation and understanding will be obtained and any consequential troubles arising will be much more readily dealt with. Disposal of waste oil is usually forbidden to any watercourse, and therefore drainage from the plant repair yard and from fuel-tank areas should be kept separate from the other drains and led to a properly watertight pit which is emptied by tank vehicle from time to time, the oil being taken off site and disposed of as the local public health authority may direct or in some location where no harm will result.

References

'Site Investigations including Boring and other Methods of Sub-surface Exploration', H. J. B. Harding. *Journal I.C.E.*, April 1949. (Precise, practical, informative despite its relatively early date.)

Site Investigations. British Standard Code of Practice C.P. 2001. B.S.I (124 pp. Two-thirds devoted to descriptive geology of soil types. Sampling techniques not covered in any detail. Informative, but only certain parts essential reading.)

Soil Mechanics in Engineering Practice. Terzaghi and Peck. John Wiley & Sons. (The engineer's 'bible'.)

'Progress of the Science of Soil Mechanics in the Past Decade', H. J. B. Harding. 58th James Forest Lecture. *Proceedings I.C.E.*, 1952. (A lucid short historical account.)

Measurement of Distance by Radio Waves, J. A. Sandover and R. Bill. *Proceedings I.C.E.*, January 1963.
'Aerial Methods of Surveying for Civil Engineering', P. G. Mott. *Proceedings I.C.E.*, December 1963.
'Setting out Tall Buildings', M. A. May. *Proceedings I.C.E.*, July 1964.
Protection of Subgrades and Granular Bases by Surface Dressing. Road Note No. 17. Road Research Laboratory. H.M.S.O. (Useful for site roads.)
Elementary Air Survey. W. K. Kilford. Pitman Publishing, 1970 (2nd Edition).
Surveying. R. H. Dugdale. MacDonald & Evans. 1970. (Elementary but practical).

CHAPTER 7

The Resident Engineer's Office Records

Importance of records

A important part of the resident engineer's work is to keep adequate records. His personal success and the assistance he can give the engineer depend much upon the efficiency of the system set up, and the way in which it is maintained to date. These records enable an appraisal to be made at any time of the progress of the work; they form the basis of fixing fair rewards to contractors; they enable all materials to be ordered in good time; they enable the designers to be assured that the assumptions made for design purposes are valid; they assist in the solving of new design problems that may arise during construction; and they form a source of information throwing light on the subsequent behaviour of the completed works. Without adequate records, the resident engineer fails in his obligations to the engineer and the employer.

Types of records

Records are of four classes:

Historical—showing progress stage by stage, as proposed and as achieved, including all relevant information having a bearing on this subject, such as records of weather, notes of discussions, decisions, and other key matters influencing the course of the job;

Quantitative and financial—measuring all that is done, the time and rate it is done, together with all relevant particulars, so as to form a basis of fair payment to contractors and for the furnishing of figures which show the cumulative cost of the job, the cost of separate parts of it, and the estimated total final cost at any time;

Qualitative—being a record of all measurements and observations of the quality and behaviour under test of the component parts of works, the raw and made-up materials used, and the foundation and other conditions whose characteristics have an influence on the behaviour of the works;

'As built' records—being a pictorial record (the Record Drawings, etc.) of all the works as completed, showing the whereabouts and dimensions of all parts as they exist at completion, together with factual descriptions of their origin, their operation as described in instruction manuals, and their performance under test.

The correspondence filing system

The first matter to be dealt with is the setting up of a correspondence and filing system. The files likely to be required are as follows.

General files for correspondence etc.

File.	*Notes on Material filed.*
1. Employer	
2. Notes of meetings	Minutes or notes of all meetings attended by resident engineer, in date order, including notes of meetings when the engineer visits site, formal meetings with the contractor, meetings with Planning Authorities, etc.
3. Contractor's head office	
4. Contractor's agent	Formal letters only
5. Weekly progress reports	Copies of the reports sent to the engineer
6. Monthly progress reports	Copies of draft reports for submission through the engineer to the employer, plus copies of report as sent
7. Planning Authorities	
8. Engineer	This will be the bulkiest correspondence file
9. Informal letters to designers	Here will be filed copies of correspondence the resident engineer may privately write to his colleagues at head office (if that practice is adopted, though most correspondence should be through the engineer)
10. Specialist advisers	Correspondence with all independent advisors, such as the geologist or landscape architect, these advisors not being on the staff of the engineer
11. Nominated sub-contractors	This file may be split into several files, each dealing with a single sub-contractor
12. Supply contractors	Subdivided into a separate file for each contractor if necessary, this being correspondence with contractors other than the main construction contractor

13. Miscellaneous suppliers	Correspondence with suppliers who will be supplying chosen materials through the main contractor, under P.C. items and the like
14. Staffing	Correspondence re the appointment of inspectors, office staff, and the like
15. Miscellaneous (job)	Re such matters as telephone, visitors to site, site services, etc.
16. Miscellaneous (personal)	Dealing with personal correspondence arising from his position as resident engineer, e.g. invitations to speak at meetings, references given to staff, and so on

Financial files.

17. Current claim from main contractor
18. Dayworks—current
19. Claims passed
20. Dayworks and extras passed
21. Engineer's certificates and correspondence thereon
22. Variation Orders passed
23. Variation Orders pending or in draft
24. Other contractor's invoices and claims (subdivided, a file to each contractor)
25. Claims pending for extra charges by main contractor
26. Estimates of future expenditure
27. Petty cash, miscellaneous

The number of separate files required will depend upon the size of the job and how many contractors are engaged on the site. A few points may be mentioned. The Notes of Meetings File (No. 2) is very useful. An extra copy should be taken of all minutes or notes of meetings, and placed on this file so that a lot of time is saved not having to hunt up particular instructions which would otherwise be hidden away in files 1, 3, 4, 8, or 10. Correspondence with contractors and sub-contractors (Files 11 and 12) should preferably be separated, a file to each contractor. The distinction under the financial files (Nos. 17–23) between that which has been done and that which is 'pending' should be noticed; there is always something pending, and it is helpful to keep this separate. Under File 21 lies that part of the correspondence with the engineer that deals purely with financial matters relating to claims and certificates for payment. This correspondence needs to be kept out of File 8, where it might otherwise be 'lost'.

No elaborate system of indexing is required by this simple filing system, and there is no need for a file reference on letters unless the resident engineer has saddled himself with a particularly dim office staff.

A register for drawings may be elaborate or simple, but is preferably the latter. The most efficient method is to set up two registers of drawings— the first recording all drawings received; the second recording all drawings made on site. The incoming drawings will need no number added to them, since they should all possess an original number. All that is necessary is to 'book' them in and mark the date received.

The register for drawings made on site should show the following details:

(i) consecutive number of drawing;
(ii) subject;
(iii) size and type of drawing;
(iv) to whom copies are sent and when.

The information under (iii) is important. A register is not consulted by a person who knows where a drawing is; it is only consulted by those who do not know. Hence a description of what one is looking for is helpful.

Historical records

The principal records that have to be kept in this category are:

inspectors' daily returns
the site diary and weather records
the resident engineer's diary
the weekly and monthly reports
instructions to contractor
sketches to contractor

The inspector's daily returns form an excellent record of the daily work on site. An example is shown in Fig. 3. The sheet shown is purposely simple; it concentrates on extracting, through the inspector, information as to:

(i) the work done during the day;
(ii) how many men were engaged on each part of the project; and
(iii) the delays.

The inspector is not asked to answer a complicated questionnaire; he is given an *aide-mémoire* at the top of the form to remind him of the separate 'parts' of the job, and he is asked to report all delays. The form not only focuses the inspector's activities for the day (he must visit all parts of the job and report thereon) but it also gives the inspector a chance to communicate with the office. An inspector will like to feel that his returns go into the office, where they can be examined and any observations he makes noticed. The daily returns also form an invaluable record, being of great help should any later dispute arise with the contractor as to progress or payment for standing time or extra work.

The site diary is a day-to-a-page diary which is built up from the

Date ..4/8/65..........

Shift: ~~Night~~/day

INSPECTOR'S REPORT

WORK DONE BY CONTRACTOR	No. of Men
(1) Valve Tower and Bellmouth, (2) Tunnel and Stilling Basin, (3) Dam, (4) Quarry and Road, (5) Road Diversions, (6) Miscellaneous.	
3/ 1 D8 dozing Rip-rap limestone up U/S slope east side. 2nd D8 and roller spreading sand in northwest corner.	1 Foreman 1 Ganger 1 Chargehand 2 D8 drivers
D6 and Hyster also spreading sand, south east of wall. Fowler D6 dozing sand up south west hillside to make up gradient to original slope, before placing filter. Small Traxcavator assisting D8 in north west corner. Rollers compacting fill both sides of wall. Dodge truck and bowser watering bank. SLDC AECs, 2 RAD AECs, 2 Euclid trucks and 2 Euclid scrapers delivering sand until 2·30 pm. Labourers directing traffic excavating for settlement apparatus north of wall and cleaning out berm drainage channel south of wall. 2nd D8 also assisted new 38 RB down quarry road.	2 D6 " 1 Traxcavator " 1 22 RB " 2 Roller " 1 Dodge " 1 Bowser " 2 SLDC AEC " 2 RAD AEC " 4 Euclid " 10 Labourers
4/ 2 38 RBs and Traxcavator loading vehicles until 2·30 pm. Drillers drilling quarry face, Shotfirer and 1 labourer blasting. New 38 RB removed to dam.	1 Ganger 1 Chargehand 2 38 RB drivers 1 Traxcavator " 2 Drillers 1 Labourer
5/ 19 RB tidying up berms at side of Green road hired lorry removing excess spoil to tip, D4 levelling berms at side of road. 13 labourers working at Middle road tidying limestone berms and 5 finished at 12·30 pm. 13 labourers working at Green road tidying up verges, helping curblayer to make curbs and channels up to gully gratings. Joiner stripped shutters from manhole where drains cross, and refixing in second ditch. 8 labourers and 1 Ganger finished at Green Road at 12·30 pm.	3 Gangers 1 19 RB driver 1 D4 " 1 Lorry " 1 Joiner 1 Curblayer 26 Labourers
6/ Men felling and burning trees in Hawthorne wood 10 finished at 12·30 pm.	1 Ganger 16 Labourers
REPORT ALL DELAYS AND BAD WORK	Time lost and No. of men Involved
1 AEC broken down all-day 1 D8 " " " 1 Euclid truck broken down from 9 am. 1 " tractor " " all day Vibrating roller and 22 RB standing all day Work closing down at 4·30 pm.	1 Euclid driver 1 22 RB "

Hours worked by Inspector .....9¼..........

Signature: ..G. Greasley..........

Fig. 3.

inspector's time sheets, notes of the weather, notes about visitors to site, engineers' operations, and any other relevant matters.

Weather records should be kept in the diary recording maximum and minimum temperatures and what time is lost due to rain or snow. It might be thought that temperature records are not really necessary, except to watch for frost when concreting or bricklaying is in progress, but sometimes inexplicable events or failures occurring later, in parts of the structure, may be traced to the weather prevailing at the time. One wall of a tank may, many months after construction, be found under test to spring an unaccountable number of leaks or damp patches in comparison with other walls, and a reference to the weather diary, which reads, 'Heavy showers throughout the day', may remind someone that a downpour of rain sent the men scattering for cover and that, in the general haste to get the wall concreted before further deluges, punning or vibrating of concrete was probably sketchily done. Similarly, efflorescent patches on brickwork may be traced to building in wet weather, and cracks in concrete found to be probably due to high temperatures and sunshine prevailing for a period after concreting.

The resident engineer's diary will be different from the site diary, as it will aim to record all major decisions made and instructions given. It is not an easy diary to keep. On busy days it is often difficult to find the time to jot down the day's activities; on 'off-days' there is apparently so little happening that nothing worth recording can be recalled. However, some effort should be made to keep to a system, and it is as well to make a list beforehand in the front of the diary of special points to be noted.

Of course, the resident engineer's own diary will be a personal record of events, and therefore in some cases confidential to himself or his firm. His main endeavour will be to note down points about which there may later be some argument. Examples are:

(*a*) the visits of all representatives to the site;

(*b*) any disputes which have arisen during the day, and particularly any verbal instructions he gave as a result;

(*c*) any particular points regarding the work which he does not necessarily wish to raise with the contractor at present;

(*d*) any notes regarding particular stages of work or operations carried out.

The weekly report will be filed in the correspondence files, and is a copy of the report sent regularly from the resident engineer to the engineer, describing in summary form all the job events of the week. A typical example is shown in Fig. 4. The *monthly report* is a more generalised summary of progress, written in a fashion which is suitable for presentation to the employer. It will not be so technical as the weekly report to the engineer, but it will still be succinct. If the report is to be submitted under the signature of the engineer to the employer (as is normally the case), then the resident engineer prepares the draft of such a report for the engineer to revise and sign before sending to the employer. Occasionally, under special arrangements—as on overseas jobs—the resident engineer submits the monthly report direct to the employer on behalf of the engineer.

XYZ CONSTRUCTION SCHEME
Weekly Report No. 80
(For week ending 26th June 1966)

Contract 52: Extension to Pumphouse
Continuous rain delayed waterproofing of roof until 25th. Plastering sub-contractors started work on 21st. They will finish next week. Installation of switchboard awaits arrival of manufacturer's fitters promised for 29th.
Labour: 2 plus 2 plasterers.

Contract 54: Electrical re-wiring
Cable laying completed but awaits connection to switchboard. Lighting wiring completed as far as possible. Contractor withdrew men from site on 24th and will return to complete after switchboard connection made.

Contract 57: Mainlaying
The extra sluice valve required at Ch. 3500 was delivered. This completes all deliveries under the valve contract (Contract 53).
Delivery of steel 600 mm diam. pipes continues. Total delivery to date 4600 m or 82 per cent order (Contract 55).
Supply of small cast-iron pipes and fittings continued. Only a few items now outstanding (Contract 56).
Approx. 260 m of pipe laid during week by two gangs working from point 'F' forward and point 'G' back; chainages 3260–3840 and 4480–4210 respectively. Suppliers are being pressed for delivery of special T-junction Ch. 3500 which is promised for next week.
The crossing under the two main-line tracks was completed successfully at Ch. 4400 and in 14 hrs. continuous working.
Labour: 1 General Foreman, 2 section foremen, 3 gangers, 3 jointers, 7 drivers, 11 labourers.
Plant: 2 19 RB back shovels; 1 19 RB crane; 3 dumpers; 2 D4 dozers; 2 concrete mixers; 4 lorries.
Testing. Testing to point F from H was satisfactory and the section left out at Point F for testing was re-inserted and the line made good. Main has now been passed from Ch. 500 to Ch. 3260.
Miscellaneous. A director of Messrs. Smith accompanied by the sports ground manager inspected the reinstated trench through the sports ground and was satisfied.

General
Weather: Wet. 2.15 in. rain
       Temp. 57° to 68° F.
Lost time: 2·men x 6 hrs. Contract 52.
       Nil   Contract 57.

Visitors
Director Messrs. Smith & Co.   25th.
District road inspector to Contract 57. 25th.
Representative pipe suppliers.   21st.

A.B.C.
Resident Engineer

Fig. 4.

Day-to-day instructions to the contractor. There are often daily occasions when it is necessary to inform, or make requests to, the contractor about the work. Some simple system of sending notes to the agent or to members of his staff is necessary. It is best to have only one book in use at a time, all staff writing their notes in it, the carbon copy which remains in the book representing a daily log of all detailed written instructions sent to the agent. Many small but important matters can be dealt with in such a manner—notes about levels set out, notes about shuttering, type of materials to be ordered, results of concrete tests, minor complaints and reminders, details of dimensions and setting out, elucidation sketches, and so on. The notes are handwritten, the sketches freehand, the signature being that of the person providing the information.

The carbon copy remaining forms a useful record in many ways. It forms a kind of 'central notebook' in which basic levels appear; the sketches and dimensions are useful for making alterations to the record drawings and for computing quantities of work done. In addition, it forms an excellent 'information bureau', enabling the resident engineer to see in a moment or two what instructions his staff are currently giving the agent's staff, enabling the resident engineer's own staff to see what instructions he is issuing.

A defect of the system is that it is not possible to send out more than two copies of each note, and the third copy remaining in the book may get faint and difficult to read if the carbons are allowed to deteriorate. For more lengthy notes to the contractor, or where more than two copies must be sent out (e.g. two for the agent and a third copy for the inspector), typed notes may be necessary, and these should be headed 'Memo to agent' rather than be put on official notepaper. It seems out of place to use officially headed notepaper for notes to the agent or his staff or for minor complaints.

Thus a note which reads:

Note to Agent   *10th February*

Concrete blinding. The concrete blinding layer appears to me to be too thin in places, so that it is breaking up under traffic before the foundation concrete is laid and the clay is coming through. Could you please see that it is not less than the specified 75 mm thickness, or let me know what the trouble is.

R.E.

—is far more acceptable to the agent if sent as a handwritten note or 'Memo' than as a formal letter of complaint.

Quantitative and Financial Records

Quantity records

The measuring up of quantities will be one of the more important tasks of the resident engineer and his staff. Many techniques of measurement may be employed, but the main essential for them all is to comply with the following two simple rules:

(1) it should be possible to ascertain immediately from the records what has been measured and what has not;

(2) the records must clearly show what has been *paid for*, as distinct from what has been *measured*. If this is not clear from the start, then endless confusion will result.

Thus, to give an instance, suppose there is a large item for 'excavation and backfill' in the contract. A contractor may have done a substantial amount of excavation, say 500 cu. m, but little or no backfill to date. The measured amount of 500 cu. m might be put in the quantities record, but for the purposes of payment the resident engineer and contractor may agree upon an arbitrary figure of 300 cu. m *for payment*, having regard to the fact that backfill has not been carried out. The records must therefore show 500 cu. m so far measured and 300 cu. m so far paid for.

The records should therefore be divided on lines which are suggested as follows:

(a) A series of notebooks containing sketches and dimensions of work as executed, where different from the contract drawings.

(b) A book or file containing the working out of the quantities.

(c) A summary of the quantities from time to time worked out, all classified under bill items.

(d) A final summary of quantities agreed for payment on each certificate.

The first records for quantities mentioned above will be in field notebooks, and the data will be placed therein from time to time as the work proceeds. This data will be collected by various inspectors and assistants to the resident engineer acting in collaboration with the contractor's quantity surveyor or measurement engineer so that the measurements are agreed on site. Accuracy, clarity, and sufficiency of measurements are essential. As the monthly date for measurement of quantities approaches, the inspectors and staff will bring their measurement notebooks up to date and ready for use in the calculation of quantities. The items of the bill will be gone through in order and the necessary calculations undertaken to find out the amount of work done during the month under each item.

At this point there are two alternative systems which can be used. In the *first* system a loose-leaf file is set up, consisting initially of a page to each item, further pages being added as necessary later. Under each item the necessary quantity calculations are inserted. Such a system is illustrated in Fig. 5. In the *second* system bound calculation books are used, the quantities for the month being calculated item by item and then the month 'ruled off'. Because extra leaves cannot be inserted when bound books are used under this system, a page reference system must be used, so that the quantity measured up to the last certificate for any item is brought forward as the starting quantity for the current month's additional measurement. This is necessary because the amount entered in the bill of quantities is always the cumulative total measurement since the job started, not just the total done for the month.

The difference between these two systems is one of convenience. The first system is physically not quite so convenient as the second, since calculations have to be inserted in a bulky loose-leaf file (or in separate

QUANTITIES REGISTER
(Loose Leaf)

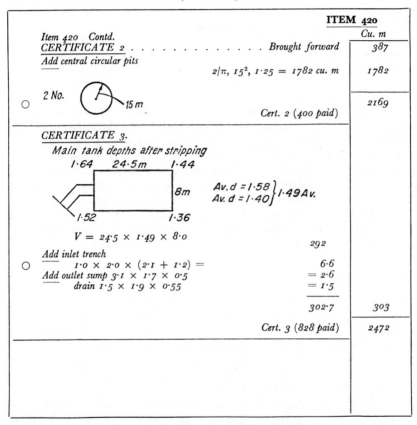

Fig. 5. A page from the quantities register.

Note. This is the working-out register of the quantities, and preferably consists of a file of loose-leaf sheets so that further sheets may be inserted as necessary for any particular item.

files) rather than in easily handled calculation books. On the other hand, under the first system *all* the quantity calculations for any one item are collected together, whereas under the second the quantities for any particular item must be referenced through the calculation books, and an error of referencing may result in quantities being missed out or being measured twice. In the hands of competent staff, however, either system works well.

Comparison of measured quantities with contractor's claim. Having calculated the quantities, they must now be compared item by item with the quantities claimed by the contractor in his monthly claim.

The monthly claim form from the contractor should be presented in the form shown in Fig. 6. The comparison required is between the contractor's quantities under the heading 'total to date' and the resident engineer's own calculations. Where differences are found, conversations with the contractor's site staff will be necessary.

It may be that quantities put forward by the contractor are less than quantities measured by the engineer, or, as previously mentioned, they may be arbitrary figures used for payment purposes only. Thus, for bulk excavation which has only been partly completed, it is a waste of time trying to compute accurately the quantity excavated to any given day. The quantity as finally excavated—to the underside of the foundations and so on—is the figure that must be exact, and this calculation need only be undertaken when foundation excavations are completed. Hence, in the meantime the resident engineer and agent (or their respective staffs) may agree on a 'round figure' representing the approximate excavation to date. This is simply a temporary arrangement to save unnecessary calculation work before the final quantity must be agreed in detail. The method is quite satisfactory. It means that the claim form will show a figure under 'Total to date', whereas in the resident engineer's quantity calculation files there will be no quantity, or perhaps only a rough pencil note showing an approximate calculation which is marked 'provisional'.

Authorisation and measurement of extra works

Clause 51 of the Standard General Conditions of Contract for work in Britain states that extra or varied works must be authorised in writing by the engineer. The same clause permits a verbal order to be given, provided this is later confirmed in writing either by the engineer sending some authorisation to the contractor or by the contractor sending a letter of confirmation to the engineer.

It is frequently impossible for the engineer to send a written variation order to the contractor in advance of the variation being undertaken. What happens is that agreement is reached between agent and resident engineer on the site that a certain matter 'shall be covered by a variation order', and it is then up to the resident engineer to submit a draft order to the engineer for his signature. A typical variation order issued is shown in Fig. 7 page 94.

Dayworks. Normally the resident engineer and agent would hope to come to an agreement as to the price to be paid for the extra or varied works, before the draft order is submitted to the engineer for signature. This price is either an *agreed rate* for payment by measurement, or *day-*

CLAIM FORMS

Section 3—Tanks								Page 6
		As Bill		As Measured			As Bill	Amount
Item No.	Description	Quantity	Unit	Last Certificate	Since Last Certificate	Total to Date	Rate £	£.p.
	Excavation							
418	*Stripping soil*	*483*	*sq. m*	*990*	—	*990*	*0·15*	*148·50*
419	*Excavation for tower*	*503*	*cu. m*	*503*	—	*503*	*0·55*	*276·65*
420	*General excav.*	*836*	*cu. m*	*400*	*428*	*828*	*0·55*	*455·40*
421	*300 mm by hand*	*12*	*cu. m*	—	*74*	*74*	*2·40*	*30·80*
422	*421 in trench*	*2*	*cu. m*	—	*2*	*2*	*2·40*	*4·80*
423	*Soiling and sowing on flat*	*210*	*sq. m*	—	—	—	*0·13*	–
424	*Soiling and sowing on slopes*	*176*	*sq. m*	—	—	—	*0·15*	–
425	*Excavation for base of ladder*	*0.10*	*cu. m*	—	—	—	*2·40*	–
				*T*otal for *excavati*on				*£916·15*
426	*Mass Concrete* *Blinding 75 m Etc.*	*17½*	*cu. m*	*10*	*6*	*16*	*12·50*	*200·00*

Section 3—Tanks—Extra Bill Items								Page 10
		Comparable Bill Item		As Measured			Agreed Rate	Amount
Item No.	Description		Unit	Last Cert.	Since Last Cert.	Total to Date		£.p.
422A	*Extra excavation by hand below trench*	*422*	*cu. m*	—	*5*	*5*	*3·00*	*15·00*
426A	*Class E mass concrete*	*426*	*cu. m*	—	*11*	*11*	*11·50*	*126·50*

Fig. 6. Claim forms as submitted by the contractor.

Note. This is the claim form as presented to the engineer for checking so that he can issue a certificate for payment. Extra Bill Items at agreed rates are frequently inserted on a separate sheet as shown. Variation orders should be issued to cover these extra items.

work 'Daywork' is a term meaning 'by the day'—or, in this particular context—reimbursement to the contractor according to the cost of labour, plant, and materials actually engaged on the varied work, charged at daily or hourly rates. The prices to be paid for dayworks may be as set out in a schedule attached to the contractor's tender; or they may be the prices as set out in the current edition of 'Schedules of Dayworks Carried out

VARIATION ORDER
No. ....

Job ....

Contract No. ....   Description ....

Contractor...

In accordance with and subject to the Conditions of Contract you are hereby instructed to execute the following work:

The prices to be allowed for the above work shall be:

This work is additional to / substituted for work hitherto included in the Contract.

You are instructed to omit items of work as follows:

ESTIMATED NET EFFECT ON THE COST OF WORKS

    This Variation Order   .... increase/decrease

    Add total effect of previous Variation Orders issued .... increase/decrease

                     Total estimated effect   increase/decrease

Signed ....   Signed ....
        Resident Engineer   Engineer

Date ....   Date ....

Fig. 7.

Incidental to Contract Work' issued by The Federation of Civil Engineering Contractors. The Federation's Schedule applies only in Britain, and for overseas civil engineering contracts there must always be a schedule of daywork rates attached to the tender documents, which have been priced by the tenderer.

The typical daywork schedule contains three parts which provide for reimbursement to the contractor on the basis of:

    (i) the cost of labour plus a percentage for overheads;
    (ii) the cost of all materials used plus a percentage for handling, etc.; and
    (iii) the cost of plant at certain rates for each type of plant.

From this it follows that as soon as the resident engineer has authorised some extra works to be carried out on a daywork basis, he must arrange that the labour, materials, and plant used to carry out the extra work are observed and checked by his staff—usually by his inspectors. It is normal practice to expect the contractors' foreman to submit daily time and

DAYWORKS ORDER

.... Contractors Ltd.

Job...   Date ....

Contract No. ....

Variation Order No. ....

Cutting hole in gable end for service pipe, temporarily plugging and forming cut-off wall.

DAYWORKS ACCOUNT

Dates carried out. *16th–24th December*

Quant.	Unit	Item	Rate	£.p.	£.p.
75	No.	Materials Bricks (Per 1000)	£25.40	1·91	
0·5	cu. m	Sand (,, cu. m)	1·25	·06	
½	50 kg	Cement (,, 50 kg)	0·65	·33	
				2·30	
		Plus 10%		·23	
					2·53
25	hrs.	Plant Compressor (See attached statement)	2·25		56·25
56½	hrs.	Labour (See statement attached) Labourers	0.40	22·60	
16½	hrs.	Bricklayer	0·45	7·42	
				30·02	
		Plus 40%		12·01	
					42·03
		Total			£100·81

Signed ....   Signed...................................
            Contractor   Resident Engineer

Fig. 8. A dayworks claim sheet.

Note. This type of sheet is submitted by contractor to the resident engineer for checking materials used and time spent. After signing by resident engineer it is returned to contractor for resubmission in his monthly claim for payment. Alternatively, the time sheets of the men on the work and the materials sheets for materials used may be presented daily by the contractor for signature by the resident engineer (or by an inspector), the full account being made up later.

materials sheets to the inspector for him to check and sign that they are correct as to hours, materials, and plant used. Later it must be the task of an engineer on the resident engineer's staff to check the 'dayworks claims' as they come in from the contractor. A typical dayworks claim sheet is shown in Fig. 8.

Extra items in the contractor's monthly claims. When the contractor's monthly claim is submitted it will probably contain not only the measurement of quantities as set out in the original bill, but:

(i) extra items at agreed rates, and
(ii) accounts for dayworks.

Some engineers do not insist that all extra items be covered by variation orders when, for instance, there are items in the original bill for trench excavation at 1 m depth and for 1·5 m depth and an extra item is added for excavation at 2 m depth. This extra item is sometimes inserted in the bill as an 'A' item, without any variation order being issued. But this is confusing, and the best method is to ensure that variation orders are issued to cover *all* variations. It is then best for the contractor to list all the extra or varied items at the end of his claim, in the same order as the variation orders are numbered because this is the order in which the bill of quantities has been extended, and it makes for ease of checking. If a rate fixed for an extra item is related to the rate quoted for another item already in the bill of quantities this can be stated on the variation order; similarly, if the extra item is in substitution of an original bill item this can also be stated on the variation order.

There is, however, one difficulty that must now be discussed, namely where a variation order covers extra work which is still measurable at bill rates. This case frequently happens. For instance, the engineer might order the contractor to undertake more excavation work, at rates which are already in the bill of quantities. Initially it is for the engineer to decide whether this is an occasion on which to issue a variation order. If he decides that no variation order need be issued, then this results in the measurement exceeding the quantity provided in the bill of quantities against certain particular items. If he decides, on the other hand, that a variation order ought to be issued, then if bill rates apply the variation order should say so, quoting the items of the bill likely to suffer extended measure as a result. It is then up to the resident engineer to decide whether he wants the 'extra measurement' charged separately under the variation order or whether it will simply be added measurement on certain bill items. The latter is probably the easiest course, since it avoids splitting the measurement into the amount which was originally intended, and that which has been added, the 'split' being sometimes very difficult to define. This kind of problem is continually cropping up where amendments are partly extra to what was originally envisaged, and partly in substitution. Where such amendments affect a number of items, it is virtually impossible to define the precise difference in cost between that which would have been done and that which has been done. In consequence, the total of the charges under the variation orders does not necessarily represent the total added cost on the job. This cannot be helped if great complexity of accounting is to be avoided. In the event the engineer wishes to know the total extra charges on a contract, these are the total of extras under the variation orders, *plus* extra measured quantities against the original bill items, *less* quantities reduced and items omitted. It is often exceedingly difficult to give a precise financial breakdown showing the causes of excess cost on a job, because even one variation order may cause many changes of quantity measurement on other items, and these changes can only be theoretically computed rather than actually measured.

Reimbursement of wage increases

A tender may have a price variation clause attached to it and be accepted on that basis. Under such a clause the contractor is reimbursed also for the cost of extra wages that he has to pay because of increases in nationally agreed rates of wages, and the extra cost due to increased prices of materials. A contract containing such a clause puts a heavy added accounting burden upon the resident engineer and his staff.

To deal with wage increases, it is first up to the contractor to submit claim sheets for the extra due. These claim sheets will be complicated and probably lengthy calculations based upon the weekly pay sheets. Thus, if there has been a £0·02 per hour increase in the basic wage-rate, then the substance of the claim will amount to the total number of man-hours shown on any given pay sheet multiplied by £0·02.

There are, however, some rather horrible complications to be taken into account which may be listed as follows:

(i) the increases apply to overtime rates as well;

(ii) building operators may get different rises on different dates from the civil engineering workers;

(iii) the plus rates for skill or conditions of working conditions (i.e. additions above the basic rate for the many workers who are not just labourers working under normal conditions) may also be varied;

(iv) the subsistence or lodging allowances may be altered;

(v) the employer's portion of the national health and insurance contributions may be altered and so may the holidays-with-pay contributions.

As if this were not enough to persuade the resident engineer that—when the problem rears its head—he could well do with some accountancy assistance to deal with this checking; there is the related problems of dayworks to consider.

The just payment to the contractor for extra works on dayworks is the actual cost of labour and materials at the time the work is carried out, plus the agreed percentages then prevailing, plus the agreed hire rates for plant also current. The extra works cannot be fairly worked out on the basic prices in the bill, with the increases in wages and cost of materials paid for separately. In this case the contractor would lose the percentage he is entitled to on the increases of wages and materials.

Actual prices and rates of wages must therefore be used for extra-work charges, and it is thus important that the resident engineer's records should show the dates on which the work is carried out so that the prices and wages ruling at that time may be checked against the daywork claims.

It follows that in working out the extra payments due on account of wage increases, the hours spent on dayworks must first be deducted. This complicates the calculations, especially when wage increases are stepped up from time to time, as one must then ensure that the relevant deductions of hours on dayworks must relate to the right time-periods between successive increases in wage-rates. However, the job must be tackled because the amounts of money involved may be substantial when the contract extends over a lengthy period.

Where further evidence is required, the resident engineer may call upon the contractor for proof of his claim. He will need to check back through the contractor's weekly pay sheets to the time sheets. A kind of elementary auditing is required, but it requires no special accounting skill. Evidence must be looked for to see that the men did actually receive and sign for the amount of money that the pay sheet states was paid out to them. The number of men paid should tally with the resident engineer's records for any week. Circumstances will guide the resident engineer as to the extent of the check he should make. He may choose to check only certain weeks in detail, and if these appear correct and the total claim reasonable, then he may pass the claim for payment.

Any contractor of standing will readily agree to furnish the necessary information, and such a degree of co-operation usually means that nothing other than a small error in accounting here and there will be found.

Increase (or decrease) in cost of materials

To check the claims made by the contractor under this heading, records must be kept of price variations since the date of tender, and the amount of materials used in the work.

A list of basic prices ruling at the date of tender should have been supplied by the contractor at the time of tendering. Where this needs to be extended later, manufacturers and suppliers must be asked to give the price that their products would have been at the date of tender. A record of all these prices should be kept in a file. The terms of the contract need to be carefully examined, however, as in some cases only those materials 'named and priced' in the list attached to the tender are to be considered, and not all the materials used on the temporary or permanent works.

In the same file running totals of the quantities of materials on which the contractor claims extra payment should be made, together with a note of the dates the consignments were bought. For preference these figures should be preceded by a figure giving the total material used prior to the date of any claim arising, so that the whole amount of that particular material used in the job can be calculated and compared with quantities measured to be sure that the quantity forming the basis of the claim is reasonable.

For making these claims the contractor should supply the actual invoices from his suppliers, together with their official receipts for the payments he made to them. These invoices should all be checked, totalled, and the total quantity related to the claims made. The invoices should then be date stamped and marked by the resident engineer or a member of his staff so that they cannot be resubmitted inadvertently.

If the resident engineer wilts at the prospect of totalling up a thousand or so invoices and checking all the pay sheets for wage increases, he may perhaps conclude that an accountant would be flattered if handed the task. Having therefore applied such general and spot checks as he is able to, the resident engineer may pass the account to the engineer, with the information as to how he has checked it. He will warn the agent that if errors are found in due course by the engineer's accountants, or by auditors acting for the employer, adjustments will have to be made to the claim accordingly. No doubt the agent will be happy enough to agree to this, as he will no more wish to use his engineering time on the minutiae of accountancy work than the resident engineer himself will.

Materials on site. The value placed upon materials on site that are not yet incorporated in the permanent structure usually represents something approximating what could be obtained for them if they then had to be resold. Thus straight reinforcing steel, being easily resold, might be paid for on 90 per cent of the invoice price excluding delivery charge. Windows, if purpose made, would be paid on a substantially lower percentage basis, and so on. The important point to note is that these payments for materials on site are temporary only, and must not be blindly continued from month to month, as the items they represent will be gradually consumed in the work and paid for under bill items. It is better to strike out such items from 'materials on site' once they start being used in the works.

Supply contract records

Supply contracts for pipes and valves must be controlled by careful book-keeping methods, whether they are sub-contracts coming under the control of the contractor, or whether they are separate contracts let by the employer and therefore coming under the control of the resident engineer. In either case it is essential to build up a stock-keeping record book in which the numbers of every type of item ordered are entered in the manner described below, the items being delivered to stockyards from whence they are issued and accounted for in the various parts of the work.

Let us take a typical small job as an example. The position may be as follows when the resident engineer arrives on the job:

(a) supply contracts have been let, one for steel pipes and specials, one for cast-iron pipes and specials, and one for valves;

(b) some items of each of the contracts have already been delivered to site and have been paid for;

(c) the main construction contractor is to collect all further items from the railway goods yard and haul to site dump;

(d) certain sections of the pipelines to be laid are 'recoverable work', i.e. work executed by the employer for another outside authority which is to be charged the final cost of that part of the pipeline, and

(e) certain further items are to be ordered under each contract.

The resident engineer will therefore need to keep clearly set out the following data:

(i) A list of what has been ordered under each contract.

(ii) A list of what was on the site when he arrived.

(iii) A record of subsequent deliveries and where delivered to.

(iv) A list showing where each item is dumped and when and where it is used.

He also needs further lists showing:

(v) Payments made to supply contractors.

(vi) Payments made to main contractor for haulage.

Not all these lists can be incorporated on one sheet of paper, and for large contracts, nothing but a proper stores record sheet (with proper stores issue and return sheets) will suffice.

In the smaller contract the following records, as illustrated in Figs. 9 and 10 should suffice. Fig. 9 shows the pipe (or valve) delivery schedule. Columns 1, 2, and 3 of this are simply copied from the relevant order or contract.

Under the title 'Deliveries' the columns permit an assessment of the delivery position at any time, and the total weight of pipes delivered to site can be known, this being used to calculate any payment due to the contractor for haulage on a tonnage rate. Under 'Payments' the corrected invoice prices are inserted by the resident engineer, and the date when he passes invoices to his head office for payment is noted.

Such invoices (usually sent by suppliers in duplicate) are collected by the resident engineer, one copy being signed and sent to the engineer when all the goods listed on that invoice have been received and examined. The remaining duplicate invoices should be retained by the resident engineer and a list kept of those sent off to the engineer. This list is essential, as duplicate copies of invoices sometimes go astray or fail to arrive. When forwarding invoices to the engineer it is always a good plan to forward them under a covering letter (a carbon copy of which is kept and filed) in which are listed the various invoices, their reference

PIPE DELIVERY SCHEDULE

Bill Item	Description	No.	Deliveries:		Weight (tonne)	Delivered	Payments:		
			Advice Note	No.			Invoice No.	Amount	Passed for Payment
D18	150 st. fl-sp (T)	3	44/5838	3	·0482	15 Oct	5838 (Overcharge £3·78 deleted. See invoice.)	£11·34	21 Oct
D19	300 × 4·5 m do. sp (T)	5	14/7953 8/2572	2 3	·6200 ·9300	29 Oct 6 Nov	7953 2572	£43·88 £65·82	15 Nov - do -
D20	300 × 525 fl-sp (T)	4	14/7953	4	·2696	29 Oct	7953	£43·68	- do -
D21	375 × 525 fl-sp (T)	2							
D22	450 × 525 fl-sp (BG)	2	14/7953	2	·2519	29 Oct	7953	£42·78	15 Nov
D23	600 × 2·20 m do-sp (BG)	1							

Fig. 9. A page of the pipe delivery book.

Notes. In the description, the pipe diameter is given first in mm, the length follows. (T) stands for 'Tyton' type joints, (BG) for bolted gland joints, etc. Where no length is given (as in Item D. 18) the item is to standard dimensions.

It may also be necessary to record the number of joints ordered and received.

The weight column is only required if the contractor is to be paid by weight of pipes hauled.

The invoice number will not necessarily always be the same as the advice note number.

It is advisable to leave a two or three-line space below each item to allow for notes as to short deliveries, incorrect invoices, pipes found faulty on delivery, etc.

numbers, and the total of the batch sent, since it can be very confusing if invoices go astray and no record remains behind of what was done with them.

Fig. 10 shows the pipe (or valve) stock book—an essential record in all but the very smallest of contracts. Columns 1, 2, and 3 are, as before, copied from the order; Column 4 is got out by the resident engineer from scrutiny of the drawings and forms a first check on the sufficiency of the order. Column 5 shows deliveries to date, and the remaining columns show where items are stored, what has been used, surplus to date, and disposal of any remainders. It is essential to complete Column 9, especially noting down any returns, as surplus pipes are valuable and their whereabouts must be known.

It can readily be seen that where the quantities of any one type of item are large, a certain amount of space must be left to show transactions with the material, and for the larger contract a loose-leaf ledger, allocating a page or more to each item and using a proper 'in and out' book-keeping system, will be required to keep matters in order.

From time to time the works dump and the various materials dumped along the line should be examined and checked to see that they agree with the book figures. Certain particular operations should be most carefully noted down, as they are frequently the cause of much head scratching if not noted down immediately knowledge of their occurrence comes in. These are:

(a) cutting pipes and making two usable pieces out of one, such as 2 No. $22\frac{1}{2}°$ bends made from cutting a 45° steel bend;

(b) borrowings (particularly collars) by one section of a job from another;

(c) 'exchanges', such as exchanging $22\frac{1}{2}°$ bend for $11\frac{1}{4}°$ bend;

(d) cut lengths of pipe brought back into the dump and then taken out again for use.

When stocktaking is carried out, the golden rule is that it is not worth doing unless it is done properly. Thus, it is no use trying to guess the class of a large cast-iron pipe because it happens to be lying with the class marking half buried in the ground and nobody is about to help turn it over. With small-diameter pipes it is quite useless to try to count up how many $\frac{1}{32}$, $\frac{1}{16}$, and $\frac{1}{8}$ bends there are in an assorted jumbled pile without pulling the pile apart. The resident engineer should send out a competent engineer to do the job of stocktaking armed with a 2 m steel tape, callipers, and a standard catalogue of pipes, and accompanied by enough labour to sort small pipes out and turn the larger ones over.

This subject has been dealt with at length. Careful and accurate records, and keeping them tied up with operations, are essential. The resident engineer is warned that if he does not take this matter seriously he will have a nightmare of trouble on his hands. Pipes are items of great value, and he will find he has the greatest difficulty in persuading the

PIPE STOCK BOOK

Pipe Stock Book

(1)	(2)	(3)	(4)	(5)		(6)	(7)	(8)	(9)
Item No.	Description	No.	Where Required:	Deliveries: Date	No.	Where Placed	Used	Surplus	Disposal
1	750 mm × 4 m S. & S.	24	Pipeline 24	On site	8	Verge by crossing 8	15 & 1 No. 2 m s.p.	2 m p.p.	Scrap
				12 Sept.	8	Verge near entrance 8		2 No. (1 cracked spigot)	3 m length in tank: 1 No. stock
				1 Oct.	8	entrance 8	6		
2	750 mm × 3 m S. & S.	1	Tank	17 Sept.	1	Site Dump 1	1 No.	—	—
3	525 mm 45° S. & S.	6	Tank inlets 2 outlets 2	1 Oct.	6	Site Dump 4	2 inlets 2 outlets	—	2 No. stock
			Pipeline (crossing) 2			Crossing 2	Not used	2 No. (This column recorded in pencil and brought to date before stock check takes place)	

Fig. 10. A page of the pipe and specials stock book.

Note. The purpose of this record (which need only be made up intermittently once the first 4 columns have been filled) is to enable the resident engineer to direct where pipe deliveries should be off-loaded, and from time to time to check the stock lying around. It is suitable only for small contracts where pipework is incidental. In pipe-laying contracts for long lengths of mains a proper loose-leaf ledger account must be kept with a separate page for each item in the bill of quantities where allocations, returns, and transfers between various portions of the job must be recorded.

employer's auditors to 'write off' from stock pipes which are 'unaccounted for'. Their value may easily add up to hundreds of pounds.

Qualitative records

Registers of test results

A file of test results needs to be opened for every kind of testing procedure adopted on site. Initially, files might be opened for the following:

  (i) Borehole: Trial Pit: Auger hole Logs.
 (ii) Grading analyses of Fill Materials, subdivided
      (a) Specified requirements
      (b) Actual results obtained.
(iii) Proctor density tests.
 (iv) *In-situ* density tests.
  (v) Concrete aggregate tests.
 (vi) Concrete cube tests.
(vii) Miscellaneous tests.

The above list presupposes that the work includes foundation testing, earth placing, concreting—which are all normal operations in connection with a civil engineering contract. Other files may be opened for other sorts of test results in connection with other types of civil engineering construction—such as well and borehole sinking and testing, pipe-laying, drain-laying, etc.

Sample register. Whenever more than a few samples of natural materials are likely to be taken for examination (and since the resident engineer will never know at the beginning of any job how many samples will be taken, he had best assume it will be a large number) it is important to open a sample register, in which every sample is booked down—no matter for what purpose. The numbering of the samples can be straight-forward, just as they come to hand, care being taken to label the sample itself with the same number.

Once this is done the sample can always be referred to later by its number in correspondence and reporting, and all the details of how it was obtained, etc., can be traced back to the sample register. If this consecutive numbering is not adopted confusion and mix-up will sooner or later break out from trying to describe samples by other systems, such as by using grid references on site; or TP/1/1, TP/1/2 . . . meaning Trial Pit No. 1, Sample 1; Trial Pit No. 1, Sample 2; and so on.

The register can consist of a ruled foolscap book which has columns ruled vertically, headed in sequence from the left to right across both pages as follows:

Col. 1. Sample number
     2. Source (e.g. borehole, trial pit, etc.)
     3. Location (e.g. chainage, grid ref.)

Col. 4. Depth
    5. Description (brief only)
    6. Container
    7. Date taken
    8. Where tested
    9. Remarks/references

To save the labour of ruling, a good stationer's will often be able to produce a suitable book ready ruled into columns as used by accountants for analysis and costing work. Each sample need take up no more than two or three lines down the page, and perhaps not all the columns need have an entry for each sample. It is important to keep the system simple and brief, so that no one has any trouble keeping it going.

'As built' records

Record drawings

Little need be said on the topic of record drawings. Every engineer has come across cases where record drawings of previously built structures have never been made, or have been inadequately made, and has known the great difficulties that arise as a result, often causing a costly amount of work to be undertaken to expose foundations or to locate buried pipes.

The work on record drawings should continue throughout the contract, a special set of contract drawings being provided on which the resident engineer marks out all deviations from the original design. From time to time, where extensive alterations are encountered, or where preliminary surveys are made, completely new record drawings will have to be made.

On numbers of occasions clarification of the existing contract drawings upon points of detail may be asked for by the contractor, such as a quick detail sketch of footing work for the bricklayer. If these freehand sketches are always drawn in a carbon-copy book the carbon copies will form an exceedingly valuable record in the resident engineer's office for record-drawing alterations, extra works, and so on. Even for such items as working out of sight rail heights for laying drains, position of holes to be left in concrete, and so on—if these and all the other odd little sketches produced in the resident engineer's office are automatically scribbled down on the carbon-copy book the record so obtained will be found to be extremely valuable. It is unnerving to find that a single copy of a sketch has been mislaid and that nobody can recall what was done.

Where pipes are laid underground special care must be taken to chart the course of these pipes accurately, marking valve and stopcock positions and hydrants. The only way to get a really permanent record of the positions of such valves, etc., is to measure the distance from buildings and 'tie-in' by two or more measurements. Measuring from frontages, or from kerb lines or road centres, gives only transitory information, as these reference lines may later be altered in position.

Other records. Where long pipelines are laid it is usual to produce a pipe-laying record book which itemises in sequence the laying of every pipe and fitting which has been laid. The invert levels of pipes are given in metres O.D. either to every pipe or at very point of change of gradient. Notes as to bedding, haunching, or surrounding in concrete are given, and each fitting or cut pipe is described. From time to time offset distances from near-by buildings or other landmarks to particular fittings, such as bends where a change of direction occurs, are noted in the record book, so that their position can be found afterwards if required. The cumulative chainage from the starting-point is given as measured on the ground. Large sewers and drains crossed by the trench are similarly logged in a record book.

It is useful, where plant or proprietary equipment has been included in the works, to make up a data file which lists the maker of such plant and equipment, the original order reference and date, and any descriptive details that might be of future use. If the plant requires attention later on the employer will find it useful to have particulars concerning the original order. Instruction manuals and plant test data, such as performance curves of pumps, turbines, and motors, should all be collected, and two sets of each, together with a set of the manufacturer's drawings in each case, should be handed over to the employer.

Conclusion

The impression might be gained that practically the whole of the resident engineer's time is occupied with paper work, but this is really not so. The size of the supervisory staff will vary with the size of the job, and it will be found that the keeping of the *essential* records outlined above will only take up intermittent time. Records that are so complex that nobody can find the time to keep them going are of no value at all, and the resident engineer should therefore first concentrate on getting down on to paper notes about things which cannot afterwards be checked. Sketches and dimensions of work which is later to be hidden and notes on the number of men and hours worked on extra works are therefore the first essential records.

CHAPTER 8

Programme and Progress Charts

THE programme of construction for the job is the contractor's responsibility, though he must comply with any special requirements laid down by the engineer or set out in any draft programme included in the contract documents. The contractor's first attempt at a detailed programme must usually be submitted shortly after the contract commences, if not before. It must then be examined by the resident engineer and discussed with the contractor if amendments are required before it is sent to the engineer for approval. One of the most important factors influencing a programme is the delivery dates required for the materials of construction.

The basic materials on which civil engineering depends, and which are likely to have extended delivery dates, are steel, cast iron, cement, bricks, and machinery. These delivery dates vary widely according to the locality of the works and the nature of the material required, but it still remains a general condition that manufactured steel, cast iron, and machinery are on such extended delivery dates that the ordering of these materials cannot be left in the hands of the general contractor. It was a widespread practice before the war, for instance, that in a contract for laying a cast iron or steel main the general contractor was the supplier as well as the layer of the pipework. Nowadays the supply of pipes and the supply of machinery are almost always the subject of separate contracts, let before the main construction or erection contract, sometimes as much as a year or eighteen months in advance.

But there are also a multitude of other ingredients of civil engineering work which it may be found necessary to place on order some while before the main construction contract is let, particularly if the work is urgent. In some cases, such as special facing bricks, the employer may be advised by the engineer to place an order for the bricks, and when the contractor comes on to the job the contractor will take over the order. This kind of arrangement needs careful mention in the specification and bill of quantities, so that the responsibilities of the various parties are strictly delineated. In the case of cement and reinforcing bars the *rate* of delivery is usually of main importance, for while firms can normally give delivery of small quantities within a reasonable time, the current commitments of the suppliers govern the maximum amount they can supply in a given time to a given job. Hence, these two materials are usually left to the contractor to supply, particularly as he may have his own personal relationships with the suppliers and will, of course, need to keep in touch with these suppliers so long as the work continues.

In addition to these main items there are numerous small items, often proprietary, which have to be incorporated in the work, such as special valves, recorder gear, lifts, and small machinery of all kinds. The variety of these products would make the separate ordering of them under separate contracts between employer and supplier unnecessarily complex, and the usual practice in this case is to put such items as prime-cost items in the main construction contract. General information about these items should have been settled in advance by the engineer, and it will be the duty of the contractor to place orders with these suppliers directly the main contract is let.

List of orders

The first essential information, therefore, when the resident engineer sets about a careful examination of a programme chart with the contractor, is to have a complete list of all such orders placed in advance and to have a complete knowledge of all the other items which may have to be placed on order forthwith. The bill of quantities must be carefully scrutinised, or else some items may be overlooked. Metal windows may be a typical example of the kind of goods, which, though not necessarily stated to be of any definite brand, may well be found to have a delivery period of nine months or longer. Having regard to the overall time of the contract and the general order of construction, an ordering list must be got out showing the dates on which various materials must be placed on order and the times that delivery must occur.

Attention is next paid to the detailed order of construction as required by the contractor to use his men and plant to the greatest efficiency, and as might be required by the employer. Where the new work is adjacent to old, particular attention will have to be paid to maintaining all rights of way to the existing building. An access road, for instance, which runs alongside a new building under construction may be difficult to keep clear at all times without unduly complicating the work of scaffolding and delivering materials for construction. It may be that the contractor would prefer to go to the expense of making a temporary alternative access road to the old building so that he can spread himself around the new works, and the consideration of this proposition may involve discussion with the engineer and the employer.

Existing sanitary arrangements cannot be cut off or interfered with until alternative temporary or permanent arrangements are made. Diversion of underground electricity cables or overhead telephone wires may be necessary. For the contractor the actual operations of excavation will have to be carefully worked out, because where mechanical excavators are used, they must 'work their way out' of a site and cannot go back to excavate isolated interior excavations. Where the site is a large and complicated one or cramped in its surroundings, the routes for laden and unladen traffic must be worked out, for at the height of construction, excavation, concreting, and other operations may be going on simultaneously. The concreting plant must be placed so that the concrete can be delivered to the work with the least possible delay.

Programme charts

The drawing up of a programme is skilled work calling for considerable experience in the art of construction. The programme may seem simple enough when presented in its final form, but inspection in detail will reveal that it represents a great deal of careful calculation. It may be quite easy for a resident engineer to suggest that, 'Part A of the works should be completed by 1st June and then the way will be clear to start part B of the works, which can conveniently follow', but as far as the contractor is concerned a much more rigorous solution may be demanded. He has to find the most economic and efficient programme. This means two things to the contractor:

(i) that once he has brought certain types of men and machines on to the job he must use them full time continuously until their tasks are completed, and
(ii) that the outputs required from men and machines must be kept as steady as possible.

A contractor cannot arrange to have thirty carpenters on the site one month, half a dozen the next, then thirty again for the third month; he wants the work so arranged that he can employ (say) twenty carpenters on steady output for the three months. Similarly, he wants the machines on steady output.

Neither is it a question of the contractor 'wanting' it so; he *must* have it so in order to be efficient and keep himself in business. Hence the resident engineer must first of all await the contractor's own proposals for a programme of working, and he must listen to and appreciate the contractor's problems before he gives his own opinions or starts reminding the contractor of certain overriding matters concerning special dates of completion that have been laid down in the specification. Of course, the contractor must comply with these specified overriding conditions, but he must be permitted to do so in his own manner, so long as his methods appear likely to give the desired end result and will not prejudice the quality of the work or the intentions of the designers.

The form in which a programme is presented may initially consist of a list of dates by which certain operations should be completed. More detailed calculations may translate these dates into a 'bar chart' which, setting out the programme in a visual form, also permits the rate and duration of working on particular operations to be written in.

The Ministry of Works have published a useful pamphlet on programme and progress charts. Though it is elementary, it contains thoroughly practical suggestions. However, the examples given, though appearing to be large, are for simple contracts. Where, in a contract, the bulk of the work both in time and expenditure is contained in a few items, the preparation of a programme chart is a simple matter, and the keeping of the records of progress is also simple. Typical examples of such contracts are the building of a reservoir or dam and the laying of pipes. For a normal reinforced- or mass-concrete reservoir the main items showing progress will be excavation, concreting, and filling. For a dam there will be half a dozen or so major items. For a pipeline, length laid is, of course, the criterion of progress.

But there are other works of civil engineering construction which are composed of separate units, each unit containing in itself a great variety of operations—e.g. excavation, foundations, concreting, bricklaying, pipe-laying, plastering, plumbing, heating and lighting, installation of machinery, decorating, glazing and woodwork, roofing, filling back, and making roads and laying drains. A programme chart for a job consisting of several units each entailing many trades would be a very complex affair, and the greater the complexity of a programme chart, the less likelihood of its being of real value. The only thing to do in this case is either to adopt one set of subdivisions into units of construction, i.e. a 'vertical' subdivision, or else to subdivide 'horizontally' into types of construction. In the latter case concreting would be one item for the whole job, further divided as necessary into the individual units or into classes, i.e. foundation, up to first floor, above first floor, and so on. The subdivision must not be excessive, or else the clarity of the programme will be affected.

Progress records

Nearly all programme charts are so arranged that the progress as compared with the programme may be marked on them. A frequent question for a resident engineer is: 'What is the progress like and how long will it take to finish?' This, even on a small job, is a difficult question to answer and, even with good records, the answer is often at best a guess. There are numerous types of combined programme and progress charts, but it depends to a large extent upon the nature of the contract which type of chart is best suited to the purpose of indicating real progress. Judgment must therefore first be exercised by choosing the correct form of chart.

The most widely advertised form of chart is also the most complicated, and part of a typical chart is shown in Fig. 11. It will be seen that the job is divided into trades, which later are divided into locality. Against each item there are two horizontal lines and two lines of figures.

The top *row of figures* indicates the cumulative quantity of any item that should be carried out week by week to conform with the proposed programme.

The *top line* (or block), shown partly full and partly shaded, shows in its

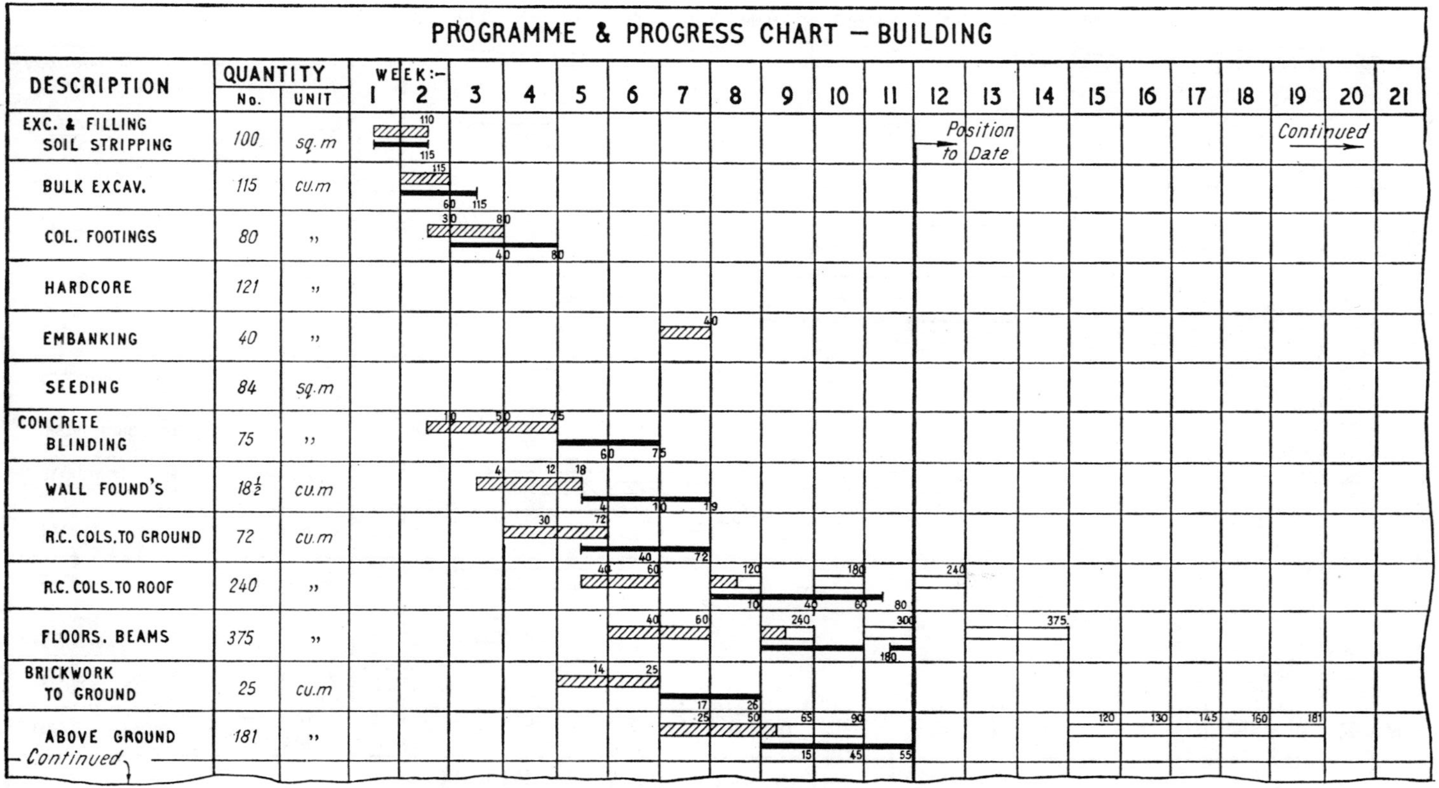
PROGRAMME & PROGRESS CHART — BUILDING
DESCRIPTION
QUANTITY
No.
UNIT
WEEK:—
1 2 3 4 5 6 7 8 9 10 11 12 13 14 15 16 17 18 19 20 21
EXC. & FILLING SOIL STRIPPING 100 sq.m
BULK EXCAV. 115 cu.m
COL. FOOTINGS 80 ,,
HARDCORE 121 ,,
EMBANKING 40 ,,
SEEDING 84 sq.m
CONCRETE BLINDING 75 ,,
WALL FOUND'S 18½ cu.m
R.C. COLS. TO GROUND 72 cu.m
R.C. COLS. TO ROOF 240 ,,
FLOORS. BEAMS 375 ,,
BRICKWORK TO GROUND 25 cu.m
ABOVE GROUND 181 ,,
Continued
Position to Date
Continued

Fig. 11. Part of a programme and progress chart for a building.

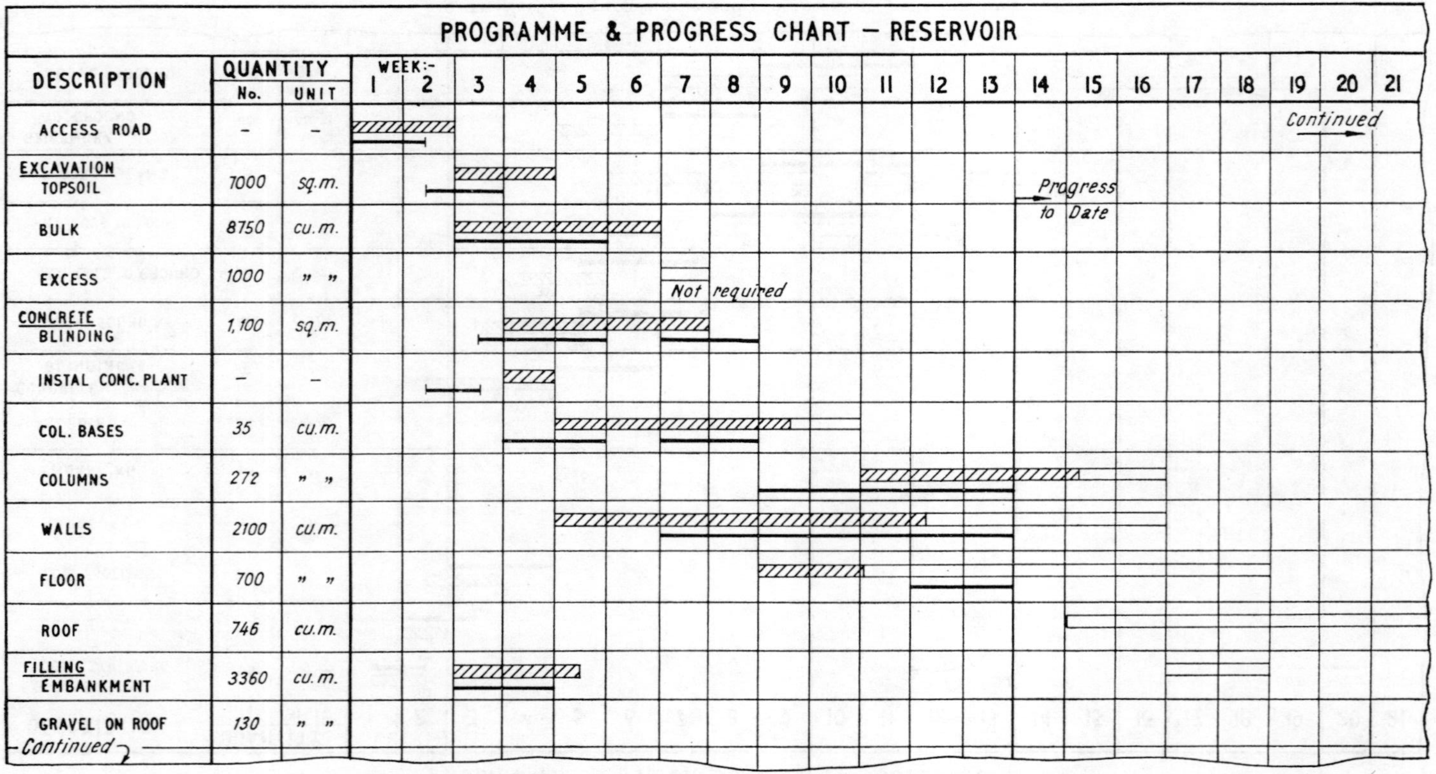

Fig. 12. Part of a programme and progress chart for a reservoir (simplified version).

full length the whole quantity to be placed, and by the shaded portion that proportion of the total quantity placed to date.

The *second line* is simply a line drawn from the date of starting work on that particular item to the finishing date.

The *second row of figures* shows the cumulative quantity actually placed week by week to date.

This chart therefore shows at a glance:

(1) the date of starting on an item relative to the estimated date of starting;
(2) the proportion of the item completed;
(3) the number of weeks at present in arrear or in advance of the estimate;
(4) the number of weeks' work remaining to be done. It also shows the time relationship between items and indicates which items must be carried out before another can be commenced.

Simplified version of a progress chart. The chart shown in Fig. 11 . . . can be quite difficult to compile for a large job, it may take considerable time to set up, and it then requires constant attention to be kept up to date. It may only be possible to bring it up to date once a month when the monthly measurement has been undertaken. Also it is rather difficult to incorporate on such a chart items which, though important for progress, cannot be extracted on a quantity basis, such as the installation of pumps, erection of plumbing, heating systems.

However, by omitting the figures of quantities a very simple time chart as shown in Fig. 12 can readily be produced. The advantage of this chart is that performance can readily be compared with intentions. This is often quite adequate as a visual reminder to both resident engineer and agent of progress, for *the aim is* to get things done *at least by the time intended* if not before.

To prepare such a chart, it is useful to draw up initially a schedule of dates for completion of sundry operations as shown in Fig. 13. This can form a useful reminder calendar for later use. It is, of course, drawn up after careful calculation to ensure that the time periods allowed for such matters as ordering, designing, and delivery are practicable.

To answer the question—'when will the job finish?'—the engineer will not only need to consult his progress chart but he must consider the season of the year, the labour force likely to be available to the contractor, and the delivery dates for materials. In estimating the time to be taken on certain work, such as concreting or bricklaying, the complexity and accessibility of the work must be taken into account, but the progress chart will not show the varying speed of concreting, bricklaying, etc., in relation to complexity, height, or shuttering area. That this is a very relevant matter is obvious, since concrete work and brickwork in a structure require more scaffolding, and become more complex and diverse in character as the foundations are left behind.

For the fairly simple job, the pictorial record of achievement to be mentioned later is of value for pipe-laying, tunnelling, and dams. For the complex building contract, a payment record chart when intelligently used often proves as good an indication of progress as anything else. It will not be of much use in a contract for the installation of plant or

TIME CHART

CONTRACT TIMES			
	Tank	*Admin. Block*	*Pumping Station*
1st Year. Jan.			
Feb.	⎫	Order roof trusses	Order windows, roof beams
Mar.	⎬ Excav.	Prelim.-heating	Founds. in
Apr.	⎭		
May	⎫		⎫ Walls
June	⎬ Walls		
July			⎫ Floors
Aug.	⎭	Order slates	
Sept.		Order guttering	Pump founds.
Oct.			
Nov.	⎫		⎫ Piping
Dec.	⎬ Cols	Roof on	⎭
2nd Year. Jan.	⎭	———	Windows
Feb.	⎫ Floor		Roof beams
Mar.	⎭		Roofing
Apr.	⎰ Main		Roof on
	⎱ laying	Plumber	———
May	⎫ Roof		Commence install.
June		Heating	machinery
July	⎱ Asphalting	⎰ Glazing	Doors. Glazing
Aug.	⎰	⎬ Electrician	⎱ Electrician
Sept.	Testing	⎱ Plastering	⎰ Plastering
Oct.	⎰ Finish embanking	Seeding	
			End install.
Nov.	⎱ Seeding	Decorating	machinery
Dec.	Manholes		Testing
3rd Year. Jan.			Painting
Feb.		Final decorating	Roads—final
Mar.			
Apr.			
May		Opening 1st May	

Fig. 13. A simple time chart for a building contract.

machinery, but for a building contract it has definite advantages, and should be one of the first graphs to be kept going. It is very simple to produce, easy to keep up to date, and its message can be read at a glance. It is also surprisingly accurate when judiciously got out. One of the reasons for this is that in a payments graph, if it is based on a properly tendered bill of quantities, the variations in complexity of work are automatically reflected in the prices. Thus, when the speed of work slows down because more complicated work is encountered, payments tend to remain steady because individual prices are higher and the payments graph tends to maintain a steady increase, which varies only slightly from the average slope.

The simple total of payments made under the contract for items scheduled in the bill of quantities may not suffice to give a true record of progress. If, however, the bill of quantities is gone through and from it is taken away all major sub-contract and prime-cost items, or relatively

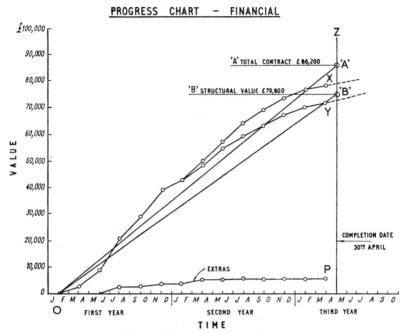

Fig. 14. A financial progress chart.

expensive items, such as windows, plumbing, heating, etc., the remaining total price will represent approximately in cash the total value of building work to be carried out by the main contractor's men. A chart similar to that shown in Fig. 14 can then be drawn up. Values A and B show the total bill price and the reduced bill price calculated as above, respectively.

By a quick analysis of each certificate of payment to get the related payment made to date, two graph lines OX and OY may be drawn showing progress as measured by finance. The vertical line through Z represents completion date, and it is obvious that OY must approach line BB' some time before reaching Z to allow time for the finishing items to go in. Extra works may be shown as a third line OP, cumulative in total from the base line. The figures adopted for lines OX and OY must, of course, be based on bill prices only, as they have to compare with contract quotations A and B. Increased costs due to increases in wages and cost of materials must be excluded.

Though it is not held that this kind of chart is absolutely accurate, it does give a fair and clear indication of the trend of progress. The slope of the lines OX and OY will clearly indicate when progress is too slow, and the causes may be quickly ascertained when the type of work done and the number of workmen engaged for that period are examined.

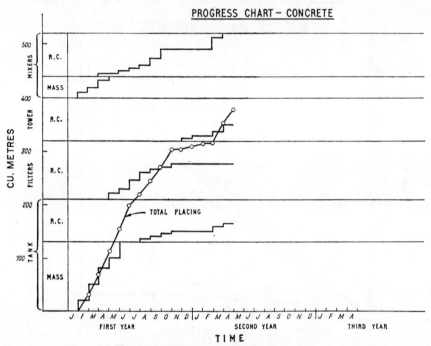

Fig. 15. A progress chart for concrete work.

Of further value to the resident engineer will be one or two additional graphs from which he can gain a good estimate as to the speed of working and progress on some of the main items of the job under different conditions. Thus, a graph for concreting as shown in Fig. 15 will be found useful. This is divided into stages showing concrete placing in different parts of the job (as in Fig. 15) or to different levels in the structure.

Other progress charts. A main-laying contract lends itself to pictorial representation of progress. A space may be left at the bottom of each contract drawing showing the sections of main, in which a block diagram is inserted to show, by colouring in and dating, the progress under the six main headings of delivery of pipes, excavation, laying and jointing, testing, backfilling, and final reinstatement. Fig. 16 shows the type of progress chart described.

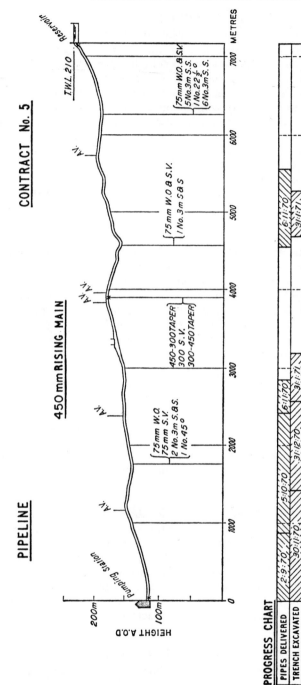

Fig. 16. Pipe-laying contract drawing showing progress chart.

Critical path method of programming

The critical path method of programming (C.P.M. programming) may be considered as a detailed form of the chart shown in Fig. 12. It sets out all the events to be achieved to complete the whole works from start to finish and links these across from one to another in a spider's web of numbered activities showing how the achievement of any event depends upon the completion or part completion of some other event. These events and their time-linkages may be shown on a large diagram: more usually they are put into a computer. The diagram is then searched (or the computer searches its data) to find those *unavoidable 'nose to tail events' which take the longest total time to achieve*. This is the *critical* path—since all other paralleling paths through other events take a shorter time.

The computer can print out a large amount of data, showing the dates by which events on the critical path must be achieved; the amount of time to spare on parallel operations; and what new critical path would emerge should times to achieve events outside the critical path take longer than supposed. The computer can repeat this for 'optimistic', 'pessimistic' or 'realistic' time-estimates for each operation and show, as a result, earliest and latest dates for completion of any event, whether on or off the critical path. (This kind of analysis is labelled P.E.R.T. programming, or 'Programme Evaluation and Review Technique'.) The information procured highlights operations which must be completed by a given time in order that the overall time for construction may be achieved; it also reveals those other operations which run second, third, etc., in regard to spare time available for them.

It is essential, however, that if the analysis is to be of practical use it must be kept continuously up to date. Actual achievements on site must be regularly reported and inserted in the computer programme which must be run through again, thus revealing new operations which have become critical, or different timings for operations, or reductions of spare time. If this is not done the work on site will depart more and more widely from the theoretical programme originally drawn up, and money spent on this will be wasted.

The chief difficulty with regard to critical path programming is the difficulty of estimating the times required for the operations; these cannot be accurately estimated without knowing the methods to be used, but the contractor cannot foresee in every instance what methods he will be using up to the end of the contract. A second difficulty is that an 'interpreter' is required to translate the computer results into real operational instructions and this, together with the cost of the initial programming, makes the method expensive. It is therefore only suitable for large complex projects where many contracts or sub-contracts are involved.

The part played by the agent in programming

It is the contractor's agent who has the primary on-the-spot responsibility for programming the work and keeping progress in line. The resident engineer's job is to assist, if asked, and provide information. As the work proceeds the resident engineer must keep watch on what is achieved and check that it matches the contractor's declared intentions, and he must advise the engineer when serious delays are being experienced. Before acting formally in this matter the resident engineer will have to put his views, perhaps several times, to the agent, and will have sought to persuade him to take the necessary steps to speed up progress, not forgetting to offer what assistance he can.

A good agent, whether he bothers to use the term or not, automatically thinks in terms of 'the critical path' that lies before him. He is able instantly to issue new 'critical-path' instructions consequent upon what he sees and what he deduces must be done. Thus, if he arrives to find a number of workers have not reported he will soon re-organise the day's work so that the best use is made of the available men.

While an agent will constantly bear in mind the major steps to be achieved in his overall programme, his main concentration is upon the present position—today, the week's aim as a whole, and the possible programme for next week. He is continually staking out the critical path ahead of him, working his way to the eventual goal with acute awareness of the need to have safety margins in hand for all sorts of difficulties and troubles that his long experience tells him will inevitably crop up, even though he cannot forecast the precise form in which they will appear.

Furthermore the good agent will be quick to detect when things are in his favour—when the weather seems to promise fine, when the spirit on the job is good—and, grasping such opportunities, he will use them to drive the job onwards knowing that one success leads to another. By this means and the force of his personality he may pull the job ahead of schedule and complete before the promised time.

References

Programme and Progress. A Pamphlet dealing with the Preparation of Charts for Civil Engineering and Building Contracts. Ministry of Works. H.M.S.O.

C.P.M. Explained. (Critical Path Method) Digest No. 53, Building Research Station. H.M.S.O. 1967.

CHAPTER 9

Specifications—General Considerations

THERE are two ways of writing specifications. One is to copy from other specifications; the other is to write directly from a full practical knowledge of the subject. A wise engineer will employ a judicious mixture of both techniques, for the good reason that there is no reasonable alternative open to him. The specification for any ordinary engineering contract frequently encompasses such a wide variety of specialised engineering experience that the engineer cannot avoid some reference to what others have written before him.

The purpose of a civil engineering specification is to tell the contractor precisely:

  (i) the extent of the work he has to carry out;
 (ii) the methods he may or may not use in order to construct the works;
(iii) the quality and type of materials and workmanship that will prove acceptable.

The achievement of the first and third items is straightforward, but there are some dangers attached to the second item.

Consider, by way of illustration, a contract for the supply and erection of machinery. The engineer will set out in his specification the work that the plant will be called upon to carry out. This section should not be difficult to write, as it will be the essence of the problem which the engineer seeks to solve by the installation of a new plant.

The engineer may, however, have definite views upon the way in which the work is to be carried out, and here he treads upon dangerous ground. He may clearly lay down certain conditions, such that no damage is caused to existing plant or structures, but he must be careful to refrain from directions to the contractor which will relieve the contractor from liabilities which are properly his. For instance, it may appear that, in order to get the plant in position, some temporary measures may need to be taken to under-pin, shore, or demolish and re-erect parts of an existing structure; there may be several alternatives. If the engineer specifies, therefore, the exact measures and apparatus to be used; then, if the contractor follows these measures and damage follows, liability for the damage lies squarely upon the engineer.

The third purpose of the specification—to specify the type and quality of materials and workmanship that will prove acceptable—appears to call upon the engineer for an immensely wide range of specialised knowledge. It is not surprising, therefore, that one of the common ways of writing a specification is for an engineer to gather all other specifications he can find that have been written on the same subject (regardless of their date) and, by a process of editing, combine relevant portions of these specifications and so produce his own. In due course, this new specification will doubtless be used by other engineers. This evolutionary system seems to have been going on for so many years that one may wonder who wrote the first specification.

Now it is easy to criticise this method, but in the event there is no real alternative. The engineer may well be able to write fully and clearly such matters in the specification of which he has had direct practical experience. But there are bound to be other matters on which he will have to obtain the guidance of past specifications and British Standard Specifications or textbooks.

In so compiling his specification from a number of sources, the engineer needs to be careful about the overall planning.

Planning the specification

One of the main faults of many specifications is that they are too jumbled up. On even a medium-sized job a specification nowadays may run to fifty to seventy-five thousand words. It is with this vast and often formless bible of instructions that a team of men on site may have to live for several years during construction, using it as their arbiter, guide, and scapegoat. With some improperly planned specifications, it is possible for the resident engineer to issue an extra-works order, only to discover at a later date that this particular extra work was so written up as to be included with another item.

There are, in general, four main sections to the usual civil engineering specification. These are:

   I. General requirements.
   II. Programme, order of construction, and liaison with other contractors.
   III. Special requirements and descriptions of works.
   IV. Materials and workmanship.

Section I—The general requirements will deal with the following matters:

1. Brief description of works	9. Protection of existing works and amenities
2. Drawings	
3. Access and land available	10. Watching, fencing
4. Easements: compensation	11. Water supply
5. Work in roads etc.	12. Power supplies
6. Setting out data	13. Drainage: discharge of water
7. Notice of other contracts	14. Engineer's office
8. Programme: priorities	15. Attendance upon Engineer

16. Telephone
17. Contractor's offices
18. Sanitation

19. Labour rates to be inclusive

20. Bonus damages
21. Forms for monthly statements
22. Contractor's orders to be approved
23. Photographs
24. Site to be kept tidy

Section II—Programme and liaison with other contractors will set out any programme required, give any special order of construction or dates of partial completion to be complied with. It will then go on to list other contractors who have been engaged to take part in the project, what their work will be, and how this is intended to be fitted in the general programme. Any nominated sub-contractors and their proposed services are listed, and such instructions as are necessary will be set out. This section may also include matters such as bonus and penalties, performance and guarantees.

Section III—Special requirements and descriptions of works will, in general, deal with all matters to be complied with that are special to certain parts of the project and which cannot be dealt with under Section IV. On some jobs this Section III will form the bulk of the specification. Within it one would find all the detailed requirements to be followed in connection with (for instance), the procuring and compacting of fill for an earth dam. This, in itself, would form a large sub-section of Section III. On other jobs, however, it may be that the work is mostly unexceptional, but extends over a wide variety of trades. In this case it may be better to omit Section III and go straight to the section dealing with workmanship and materials, mentioning any special requirements as they crop up under the various trades.

Section IV—Workmanship and materials should deal with the detailed requirements to be followed in every trade, the trades being listed more or less in the traditional order as follows:

Demolition work
Excavation and filling
Pipe-laying (if a major item in the contract)
Roads (if a major item in the contract)
Concrete—*in situ*
      —reinforcement
      —shuttering
      —pre-cast
      —pre-stressed
Brickwork

Masonry
Waterproofing work (asphalt etc.)
Steelwork and ironwork
Roofing and carpentry
Joinery
Flooring
Plastering
Glazing
Electrical
Plumbing
Painting
Fencing

The order given is not strictly in accordance with the building or civil engineering listed order of trades, and it may be changed as seems reasonable. Any list should be generally in the order in which the work will be undertaken, so that, in writing the specification, ideas can be developed consecutively one after the other—e.g. by putting steelwork before roofing (which is contrary to both building and civil engineering codes) one can describe the steel trusses required for a roof before one goes on to describe the finish of the roof. Perhaps in another contract, if the building is steel framed, it would be advantageous instead to describe steelwork before brickwork. Rules do not need to be followed so rigidly that a logical approach is lost.

Site and access

The location of the proposed works having been given, the specification should state which means of access can be used, and which, if any, cannot. The general conditions of contract usually state that the contractor is to bear all expenses and charges for special or temporary wayleaves required by him in connection with access to the site, and further, that he is to negotiate for these himself and conform with all local authority and highway authority byelaws. Where permanent easements for pipes or other works are required, the employer undertakes to acquire and pay for these and also to pay such compensation for damage within certain specified limits of ground as must necessarily result from the execution of the work in a reasonable manner. The employer may undertake to pay such compensation for a 10–20 m strip of land along the pipeline route.

It is usual to mark on the drawing, areas which the contractor may use for work-sheds, storage of equipment, etc., and to describe these in the specification, informing the contractor that if he requires further land elsewhere he must make provision and arrangement for it at his own expense.

Possession of the site is usually given to the contractor on the starting date, though it may be possible only to give part possession, extending the portions of site available as the contract proceeds. This question is usually dealt with in the early part of the specification, and there must also be made provision for dealing with claims from the contractor for time or expense caused to him by the inability of the employer to allow access to any given portion at the time when the contractor asks for it.

Some contracts expressly exclude claims under this heading, but this would seem unfair. A fair contract will at least grant an extension of time to the contractor for delays caused by the employer refusing access.

Special mention will have to be made of any particular arrangements which must be made to keep a way of entry open to existing works.

It is also of interest to the contractor to know the location of the nearest railway station, and whether at this station there is a crane for off-loading out of railway trucks, though the contractor must expressly be left to make any arrangements he requires himself. He should, in any case, be instructed in the specification to visit the site and inspect the conditions of erection for himself.

Describing the extent of the work

The extent of the contract must be clearly defined. The actual physical boundaries of the beginning and end of the constructional work should be stated in words. The overall purpose of the work required should be stated, so that the contractor can get a definite picture of what is required from him. For constructional contracts this section of the specification will be a brief description of the various structures, their position, relation to each other, and purpose.

In some contracts a valiant effort is made by the specifier to bind the contractor to do everything necessary to make the works complete and finished. The following example, taken from an actual contract, is rather breathtaking:

> The work hereinafter specified shall include all the general work preparatory to its execution, and the compliance by the contractor with all the Conditions of Contract, materials, apparatus, together with water, machinery, pumps, shoring, timbering, moulds, templates, centres, tools, tackle, utensils and plant of every description, also labour, wages, salaries, carriage, transport, carting, offices, sheds, coverings, matters and requisites of every sort and kind that may be necessary for the due and perfect construction and completion of the work; the provision of proper and sufficient protective works, including all necessary temporary fencing, lighting and watching required for the safety of the public and the protection of the works and of adjoining lands; the execution of all necessary contingent works; the payment of all fees to highway and other authorities and persons, and of all charges in respect of damage to roads by extraordinary traffic rising from or out of the execution of the works; the effecting and maintenance of fire, workmen's, third party, and all other insurances, the provision of mess, sanitary and all other accommodation for workmen, the regular clearance of rubbish and any reinstatement; clearing up and leaving perfect on completion that may be necessary, and all other matters, things and requisites of any kind whatever necessary for the due and perfect construction and completion of the several works in accordance with the Conditions of Contract, and according to the true intent and meaning of the Drawings and of this Specification and of the further drawings and instructions that may be issued by the Engineer from time to time.

The clause merits some attention, because it illustrates so well the dangers that beset the engineer while writing a specification. However large the clause becomes, there is always the danger of incompleteness which results in tailing-off into lame phrases such as, 'and plant of every description' or 'matters and requisites of every sort and kind'. The aim in writing the clause is laudable, but it is nevertheless a waste of time. To the tendered figure, appended to the summary of the bill of quantities, will be attached a brief description of what it is intended that the figure shall include, and this description should be short and in sufficiently general terms that it will include everything necessary for the 'proper completion' of the work. In the event of a dispute, 'proper completion' requires legal definition.

It becomes clear that, in the part of the specification dealing with the extent of the contract, the description should relate to the physical extent of the works to be constructed, and the defining of the full liabilities of the contractor should be left to the legal department in their drafting of the general conditions, and the contract between employer and contractor.

Covering the question of wages

It is important that a clause is included in the specification, making the contractor responsible for all necessary payments to his men; otherwise, he may refuse to pay a bonus or travelling time or subsistence money, or may refuse them the opportunity to work overtime unless he recovers his payments under such headings from the employer as an extra on the contract. The contractor's obligations under the contract include the supply of all labour and materials and plant necessary to get the work done. The specification should make clear that, as with materials and plant, what the contractor has actually to pay for labour is no concern of the employer's, save that it must be at least the minimum rates laid down by national agreements between federations of contractors and their employees. A bonus payment or a certain amount of overtime may have to be given to the workmen by the contractor in order to ensure a supply of labour on the site. Similarly, travelling time and subsistence allowances may have to be paid. The choice of such payments lies with the contractor.

The specification should clearly indicate that the tendered prices are to include all labour payments: wages, overtime, bonus, subsistence, travelling, insurances, holidays with pay, pensions, lost time, plus rates for skill, and so on. The only extra payments in relation to labour the employer should undertake to pay are:

(i) overtime rates of pay for *overtime ordered* by the engineer, and

(ii) *increases in the rates* applicable if such increases are nationally agreed after the date of submission of the tender and provided the contract permits such increases to be claimed.

Special contracts

What has been said so far applies primarily to construction contracts. There are, of course, many other types of contracts which the resident engineer will be expected to supervise, for instance, for the supply and erection of machinery, water- or sewage-treatment equipment, or for sinking wells and boreholes. The description of the extent of these contracts will probably need close attention. The drawings for these contracts may be merely suggestions for the consideration of the contractor, who is at liberty to make alternative recommendations. Indeed, in order to call forth the best that contractors are able to offer, it is essential that alternatives should be left open to the contractor. None the less, it is of great benefit to the contractor for the specification to set out the prime considerations in making a choice from the tenders submitted. For instance, a specification for machinery might state that in selecting a tender the authority will have regard to the following factors:

(*a*) capital cost;
(*b*) operating cost;
(*c*) reliability; and
(*d*) ease of operation and maintenance.

Tenderers will therefore have clearly in their minds the main points on which they are in competition with one another.

A list of the drawings should be inserted in this part of the specification.

Co-ordination of several contracts

Under a construction contract it is frequently necessary for the contractor to carry out certain building work in connection with the other contracts, under which machinery of all kinds may be supplied and erected. Many examples spring to mind—the building of foundation blocks for machinery, the building in of pipes into structures, the excavation and backfilling for pipework supplied and laid by machinery contractors, and all the numerous tasks of building in, or concreting in, of rag bolts, supporting blocks, hangers, etc., for a great variety of equipment.

All these items must, of course, occur individually in the bill of quantities and, even where exact details are not available, some rates for provisional quantities should be obtained in the bill. The specification must, for its part, state clearly the extent of the work that will be required and the extreme importance of the building contractor carrying out this work as and when required.

This question of the 'marrying up' of several contracts on the site is one of the most difficult problems that the resident engineer has to face, and he is entitled to receive clear guidance from the specification as to the exact responsibility of each contractor.

The specification for the building contractor must therefore clearly state that he is called upon to exercise the most careful liaison with other firms installing plant and machinery, and he must be prepared, given reasonable notice, to carry out from time to time such building work as these other contractors may require to enable them to proceed with their contracts.

The building contract specification, having commenced by emphasising the importance of liaison at all times, should continue by stating the nature of the other contracts which are being let in connection with the work, and the extent these other contractors will be entitled to call upon the building contractor. Such points as the following will need to be considered:

(*a*) Whether the building contractor will be expected to off-load on the site deliveries of materials for the other contracts. (If so, items in the bill must be provided.) If it is not so expected, then it may be inferred that the other contractors are to make their own arrangements with the building contractor, if they wish, for off-loading.

(*b*) Whether the building contractor will be expected to take charge of and keep safe materials on site which belong to other contractors and which are delivered to the site before these contractors commence work. If this is so, an item, or items, must be placed in the bill for the building contractor taking charge of these materials, storing, keeping under supervision, and insuring if necessary.

(*c*) Whether the building contractor will be expected to loan scaffolding, hoisting equipment, etc., to the other contractors. If this is so, then the normal method of charging for this equipment is by the standard rates set out in the *Schedule of Dayworks Carried out Incidental to Contract Work* published by the Federation of Civil Engineering Contractors.

(*d*) Whether the contractor is to supply unskilled labour for the erection of machinery, plant, etc., of the other contractors, and if so, by what method he is to be paid. This may be on a labour plus percentage cost or by a lump-sum quotation.

(*e*) A definition of the words 'building in', especially in relation to pipework, could usefully be made in this part of the specification. It should be taken to mean any one of three things. Firstly, for example, the machinery or plant contractors may place in exact position a pipe which is required to be built into a tank. The building contractor is then expected to shape his shuttering around the pipe and pour concrete in. Or, secondly, the term should cover the case where a hole is left in the concrete, and later, when the pipe has been placed in position by the machinery contractors, the building contractor is to fill up the space remaining outside the pipe. And thirdly, the case must be covered where a hole has to be cut or knocked out, the pipe placed, and the remaining space outside it filled up. All these three cases should, for the sake of forestalling future arguments, be considered as being implied by the term 'building in' or 'making hole for and/or building in', and should apply to bolts, pipes, fixing lugs, etc.

It may be thought, looking back over points (*a*), (*b*), and (*c*), that these might well be left for arrangement on the site. Frequently this is done, but equally frequently difficulties arise. The building contractor finds himself first to arrive on the site, and directly knowledge spreads that work has begun, the engine manufacturers, pipe suppliers, electricians, heating engineers, and others concerned start sending off their materials. A lorry load of pipes may arrive, perhaps part of a pump contract. The building contractor will be quite within his rights if he refuses to touch them or allow his crane to be used for off-loading. He will more usually be inclined to give a helping hand, but what if one of the pipes is later found to be cracked? Naturally, forseeing this possibility, he will not be willing to sign the delivery note.

It will help, therefore, if the specification can lay down in advance what unloading and storage the building contractor is to undertake.

Scaffolding. On the question of scaffolding, hoisting gear, and the like, particularly scaffolding, the specification for the building contract will depend on what is laid down by the terms of plant suppliers. Most of these will usually be for 'supply and erection and setting to work, including all skilled and unskilled labour, but excluding any builder's work, such as foundations, excavation of trenches, building in of pipes, bolts, hangers, lugs, etc.', and it may be understood from the use of the word 'erection' that the plant contractor will obtain the scaffolding he requires himself. But sometimes scaffolding is expressly excluded from the plant contract, and must therefore be supplied by the building contractor.

Summing up, this part of the specification has two main aims; firstly, to require the building contractor to work in with the other contractors, and secondly, to fit together the responsibilities of the various contractors so that they neither overlap nor leave gaps.

Specifying workmanship and materials

The classification of basic materials, either by trades or alphabetically, is fairly easy. To obtain some order among the various methods specified often presents problems, as some methods apply generally throughout the contract, such as concreting, while other items refer to particular parts of the structure.

The general clauses can deal with many subjects, such as concreting, shuttering, reinforcement, brickwork, renderings, plastering, windows, doors, plumbing, roofing, timber, etc. It is valueless to list them unless the list is complete; the specifier will need to draw up his own list to make it apply to the specification he has on hand. He will again have to resort to textbook information, and be guided in his selection of the points he mentions both by his own practical knowledge and the special conditions of the contract. British Standard Specifications are a valuable aid, and much advice is contained in the various British Standard Codes of Practice. A list of these codes may be obtained from the British Standards Institution. It is important to notice that it is not possible to specify that, say, brickwork is to be erected in accordance with British Standard Code of Practice 121 : 101. The latter Code is a lengthy document and this would be rather like specifying the brickwork to be built according to a given textbook on building construction.

Most specifications include a clause stating that all materials used in the works shall comply with the latest edition of the appropriate British Standard Specification. However, the specifier must always bear in mind that:

(*a*) the quality of certain materials is sometimes not covered by any standard specification (e.g. there is no standard specification for the quality of ordinary bricks), and

(*b*) many specifications cover several grades of a given material.

Hence when writing the section on materials and workmanship the specifier must check that what he is writing makes sense in relation to the standard specification he is quoting.

It must be admitted that the specifier must have access to many standard specifications, the number of which is increasing year by year. One further point must be made in regard to specifying materials. Words such as 'best', 'perfect', 'highest quality' in describing materials in a specification should be avoided. Only the terms mentioned in the British Standards should be used; such as 'Light', 'Medium', or 'Heavy Grade', 'Ordinary', 'Second Class', or 'First Class'—and then only with reference to the specific standard mentioned.

Writing a good specification

Three overriding principles should be followed producing a sound and practical specification:

1. The layout and ideas expressed should be logical and clear.
2. The English should be clear.
3. The specification should be as short as can reasonably be expected in relation to the amount of work to be covered.

It is necessary to take a little thought before writing and have a clear idea of what one needs to say. Sometimes the writing is a muddle because the engineer wanders from one subject to another, or because something has been added without reference to what was written earlier. A good starting sentence will aim to give the main facts or arguments which are amplified in the following material. This acts as a guide for both reader and writer. Legal terms should be avoided as far as possible; they often sound unnatural when used, and more than likely some simple phrases can be used instead which will more easily be understood.

The need for keeping the specification as short as possible is important in the interests of saving time for all concerned. There is no point in specifying in detail matters which are of so little consequence to a contractor that he will not mind being given more detailed instructions as the work proceeds. There is also no point in specifying in great detail operations under which little contract work is to be carried out. Thus, it is rather silly to write a long description of the concrete work, if the only concrete to be placed relates to thrust blocks for a pipeline. Similarly, only a few notes about pipe-laying will be needed if only a few yards of pipe have to be laid in connection with a building. Another matter that needs to be watched is describing things that are quite clearly shown on the contract drawings. A good deal of space can also be saved by describing in the bill of quantities what is wanted in regard to the supply of single small items not repeated elsewhere. This saves cross-referencing between bill and specification.

Perhaps the most important point to remember is that, if the contract is to go out to selected tenderers for pricing, then some of the more obvious and well-accepted trade practices can be more succinctly described than might be the case if open tendering is adopted. To take an example, to say—'shuttering shall be true to line, rigid and properly supported' may be a sufficient description for that topic alone if the engineer thinks there is no risk of having an inexperienced contractor on the job.

If a contractor aims to cause trouble there is little hope of any specification, however large, being found without fault. To safeguard the position that would then arise, it is important to spend much time and care when drafting those parts of the specification which describe materials and work of substantial cost. The specification needs checking again when the bill of quantities has been produced. The most important and expensive items must be taken in the bill, one by one, and the relevant parts of the specification must be tested against the items and against the question—'What precisely is the contractor called upon to do under this item; does this describe the complete and whole of the work we want him to do?' The damage is not great if a £100 item has been tendered on the basis of 'medium grade' material when 'first grade' should have been specified. But the damage can be very great if, under an item such as excavation, the specifier forgets to include backfill or forgets to say where the excavated material is to be carted to, if this is some distance from the site. More often than not, the earlier parts of a specification which deal with the major items of construction and the more expensive trades are those which need to be written, rewritten, and checked with the greatest possible care.

CHAPTER 10

Bills of Quantities and Costing

CLAUSE 57 of the Conditions of Contract currently provides (1978) that, except where any statement is made in the Bill of Quantities to the contrary, the quantities shall be deemed to have been measured in accordance with the Standard Method of Measurement reprinted in 1973 by the Institution of Civil Engineers—'or such later or amended edition thereof as may be stated in the Appendix to the Tender.' The engineer should note the need for a statement in the preamble to the bills of quantities if the Standard Method is not followed.

A new Standard Method was published in 1976, but it is not mandatory and many engineers have not adopted it because it seems unnecessarily complicated, lacks clarity and practicability. Considerable publicity has been given to 'Method-Related Charges' proposed in the new Standard. These are defined, rather confusingly, as (i) *Time-Related Charges*, meaning method-related charges for work, the cost of which is proportional to time; and (ii) *Fixed Charges*, meaning method-related charges which are not time-related charges.

Both these charges are no more than items in a preliminary bill of quantities to cover such matters as site offices, water supply, power, temporary works, plant, access, supervision, etc. There is nothing new in this practice: items of this sort have appeared in contracts for many years, and they should always be divided into once-only charges of a 'set-up' nature, and charges which are related to the contract period.

In the material which follows, only the reprinted 1973 Standard Method is referred to, as it still forms a reasonable and practicable guide.

Arrangement of items

For large works it may be necessary to divide bills of quantities into separate groups relating to separate parts of the job, each group being subdivided into its various trades as listed in the 1973 Standard, or perhaps as listed on p. 122 above.

The usual practical answer is to divide the job up into its main sections. Thus, the main bill sections for a bridge might consist of:

(i) abutments;
(ii) piers;
(iii) superstructure;
(iv) approach roads and surfacings;
(v) miscellaneous.

Within each section the items would be taken in order grouped under trades—excavation, concreting, etc. However, within such a section as 'miscellaneous' it may be necessary to include a number of small operations or structures, each of which involves several different trades. It would then be usual to take the various items in some logical sequence, applying the trades to each in turn, but not sectionalising the bill further. A typical sequence might be—excavation for drainpipes; concrete bedding to pipes; laying and jointing pipes; excavation for manholes; concrete to manhole bases; brickwork to walls of manholes; providing and setting manhole covers; excavation for fence posts; concrete for fence posts; etc., etc.

A sense of proportion must be retained when billing quantities. If the main civil engineering work for a bridge (say) is likely to cost a million pounds it is a waste of everyone's time to bill every little quantity involved in constructing a few ancillary roadside manholes on the approach roads. If these manholes are more or less similar they should be specified comprehensively in the specification and shown on the drawings, and can then be billed in a single item: 'Construct manholes as specified in Clause . . . and shown on the Drawings—5 No.—'

If the manholes vary in dimensions such that a uniform price for all of them could not fairly be called for, then the best method to deal with this situation is to 'lump the quantities together' and bill as follows: excavation and backfill to manholes; concrete to manhole bases; brickwork to manhole walls, etc.

In very large civil engineering contracts it would be quite usual to make a single item cover a whole minor structure in its entirety, provided that such a structure is specified in detail and shown adequately on the drawings. An instance of this would be a small gauge house which might form a relatively low-cost item in comparison with (say) a dam, which forms the main subject of a contract. Alternatively—and this is probably somewhat fairer to tenderers—a provisional sum can be provided for this kind of item, so that a subsidiary bill of quantities can be produced at a later date and rates agreed for the construction.

Number of items: accuracy of quantities

Some civil engineering bills of quantities contain upwards of a thousand items because many types of differing operations in building and civil engineering construction are involved. Nevertheless, the number of items should never be more than need be, because the more items there are, the more complex is the measuring and accountancy work throughout the whole period of construction.

On the other hand, if tenderers are to be given a proper chance of submitting fair prices it is no use adding together items which involve the contractor in different and unrelated costs. Thus, to include several concreting operations under one item when some of the concrete must be placed above ground, and some below, or some in small quantities and some in large quantities, may be unfair to the tenderer and thus to the employer. Either tenderers must waste time working out the subdivision of quantities or they may have to hazard a guess as to what a fair average price should be. Hence, not only the types of material and the varieties of trade involved influence the number of items in a bill but also the location, height, quantity, access to the work, and many other aspects of the separate portions of work.

The stated quantities should accurately represent the quantities as measured from the drawings to certain specific and clearly stated limits. These limits should be marked on the drawings as—'Line showing depth (or width) to which quantities have been measured for the purpose of the bill of quantities'—or some similar phrase. If below or beyond such boundaries the engineer thinks that further work might possibly be required, he can enter a further provisional quantity under items in the bill which are labelled provisional.

It has been stated that—'civil engineering work is normally based on an approximate bill or schedule of prices'. This is not true. The quantities given in the bill must accurately reflect the amount of work shown on the drawings. If this were not so, no reliance could be placed on the tendered price as a proper estimate of the cost of the works, and untold confusion would result. The confusion may arise because the quantities are *not fixed*; this is an entirely different matter from their being inaccurate. If, as does happen occasionally, the whole works are constructed exactly as shown on the drawings, then the amount paid to the contractor should be exactly the tendered sum.

Hidden reserves in quantities. The point discussed above can be further elucidated by considering the troubles that can follow 'over-measuring' quantities when preparing a bill. The temptation to do this can arise, for instance, when billing trench excavation for a pipeline. Perhaps it is expected that there will be longer lengths of pipe trench excavated at lower depth than the drawings show. If the engineer adds a guessed quantity extra to each length of deep excavation his quantities will show a longer length of pipe trench than pipeline; this is confusing, to say the least. If, alternatively, the engineer increases the length at lower depth and decreases equivalently the lengths at shallow depth he may, if he overdoes this adjustment, give a false impression of the nature of the work.

Thus, there may possibly arise a claim from the contractor for 'changed conditions' which, in truth, is a claim because the quantities billed have been misleading. If, however, the quantities were marked 'provisional' such a claim would have no chance of success because the contractor would have been forewarned of a possible wide variation in the quantities; but this practice must not include too many important items, or the whole bill of quantities becomes so vague that tenderers are unable to submit properly judged prices. If the quantities for the major items cannot be estimated with reasonable accuracy in advance, then the bill of quantities method should not be used. Instead a schedule of rates type of contract (see p. 10) should form the basis of tender, the items of which are different from those in a normal bill.

The best answer in preparing bills of quantities is to compute the quantities accurately, to adjust them intelligently if it is expected from past experience that measurements will tend to be slightly more or less than the theoretical computations show, and then to leave them as they stand. They will represent the engineer's best appraisal of the actual amount of work to be done in constructing the works as shown on the drawings. In this manner, contractor's claims arising from inaccurate quantities are most likely to be avoided. To provide against foreseeable risks provisional items can be inserted for further work that might be necessary.

Quantities for building work in a civil engineering contract

The *Standard Method of Measurement* of civil engineering work does not specify a number of operations which are more appropriately classified under building work, but which will nevertheless be frequently encountered on a civil engineering project. The civil engineer is then faced with the problem of how to bill these items of a building nature. One procedure must certainly be avoided, namely measuring an operation in one manner under certain items of the bill and measuring the same type of operation in a different manner under other items of the bill.

The most workable method in practice is to measure certain trades (e.g. excavation, concrete, steelwork, etc.) in accordance with the civil engineering standard method, and the other trades (e.g. brickwork, masonry, timberwork, etc.) in accordance with the standard methods of measuring building work. This division should run right through the whole bill of quantities, and the preamble can make a statement to this effect.

While the Standard Method of measuring civil engineering work can generally be adhered to, measurement in accordance with the standard methods for building work may have to be modified, in order to make such measurements acceptable to civil engineering contractors. A civil engineering contractor is not normally interested in the detailed measurement to be found in the standard methods for measuring building work; he prefers that rates shall be inclusive of minor matters; e.g. the painting of small equipment can be included in with the supply and fixing of the equipment, or many minor extra labours in regard to brickwork may be included in the price of brickwork per sq. m or cu. m, and so on.

The list of trades contained in the building methods of measurement is more comprehensive than the civil engineering list of trades, and forms a useful guide for producing an orderly arrangement of the items in the bill.

Numbering of items

The engineer who sets out to take off quantities and write up a bill may find, having written the whole bill, numbered the items, and completed matching the cross-references with the specification, that an item or two has been missed out. Even if his work is perfect, others may produce amendments involving addition to the quantities.

If the items have been numbered right through from beginning to end it is then difficult to add a further item which has been forgotten at the proof stage of producing the bill of quantities because this would involve renumbering all items subsequent to the insertion and checking to see that all cross-references are corrected. The only possible way to avoid this difficulty is to insert the forgotten item as an 'A' item—e.g. Item 38A or to collect these as 'Late Items' at the end of a bill.

A useful way of numbering the original bill items is to use a letter prefix to each number, using a different letter for each section of the bill. Thus Excavation items are numbered A1, A2, . . . etc.; Concreting items B1, B2, . . . etc.; Reinforcement items C1, C2, . . . etc., and so on. Hence if, before the bill is printed, additions have to be made to it the additional items can at least be added at the end of their correct section without disturbing the numbering.

An extension of this idea may sometimes be useful by similarly labelling the specification sections Section A—Excavation; Section B—Concrete; and so on—the specification paragraphs starting at number 1 under each section, thus permitting the addition of further clauses in the specification without complete disruption of the whole numbering system, the cross-references, and index. It is also useful, in that the letter prefix to the bill items refers to the relevant part of the specification, which is similarly labelled.

Taking off quantities

Some simple rules for taking off quantities were given in the 1973 edition of the *Standard Method of Measurement*. These can be followed with profit, but the civil engineer can also, within reason, use any logical and accurate method that is sufficiently clear for others to follow who may have to check his work. Of course, a systematic approach is needed, and the complicated shapes of civil engineering works demand intelligence in working out suitable methods.

Particular attention should be paid to the title of a drawing, and the quantifier should take care to remember in what units he is working. It is all too easy to get the arithmetic right but fail to notice that all quantities must be multiplied by two because the drawing is headed—'2 No. off identical'; or to confuse cubic feet with cubic yards. Such errors tend to slip past any checking.

Use of quantity surveyors

It is unnecessary for an engineer to employ quantity surveyors for civil engineering bills of quantities. Architects, however, employ quantity surveyors for building work, the surveyor then having wide powers to detail and specify the work, prepare estimates and valuations, and issue certificates. Under an engineer the quantity surveyor would not have such powers, and would therefore act simply as a measurer for the engineer.

Nevertheless, quantity surveyors are increasingly being employed by contractors, probably because of the increased building of large blocks of offices and flats. Thus, in turn, the engineer may tend to employ quantity surveyors in the future in order to match the increasing number of contractors who employ them.

In civil engineering many contractors consider that bills prepared by quantity surveyors are a positive disadvantage. This arises from the tendency of the quantity surveyor's bill to describe a finished job, whereas an engineer's bill is a description of the work as it is done. Far from wanting bills of quantities broken down into ever more minute operations, most civil engineering contractors prefer to see items described as inclusive of small details which add little to the price. If detailed building work must be billed in quantity surveyor's style, then it should be kept separate from the rest of the work, as the civil contractor's costing system is not always set up to cope with such details.

Measuring and billing items

The recommendations of the *Standard Method of Measurement* should be followed carefully and any different methods used should be drawn to the tenderer's notice. Where quantities are small, or operations are unusual, departures from the recommended units of measurement may be quite sensible. Furthermore, regard should be paid to the way suppliers invoice their materials to the contractor. It is annoying to the contractor to find some small item measured in cubic metres in the bill, when all suppliers quote by weight. A typical example is the billing of sheet piles by square metres, when suppliers invariably quote for supply in Mg weight.

The guiding principle in deciding how to deal with quantities is to consider how the contractor is most likely to tackle the work, how he himself will be charged for the materials involved, and how the quantities should therefore be divided and measured so that he can easily price the separate items.

Excavation

An early problem usually concerns what amount of excavation is to be billed under the heading of 'bulk excavation' and what is to be billed as 'trench excavation' or 'excavation in pits'. The general rule is, of course, that the amount which will be excavated in bulk should be described as such; the rest is bound to be 'special' by reason of its extra depth, small size, or remoteness from the major site of excavation. It follows that 'special' excavation is always measured as the net amount below, or beyond, or detached from the bulk excavation—e.g. a trench in the bottom of a bulk excavation is measured as the volume below the bottom level of the bulk excavation, and not as the amount vertically above the trench bottom to the original ground surface. It is for the engineer to decide what he considers is 'bulk excavation'—he may think in terms of the amount that it is possible to excavate with a scraper, face-shovel, or dragline. He may be faced with doubts about this. A simple instance is what to designate as the 'bulk excavation' for a service reservoir where the wall foundations may have to be excavated to 0·50 m to 1·0 m lower depth than the floor for a 4·5 m width all round the perimeter. Is this extra 0·5 m by 4·5 m excavation in trench, or bulk excavation? This is a question that only the engineer can answer; and to answer it he should have regard to what is fair to the contrator. If the depth and width of the extra excavation are such as to lead the engineer to expect that something extra will be required from the contractor to get the material out (such as timbering, use of a different type of plant, etc.), then the item ought to be billed separately.

As against this, even if it is expected that the contractor will dig the outer perimeter trench to wall foundation full depth first, from ground surface, leaving the middle 'dumpling' to excavate in bulk—the engineer need not bill the quantities so, unless he wishes (for some reason) to specify this method of excavation. It is better not to assume (or specify) special methods of attack by the contractor, but to assume 'normal' methods and let the contractor submit his own price for doing the work his own way.

The 1973 *Standard Method of Measurement* requires trench excavation for pipes and drains to be measured in separate items for each 1·5 m depth, average depth being stated. For deep pipe trenches, steps of 3 m are stipulated. Such steps can be rather large in practice and can result in under or over-payment to a contractor where actual depths for long lengths are just under or over a given step. It is more convenient to take the first depth as that which is normally to be expected, i.e. 1·5 m (say) for pipes up to 300 mm diameter (2·0 m or 2·5 m for larger pipes) and thereafter to provide separate items for lengths at every extra 0·5 m depth. This avoids the need for having to calculate average depths in most cases, and avoids disputes arising when the actual depth proves different from the estimated average depth, as it frequently does.

Care needs to be exercised in describing how the quantities at different depths are to be measured. The unit of measurement for pipe trench excavation is the linear metre, for a given diameter of pipe. The normal practice in measuring trenching for pipes is to measure from the ground surface. Thus a 150-metre trench, 100 m of which is not deeper than 1·5 m, and 50 m of which exceeds 1·5 m but does not exceed 2 m depth, is billed as two items:

> *Item a.* Trench excavation not exceeding 1·5 m depth ... 100 metre
> *Item b.* Trench excavation exceeding 1·5 m depth but not exceeding
> 2m   ...   .   50 metre

The intention of this method is readily made clear by the fact that the total billed length of excavation equals the total length of the pipeline. The method, it should be noted, is different from that adopted when excavation is measured by cubic metres. Taking the trench width as 1 metre the above items would read:

> *Item a.* Trench excavation not exeeding 1·5 m depth from ground
> surface ...   .   225 cu. m
> *Item b.* Trench excavation exceeding 1·5 m depth but not exceeding
> 2·0 m ...   .   25 cu. m

The same kind of care needs to be taken when billing boring items, and which should read similar to the following:

> *Item a.* Boring — mm diameter from 0 to 10 m below ground sur-
> face   ...   .   lin. m
> *Item b.* Boring — mm diameter from 10 m to 15 m below ground
> surface ...   .   lin. m

Net measurement of excavations. The 1973 *Standard Method of Measurement* states that 'it may be necessary' in the case of trenches (other than for pipes), and in the case of pits, pier holes, etc., to provide a separate item in the bill of quantities for excavation beyond the net width of the structure for working space, timbering, shuttering, etc. This item, if provided, is to be billed as the area of the sides of the excavation in square metres. However, it is frequent practice to measure excavations of this type as 'the net volume vertically above the plan area of the foundations', and to make the contractor allow in his rates for such excavation for any further excavation he has to do for working space, etc. When this is done it is essential to draw the contractor's attention to this method of net measurement at the time of tender, by putting the matter out clearly in the preamble to the Bill of Quantities and, preferably, also in the Specification.

Filling. Filling is the net volume of the void or structure to be filled, and not the 'bulked volume' of the loose filling that must be handled to fill such a void or structure. The contractor usually has a very good appreciation of the bulking or compaction factors applicable to certain types of fill. (The bulking factor is the ratio of the volume of loose material to its volume when fully compacted or *in situ*). On very large earthworks it is vitally important to a contractor that he estimates the bulking factor correctly, or he may lose money heavily. On such contracts the engineer should assist tenderers to arrive at a correct estimation by providing the results of laboratory or field tests for examination. When four or five million cubic metres of filling (or excavation) are involved—as in the construction of a dam—a difference of only 2 per cent in the bulking factor can produce a large error in estimating the number of lorry loads of fill that are required. When the filling has to be bought (as from a commercial quarry, for instance) the error may be extremely costly.

It would seem fairer to contractors engaged on building large earthworks to tie the unit rates for filling and compacting to a given bulking factor, permitting a proportionate increase or decrease in the rate should the factor experienced in practice depart more than a certain amount from the stated factor—particularly where fill has to be bought by the contractor by the ton. The engineer himself is by no means always able to foretell what the bulking factor will be, especially if he has only the results of laboratory 'Proctor' tests to go on, and if he is unable to forecast the bulking factor it hardly seems fair to expect the contractor to do with lesser facilities what the engineer cannot do.

The measurement of filling by the cubic metre, though universal, reflects another aspect of this subject where the need to find an easy method of measuring runs contrary to what happens in practice. The reader can find this out for himself if he tries to phone any quarry owner or haulier and asks him to quote a price for the supply or haulage of any type of filling per cubic metre. He will invariably be quoted per tonne (1000 kg). Every quarry owner weighs his material out; every truck driver or haulier is concerned with the weight his truck can carry, because the performance and life of his vehicle depends upon the weight it is carrying in relation to its braking power and the gradients and surface of the haulage roads it has to travel. However, until the *Standard Method of Measurement* permits measurement of filling by weight the present illogical method of measuring by the cubic metre must be followed.

Concrete

In billing items for concreting—apart from the main divisions into mass and reinforced concrete of different classes—the general principle in subdivision is to classify items into types of work where the operations are similar, i.e. approximately the same complexity, similar in bulk, and having similar type of access. Thus, it is not necessary to take out individual items of construction.

Where there is repetition work the 1973 *Standard Method* allows shuttering to be included in the rate for concrete, and is not an item measured separately. This would apply to items such as reservoir columns, roofs, and walls, but would not apply to varying depths of beam ribs in a framed building; or even to floor areas in a building. Generally, unless the concrete items really are repetitive, it is better to separate out the shuttering.

When trying to decide how items of concrete shall be collected together, the engineer often overemphasises the physical separateness of various portions of the concrete, as compared with the differences between the placing methods to be used. Thus, suppose a number of foundation footings of different shapes must be concreted over a wide area of the job, but generally at or about the same level below ground. Then, so far as the contractor is concerned, all these items of concrete could be lumped together and so described, because the method of placing them all will be very similar. The concrete will have to come in relatively small quantities, and it will have to be distributed (which costs money) either by pipeline, monorail, dumper, or crane skip. But suppose some of those footings are in a somewhat inaccessible place, where the concrete has to be lowered down a considerable depth, or raised up, then that concrete should be billed separately. To place concrete to a footing which is half-way up a bank may be twice as costly as to place the same amount of concrete in the bottom of a general excavation area. It is the *location* of concrete which often has the heaviest influence on its cost.

Confusion often occurs in the billing of items extra over concrete or shuttering for openings, for leaving holes, or for building in bolts, pipes, etc. Perhaps the best guidance can be given by taking examples:

Rag bolts. Take an item 'extra over concrete and shuttering in items . . . for forming hole for and/or building in' rag bolts. (By number classifying roughly by depth.)

Step irons. Separate item treated similarly to rag bolts.

Holes for spindles, electric conduit, heating pipes. Take an item 'extra over concrete and shuttering for forming holes for valve spindles, etc., up to 75 mm diameter. Ditto over 75 mm up to 150 mm . . . and so on.

Building in pipes. Treat exactly as rag bolts, but classify according to diameter—up to 300 mm, 300–600 mm, etc., and relate if necessary to differing parts of structure—i.e. walls, floor, and roof.

All the items above should have no deduction made from concrete or shuttering for volume occupied by built-in material. They need not usually be subdivided into the various classes of concrete, as the work does not vary in relation to the class of concrete, but where thickness of concrete is very variable some classification on thickness may also be necessary.

Forming manhole openings. Take separate items for each size of manhole 'extra over shuttering in item . . . for forming manhole opening 900 × 600 mm in roof'.

Ditto for 750 × 750 mm opening and so on.

The concrete payment will, of course, be net, i.e. after deducting the volume of the opening.

When it comes to billing the supply and fixing of ladders, angle irons, hand-railing, etc., these will be taken as 'supply and fix in position ready for grouting in bolts, etc.'

Any other methods which are adopted will be found to be much more complicated, resulting in a multiplicity of items, the true intention of which may not be very clear.

Brickwork

The Standard Method provisions for measuring brickwork are more appropriate to the measurement of massive engineering brickwork structures than to the measurement of brickwork in an engineering contract. The unit of measurement proposed—namely square metres, the thickness of wall being stated—is, however, convenient and should be adopted. For other matters, such as the measurement of cavity walls, piers, fair facing, etc., the Building Method of measurement can be referred to for guidance. The various innumerable extra overs allowed for in the Building Method would not, however, be separately itemised in civil engineering work, but they act as a useful reminder to the specifier as to matters which he should specify should be included in the general rates called for.

Brickwork should be classified according to height above ground. No fixed rules regarding this are laid down in either Standard Method, but in general it is appropriate to measure external brickwork in one- or two-storey heights, brickwork from footings to d.p.c. level always being measured separately. Internal walls would be measured from floor to ceiling, the floor level being stated. Where, in a tall building, there may be no natural storey-breaks to external or internal walls, quantities should be taken out for heights not exceeding a rise of 7 to 8 m at a time.

Except where large quantities of plain walling have to be constructed, extra-overs for facing of brickwork should follow each main item of measurement. This facing work may consist of fair facing one or both sides (including the type of pointing required), or for use of facing bricks, or for any special patterning effect required, or for leaving rough for rendering. But common sense should be used when deciding how to subdivide the items. If, for instance, a fair amount of cavity walling is to be built of uniform thickness the interior wall of common bricks being left rough for plastering, the outside wall being of special facing bricks carefully pointed, then it is just as well to bill this item 'complete' per square metre and so make one item cover what would otherwise amount to four or five items, of which most are extra-overs.

Where brickwork has to be stepped out, as in foundations, it is best not to try to measure the quantity of brickwork in cubic metres or to attempt to measure it as 'reduced brickwork one-brick thick' with a number of complicated extra-overs, but to measure the quantity of brickwork at its normal wall thickness right down to the top of the foundations, then to give extra-overs in linear metres for stepping or corbelling out, as follows:

Extra over Item . . . for labour *and* materials for 3 No. courses, stepped out 30 mm each course at base of wall, measured both sides of wall.

Steel and ironwork

Where a building contains only a few miscellaneous pieces of ironwork, such as supporting angle irons for valve-spindle guides, small rolled-steel joists, and the like it is better to give an item for 'supply and fix in position . . . complete with bolts, etc.' and state the approximate unit weight for each and to bill by number.

Pipelines

The 1973 *Standard Method of Measurement* states that laying pipelines is to be measured per linear metre; but adds that where the pipeline forms a substantial part of the work to be carried out the pipes and pipe fittings may be entered by number, 'the diameter, length, thickness, and weight of metal in each class of pipe or pipe fitting being given'. Either method would be satisfactory, but where long pipelines have to be laid, measurement by the linear metre would be the more usual method. The measurement is usually through all valves and fittings, even though these valves and fittings may be separately itemised, as 'Supply and lay in position ready for jointing', or (where the pipes and fittings are supplied by the employer) 'Take delivery of, haul and lay ready for jointing . . .'

When pipes and fittings are supplied by the employer under a separate contract the unit weight of each of the pipes and fittings should be given in the bill of quantities.

Measurement by numbers of pipes and numbers of fittings is usual where large-diameter pipework has to be laid in short lengths, or where the pipeline contains many fittings, or where it is to be joined to other pipework. Thus, if 50 m of 900 mm-diameter pipework has to be laid through the foundations of a building and contains a number of tees and bends and so on it is much fairer to the contractor to itemise the pipes and fittings separately by number. The setting of a single large bend, or taper, or tee in its correct position, ready for jointing, may be a lengthy and difficult operation.

Jointing and cutting are measured separately for cast iron, steel, and concrete pipes, but the linear measurement for sewers and drains may be inclusive of the jointing and cutting.

Costing

Accurate costing of civil engineering construction work is very difficult to carry out. By 'costing' is meant finding the cost of undertaking separate classes of work—such as concreting, bricklaying, shuttering, etc.; or finding out the cost of undertaking separate portions of the work—such as the cost of access roads, subsidiary buildings, main building, installation of machinery, etc.

Means have to be found to correctly apportion the desired heads of costing the charges for labour, materials, plant, and overheads.

To apportion labour charges it is necessary for the workmen, or the section foreman acting on behalf of the men in his team, to fill up time sheets showing the hours spent each day by each man on the various types of work. The hours entered on these sheets must be priced out so that the labour cost can then be allocated under the different headings by the cost clerk. Difficulties arise in dealing with: (i) overtime and other miscellaneous wage payments, and (ii) the time sheets of men such as fitters, time-checkers, flag-men, night-watchmen, chainmen, storekeepers, etc., whose work cannot be *directly* allocated to a specific site operation. Decisions have to be made (in advance of setting up the costing system) as to how such men's time sheets are to be allocated. They may be separated out into different categories, or they may all be put under the heading 'site on-costs'.

The allocation of charges for materials presents further difficulties, since the paper work on site is usually concerned only with checking the inflow of materials against the suppliers' invoices, and none of the basic records may show where the materials have been used in the separate parts of the job. The bill-of-quantities measurements can be of assistance for calculating quantities (and therefore price) of materials used in the permanent works, but there are many more materials, such as timber for shuttering, scaffolding, small tools, diesel oil and fuel oil, nuts and bolts, etc., which are not used in the measurement records. As with wages which cannot be directly charged to any specific operation, so materials which cannot be costed out to particular parts of the job will have to be charged as part of 'site on-costs'.

Provided the plant-hire charges are known, the allocation of plant charges is relatively easy on the basis of the daily returns of plant usage provided by the plant foreman.

In addition to the items already mentioned, it is necessary to add in the various site administration charges to the account for site on-costs,—wages of general foreman, engineers, site clerk, wages clerk, agent and sub-agents, etc., together with all such other charges as telephone, water supply, messing, sanitation, insurance of works, petty cash, etc., etc.

The result of all this is that a heavy proportion of the total cost virtually cannot be analysed and has to be put under the general heading of 'site on-costs'. A further difficulty then reveals itself, namely that the ratio of these site on-costs to the direct charges varies from week to week of the job according to the output, amount of overtime worked, amount of temporary works being built at any one time, and so on. On-cost expenditure at the beginning of a job may be several times the cost of the direct (or productive) expenditure because of the large proportion of labour and materials used on preliminary works, such as access roads, power and water supply, etc., etc. When productive effort is in full swing the on-costs drop to their lowest, but they tend to rise again towards the end of the job as productive work tails off and site clearance, removing sheds, transporting plant off the site, etc., takes place.

The reader will not be surprised to learn that in consequence few, if any, contractors cost works in the manner outlined above. The actual cost of a portion of a job, or of a particular operation, is never known. What is known is the *estimated* charge as set out in the bill of quantities according to the quantity of work actually done and measured.

It is only possible to find out the 'cost' of separate parts or operations on a job by using the estimator's figures put in the bill of quantities, and the only way these estimated figures can be checked against the real figures of actual expenditure is by comparing the total estimate against the total expenditure. Of course, the direct costs involved in any particular operation can be ascertained without difficulty. The number of men and the hours they spend on that operation, together with the materials and plant they have used, can be carefully noted down and priced according to the prices for labour, material, and plant that apply; but the indirect costs, representing a heavy percentage addition, can never be exactly apportioned out; they can only be applied as a general percentage added to all the operations. Hence contractors, if they do costing at all, carry it out on a different basis from what the layout of a bill of quantities seems to imply.

The practicable headings under which a contractor can expect to analyse his expenditure are more likely to be: gross wages paid, transport of men, 'non-productive' hours (i.e. plus rates for overtime), cost of wet-time; materials used in permanent works, materials used in temporary works, materials used in shuttering; equipment, scaffolding, small stores; fuel and power; plant hire, plant repairs; temporary offices and services; site staff and administration expenses. To check any estimate submitted against a bill of quantities, the sum total of the tendered prices in the bill will be compared with an estimate based on the expected number of men and machines required for the job, together with a calculation of the cost of the materials to be used in the permanent works, to which are added all the other on-costs applicable, as judged from costing records of other jobs undertaken as outlined above.

Thus, the prices submitted individually in a bill-of-quantities contract may not represent the actual separate cost to the contractor of each such item, but they should in total represent the total expenditure to be incurred, including an allowance for profit.

Some rough guide rules for costing

Some general (though rather rough) rules for guidance in estimating total costs of a job might be of interest.

On a large civil engineering site where the work covers the usual range of activities a first, and very approximate, guide is that the costs of labour, plant, and materials each come to about $33\frac{1}{3}$ per cent of the total on-the-site costs, the site overheads having been spread over the three items. Variations from these figures are rather large; the labour cost can rise to 40 per cent (50 per cent in tunnelling work), but is seldom lower than 30 per cent.

The rule above is useful only when a little mental arithmetic is required to get an idea of the possible cost of a job. It would not be used by a contractor for checking his tender. The following more accurate guide may be found useful to the resident engineer if he wishes to estimate what a contractor has spent on the job to a given date. It is a method more nearly akin to the contractor's method when checking a tender, except that when the contractor tenders he must necessarily use estimated figures for the number of men and the plant required, whereas the resident engineer should have records of men and machines actually employed.

(a) Take off all quantities of materials used in the permanent works and find total current market charge for supply ... ... £ X

(b) Add 5 per cent to (a) for wastage, etc.... ... ... £ 5%X

(c) Compute total gross wages including allowances and employer's insurance contributions, etc., paid to *all* wage-earners and salaried employees on site ... ... £ Y

(d) Compute hours worked by plant on site of each sort (whether hired or owned by contractor) and multiply by unit rates charged as per Contractors Plant Hire Association (*Note: not* the dayworks hire rate.)... ... £ Z

(e) If the contractor's *own* plant has been extensively idle on site exclude this idle time from (d) above and cost the idle time separately at two-thirds the unit rates charged under (d) ... ... £ W

(f) Take charge for fuel for plant at $12\frac{1}{2}\%$ of (d)... ... £$12\frac{1}{2}\%$Z

(g) Take charge for all *normal* equipment, tools, etc. as 10% of (c) £10%Y

(h) Take miscellaneous charges as 5% of (c) ... ... £ 5%Y

Sum total cost up to and including site on-costs, but excluding head office charges, financing and profit. }

Special items of equipment of an exceptional value and cost should be added to item (g). The cost of repairs to plant is covered by the rates allowed for under (d).

References

Standard Method of Measurement of Civil Engineering Quantities. I.C.E.

Standard Method of Measurement of Building Works. Royal Institution of Chartered Surveyors.

Schedule of Rates of Hire (for Plant). Contractors Plant Association.

Schedules of Dayworks carried out incidental to Contract Work. Federation of Civil Engineering Contractors.

CHAPTER 11

Sub-contracts and Services

Definitions

A clear distinction must be made in both the specification and in the resident engineer's mind as to the difference between the three terms *sub-contract, prime-cost item,* and *provisional sum.*

By *sub-contracting* is meant the undertaking of certain work by a contractor who is subsidiary to the main contractor. The main contractor engages the sub-contractor to carry out part of the work of the main contract. Normally a contractor cannot let out part of the work on sub-contract unless he obtains the permission of the engineer to do so. Alternatively, he may be required by the terms of the specification to sub-let certain particular items to 'any specialist firm' or to a given firm in particular. In the latter case this sub-contractor is usually called a 'nominated sub-contractor'. The main contractor may be paid for work let under sub-contract either by bill rates on measurement, by actual cost plus percentage, or by lump sum.

A prime-cost item consists of a sum provided in the bill of quantities to cover work or services to be executed by a nominated sub-contractor or for the supply of goods from a nominated supplier, together with an opportunity for the contractor to add a percentage or lump sum (or both) to cover his related work and profit. Usually, the prime-cost item covers the supply and installation of certain materials. A typical instance is:

	£
P.C. sum for supply of heating boiler	30·00
Add . . . per cent for delivery, overheads, and profit ...	
Add Lump Sum for all fixing work as Specification ...	
Total to end col. ...	

The sum of £30 (or whatever is the estimated cost of purchasing the item) is inserted in the bill; it is for the tenderer to price the percentage addition and lump sum. Thus the need to detail the exact type of boiler required before the contract can be let is avoided. Also the employer can later choose any sort of boiler, and if he wants a high-quality one this does not inflate the price to him unduly. The percentage addition is normally between 5 and 15 per cent. The lump sum, which remains fixed whatever the price paid for the boiler, acknowledges that the

146

contractor's work in fixing is no different whether a cheap boiler or an expensive one is installed. A lot of small items such as door furniture, fireplaces, lighting fittings, sink units, meters, covers, etc., can be dealt with in this manner. Sometimes the lump-sum portion of the item is omitted where the fixing work represents a very small portion of the cost of the work, as, for instance, in the supply and fixing of lamp fittings. The specification should always make precisely clear the extent of the work to be carried out by the main contractor under the lump-sum addition.

A provisional sum is usually a round figure quoted by the engineer against an item in the bill which the contractor is not called upon to price himself. It is a kind of reserve fund to pay for doing that particular item, which may or may not be spent, wholly or in part. The amount to be paid to the contractor for carrying out the item will be that agreed upon later, either by reference to bill rates for work actually carried out, or by a lump-sum agreement, or on a cost plus percentage basis.

The rights of the contractor and the choice of the engineer of who shall do the work under each of the three types of items vary. A main contractor may himself tender for the work that he is required to sub-let, and the engineer may accept or reject this tender just as he pleases, *provided that* he has not already promised the sub-contract to some nominated firm. If the main contractor's tender is accepted he is entitled to both the tender price and the percentage and/or lump-sum addition he added in his main contract.

The main contractor is not normally able to tender for items of prime cost that are for specialist apparatus, such as clocks, fireplaces, heaters, etc., or a particular brand of manufacture.

The main contractor is entitled to carry out the work included in a provisional sum if this work is of the general type he would normally expect to undertake. If the work is to be carried out by sub-contract the main contractor will expect to have this work done under his supervision, though he has no proper ground for complaint if the whole of the work under a provisional sum is taken from him and given to others or is not done at all.

Sub-contracts

The resident engineer should be wary over these questions, particularly that of sub-contracts. They are a fruitful source of trouble on the job, and the resident engineer must be prepared if necessary to back up the main contractor. The difficulty is that the sub-contractors are frequently not of the main contractor's choosing. For heating equipment, for instance, for a lift, or electric wiring, it often happens that it is the employer or engineer who chooses the sub-contractor to undertake this work. The employer is, of course, guided by the advice of the engineer, but the contractor has no choice in the matter. He simply finds that Messrs. A & B have been chosen to put in the heating plant, for instance.

This may be all very well, but the main contractor may, for a variety of reasons, dislike Messrs. A & B. With just reasons on his side the main contractor may accumulate a considerable number of grievances in a short time. He might declare, and prove, that the sub-contractors forced upon him were unco-operative, frequently requiring ladders and scaffolding, holes knocked out, bits of plastering done, rag bolts plugged in, work covered up, other work stopped, and so on. It is safe to say that hardly any job of magnitude can be completed without some minor or major squabble occurring. A simple case of friction occurs where the main contractor is either a small contractor with few men or has reached a stage where he has few men on the site. The sub-contractor may arrive with an army of men, who swarm over the building trying to do everything under the sub-contract at once, speed of execution being often of major importance to a sub-contractor to enable him to make a profit. The result is that the main contractor finds he can do practically nothing of his own work while the sub-contractor is on the site. It is certain that the main contractor will grumble as a result.

It is clear that the resident engineer must do everything in his power to ease the lot of both contractors. He must take a just line, and, as always in these matters, decide upon a fair compromise between the conflicting claims of the parties. While it is true that the main contractor has undertaken to carry out the work as a whole, if he has not been forewarned of the firms he is to work with as sub-contractors, then he has a fair claim for extra time, or for lost time if he is delayed or has to stand by while they do their work. But if they are sub-contractors of his own choosing or he was forewarned through the specification or bill of quantities as to who would be these sub-contractors, then, of course, he has no such claim. Further troubles may well arise over standards of workmanship. A sub-contractor, who, by knocking holes, makes a grievous and unnecessary mess of plastering work, or who carelessly knocks bits off doorframes, or who will not clear up properly after him is a nuisance to everyone. On the other hand, sub-contractors frequently have legitimate grumbles against main contractors, who will not supply enough scaffolding, nor knock holes or plug in bolts as and when required. In addition, one of the chief worries of sub-contractors is the question of payment. They are frequently uneasy on this score, since they can only get payment through the main contractor, who may tend to be dilatory in this matter.

The resident engineer's duties in regard to sub-contracts are therefore important. His first task is to see that the sub-contractors are absolutely clear as to the amount of work they are to undertake. Sub-contracts are usually quoted 'builder's work excluded'. It is therefore most important that all parties should know beforehand exactly what is meant by the term 'builder's work'. Does it include scaffolding and ladders? Does it include the actual fixing and plugging in of holding bolts, as well as the knocking of holes for these bolts? Does it include the use of cranes, ropes, hoisting, and temporary supporting gear for the sub-contractor's apparatus? These are vital points.

Conditions of sub-contracts

The precise terms and conditions of any nominated sub-contractor's contract should have been described in the specification, and the engineer should have seen that the terms applying to the sub-contractor do not conflict with the terms applying to the main contractor. Mistakes can sometimes arise, principally concerning the period of maintenance and the release of retention money. Usually the period of maintenance for the main contractor is twelve months; but it is sometimes not possible to get a sub-contractor to agree to this, especially if his work terminates many months before the period of maintenance for the main contract commences. Similarly, retention money may be applied to payments made to the main contractor for the sub-contracted work, in which case the nominated sub-contractor's contract must contain the same provision.

The Institution of Civil Engineers and Federation of Civil Engineering Contractors have approved a form of sub-contract designed to be used in conjunction with the approved *General Conditions of Contract* for the main contract. In this form of sub-contract between main contractor and sub-contractor, the latter is deemed to have full knowledge of the provisions of the main contract, a copy of which (excluding the prices) must be provided to him if he requests. Other clauses provide that the sub-contractor is required to take over, in relation to his work, all the liabilities and duties held by the main contractor, including maintenance of the sub-contracted works until the main contractor's liability for their maintenance has ceased. As mentioned above, however, the latter cannot always be demanded of a sub-contractor. In regard to payments, the main contractor has to pay to the sub-contractor any money due to him within seven days of the main contractor receiving payment for the sub-contracted work from the employer.

Where conflicts occur between the provisions of the main contract and acceptable provisions to sub-contractors, the resident engineer must do his best to find an equitable solution and put this solution up to the engineer for approval. If the nominated sub-contractor has not yet been appointed when work on site starts, then it is up to the resident engineer to make provision for the sub-contractor's terms to fit in with the main contractor's terms.

With the actual progress of the work he must try to keep both contractor and sub-contractor happy and restrain them from making unreasonable demands on each other.

Payments. With regard to payments to sub-contractors this is the contractor's responsibility. It must be borne in mind, that except in certain special cases, a sub-contract is a contractual agreement between the main contractor and the sub-contractor and that the engineer and the employer are no party to this contract. Hence sub-contractor's work is measured and certified for payment in accordance with the bill rates for the main contract. In measuring up for a certificate for payment, however, the engineer may call for evidence from the contractor that he has paid his sub-contractor for the work previously measured. If he has not, and if he persists in refusing to pay his sub-contractor, the approved General Conditions of Contract give power under Clause 59 (2) for the amount owing to the sub-contractor to be deducted from payments due, so that the employer may reimburse the sub-contractor direct. This action is, of course, only taken in extreme circumstances.

It would seem wise that, where a sub-contract is called for, the main contractor should first be allowed to suggest which sub-contracting firms he would care to work with. Where there is freedom to choose the sub-contractor (for such items as plastering or painting, for instance), the sub-contractor finally chosen should preferably be from those suggested by the main contractor, provided that the workmanship and price seems reasonable. The results should have a much greater chance of being satisfactory, because, quite probably, the two contractors will know each other and have worked together before to their mutual satisfaction. Where payment for work by sub-contract is on bill rates there will be even less reason to interfere with the choice of sub-contractor. The resident engineer will only have to satisfy himself that the sub-contractor will turn out the necessary standard of workmanship.

Heating

Heating work is usually designed and specified separately from the main contract for erection of a building, and is therefore let out to a nominated sub-contractor. It may be that the engineer permits the main contractor to call for the necessary quotations. This permits the main contractor to put forward the names of sub-contractors whom he is satisfied he can work with. The specification drawn up by the engineer may be a complete engineering design or, for small installations, he may leave the particulars of the design to the heating sub-contractor, calling for a guarantee that the temperature inside the building shall be not less than a given figure for a given outside air temperature of say 32° F. Tenders submitted will be compared on the basis of both capital cost and running costs, together with the quality of materials offered and the type of design submitted.

A tender of a sort may have been submitted during the preliminary design stages of the scheme, and the price then given will be the basis of any provisional sum inserted in the bill of quantities. It is not likely, however, that the information given in these early stages will be adequate. The resident engineer should therefore, very early in the work, follow the original quotation up, asking for a revised up-to-date quotation and for details of the equipment proposed. Heating engineers usually mark their runs of pipe as ink lines over 1 : 100 scale drawings, and from that the resident engineer is supposed to deduce or make provision for the run of pipes.

In practice, things may not work out so simply as they appeared on the plan. Although it would be nice to have every detail fixed in advance of erecting the structure, this is not always possible, but at least a preliminary talk should take place with the heating engineers as soon as possible. Certainly the runs of pipe should be decided upon before the internal walls and ceilings are erected. Not all the pipes may be shown on the small-scale drawing submitted. Such things as thermostat controls, air-release valves, and shut-off cocks have a habit of coming in very awkward positions. Heating engineers have also to lay their pipes to gentle grades, which, while unnoticeable in some places, may in other places have startlingly ugly results. Thus, a flow pipe which, on first appearance on the plan, looks as if it will tuck away neatly along the junction of ceiling and wall will, in practice, be found to have a fall one way, making it look most ugly and tending to make the lines of the building appear out of true. In addition, such a pipe, which may neatly clear an obstacle at one end of a room (such as a beam), will foul the same-dimensioned obstacle at the other end. Vertical runs of pipe may also seem well in plan, but in practice will be found to need diversion around beam ribs in the ceiling, or perhaps it may be found that there is insufficient room to run all the pipes together because of encroachment upon a window area.

With radiators it will be important to know the exact positions of them and at what level the feed pipe will be run. If the feed pipe runs along a few inches above the floor, as is most likely, how is this pipe to be supported? It can be supported either by stays from the wall or stays from the floor. If there is to be a skirting to the wall the pipe should be placed in relation to the depth of the skirting so that the best appearance is achieved.

The heating work should therefore commence as soon as sufficient structural work has been completed. This will be when the completion of the internal walling is in sight and before the plastering. The heating engineers usually include for erecting their radiators complete in the first instance, and then taking down once and re-erecting after plastering and decorating has been carried out. The question of who is to carry out the painting of the heating apparatus must not be forgotten.

Electricity supply, lighting, and power

Without being an expert in electrical engineering, the resident engineer may still successfully control this work. Of all sub-contracts, this is the one most likely to be extensively varied in detail from the original quotation. The amount to be paid extra on account of such variations is a difficult matter to determine. Such alterations as two power points in a room instead of one, the addition of two-way instead of single landing switches for lighting of staircases, extra feeds required for small machinery, 'wiring up to' and setting to work small motors, such as fan motors—all these things will come along as alterations to the original tender. If the resident engineer does not know what would be a fair price to charge for such alterations (and he is very unlikely to know unless he has had extensive experience of this type of work himself), the simple method of controlling such work is to call for a separate quotation of the amount to be added to or deducted from the original tender for each alteration made. He should not approve the alteration until he has received the quotation and sent it to his head office for their comments.

An alternative method is to allow the contractor to charge on a labour-and-materials basis, but this is not to be recommended. In the first place it will be found very difficult to observe and note down the time the electrician actually works on the extra item; and secondly, it may be even more difficult to arrive at an estimate of the time and materials saved in part on the original quotation. Where the item is wholly additional and clear cut in relation to the rest of the contract, a time-and-materials basis may be safely used. An example of this is where the electricians are required to carry out the extra work of running a cable to an electric motor, wiring up starter and control connections, and generally setting to work.

For lighting, proprietary types of lighting fittings can be specified. In fact, for a proper comparison of original tenders the lighting fittings should have been definitely specified or be on prime cost, even if they are altered afterwards. The type of switches to be used should also be given and the type of lighting conduit.

Cable runs.   In civil engineering building the structures erected are often of solid walling—either reinforced concrete or solid brickwork. Cable runs are usually enclosed in galvanised or enamelled iron conduit, which is screwed and jointed together. Galvanised conduit is the better class. These runs of conduit will all have to be worked out, and the electrician may wish to 'book' certain localities for the line of his conduit. If this layout is not considered early in the work the result may be very ugly. To attempt to consider this work after the plastering has been commenced is too late. Runs of surface conduit can be extremely ugly, spoiling completely the appearance of a room. If they are to be laid sunk in the surface of the wall, then consideration in detail will have to be given to them in the early stages of the work.

In domestic dwellings the electricity cables are frequently run between the floors and ceilings, or, on the ground floor, below the flooring boards. It is a simple matter to conceal the vertical conduits in chases cut in the interior walls, and the switches can be cut in the wall so that they are flush to the finished surface. But where, as in civil engineering, the framework is of reinforced concrete or rolled-steel joists embedded in concrete it will be found difficult, even impossible, to lay the conduit in chases cut in the walls for the full height unless special provision has been made. Hollow clay blocks for the walls can be obtained with grooves for conduit already cast in them. These are necessary, as it would otherwise seriously weaken these hollow block walls to cut a chase in them. But again, where there are reinforced-concrete beam ribs and reinforced-concrete ceilings it is not usually possible to cut chases of the necessary depth to conceal the conduit without coming up against the reinforcement. A chase of about 38 mm depth is required, and as plastering is normally 19 mm thick, this implies that 25 mm of concrete must be cut out. This means thereafter that the line of runs of electrical conduit and the special provisions for them should be worked out in the design stages of the work.

If the resident engineer sees no sign of such special provision on the drawings he should early consult with the electrical contractors and the engineer to see how the runs of conduit may best be laid out. To hope that such matters will probably 'come out all right in the end' is to invite disappointment at a later stage.

Planning service routes

In good architectural work the routes for such services as gas, water, heating pipes, electricity cables, and telephone lines will all be pre-planned. In civil engineering work less attention is sometimes paid to these matters because of the industrial nature of the structures erected, in which it may be neither necessary nor desirable that pipes and cables should be hidden away in ducting. However, there is always some pre-planning required, if only to get over the difficulty of routing services through an R.C. framed structure with solid concrete floors and for providing tidiness and ease of access. Where even a small building is to be erected, it much improves the interior appearance to plan the routes of services out beforehand and, if this has not been already done, the resident engineer might as well take on this task himself.

It is most important in the planning of service routes to act early—preferably before the foundation work to the structure is anywhere near completion. The sub-contractors for heating, lighting, and plumbing, and any other sub-contractors providing services, should be called to site, and each should be given a copy of the building plans and asked to show their proposed routes on these plans. It will then be necessary for the engineer to draw up one master plan showing all the services and the routes they must follow, and this master plan is then re-issued to the sub-contractors for any further comments and alterations. It may even be necessary to commence some of the sub-contract work forthwith, before the foundations are completed, e.g. drain and sewer connections, water mains, and gas mains may have to be laid through the foundations and then temporarily blanked off for later extension within the building.

Plumbing

Plumbing work should always be carried out by a specialist firm unless the contractor himself employs experienced plumbers. A good plumber can make an altogether more pleasing and neat job of the work than an inexperienced man—the difference being immediately apparent to the eye but practically impossible to describe in the specification. In civil engineering work plumbing is often more complicated than in traditional buildings, because the walls and floors may all be of much heavier construction. Whereas a plumber will normally find no difficulty in running pipes through traditional house or flat construction, he may find great difficulty in getting pipes through reinforced-concrete floors and, in particular, he may not be able to run his pipes up neatly, close to the interior corner of a room, because of the reinforced-concrete framing to a building.

There are usually four main feed pipes for a hot- and cold-water system— the cold riser main under pressure feeding the main supply tanks at the top of the building; the cold main down feeding urinals and w.c.s; and the hot and cold-return pipes of the heating system. Cold taps to washbasins and sinks will be taken off the main riser under pressure, as this water will be used for drinking. The hot taps to basins and sinks will be taken from the up hot flow from the boiler or from the hot-water storage tank. The sizes of mains will depend on the range of apparatus to be fed.

The positioning of urinals and w.c.s in a reinforced-concrete building often presents some difficulty. For w.c.s the P-trap type will probably be found more suitable, as use of this will enable the soil pipe to be brought out through the outer wall at sufficient height to clear the reinforced-concrete frame of the building—provided the wall is not too thick. In the case of the urinal, however, the trap is situated wholly below the outlet grating, and it may be necessary either to raise the urinal as a whole above floor level to get the trap in or else the soil pipe will have to be taken through a hole cut in the floor and taken to the outside of the building just below the ceiling of the room below. This latter proposal may, however, be vitiated by finding that the outer support beam of the floor is very deep, so that the soil pipe has to hang down a foot or so before it can bend to pass out through the wall, or it may be that a window comes in the required position for exit of the soil pipe. In such cases it is necessary to replan, taking the soil pipe down inside the building and walling it off from offices and similar rooms in a conduit of its own. It will be seen that all this needs to be planned out at a very early stage in the job so that drains and collecting chambers can all be constructed in their right ultimate positions during the construction of the foundations.

Soil pipes are usually of cast iron, sometimes they are of asbestos cement, subject to what the byelaws of the local authority will permit. Jointing of cast-iron pipes is with yarn and run lead or lead wool caulked hard. Sometimes a proprietary compound such as Philplug is permitted. Jointing of asbestos-cement pipes is by tarred rope followed by a stiff mortar mix or Philplug or similar.

Water services are usually run in copper nowadays, as copper pipes will sustain high pressures, are very durable, easy to cut and joint, and present a pleasing appearance. Galvanised steel piping is cheaper and is used for heating systems, and may also be used for water supply if the character of the water enables the local water authority to permit this under their byelaws. Joints for copper piping are either compression-type joints or capillary-type solder couplings. Joints for galvanised-steel tubes are screwed couplings. Plastic piping is now permitted by many water authorities where the water pressure is not excessive. The resident engineer will need to consult the local water authority's byelaws to find what types and grades of piping are permitted.

Plumbing work is paid for on measure according to metre run of pipe, fittings used, etc. Alternatively, a lump-sum quotation may be called for if the extent of the work can be precisely defined before tenders are submitted.

Other sub-contracts

The installation of a lift is a typical example of a mechanical engineering sub-contract. The sub-contractor will usually include in his quotation for the supply of a skilled erector to take charge of the erection of the equipment, and he will either charge additionally for any unskilled labour he has to take on to assist in the erection, or he may expect the main contractor to supply the unskilled labour. The latter is often the most convenient method, as the unskilled labour requirements may at one time be half a dozen men needed to shift some large piece of equipment or off-load some machinery, and at another time only one man may be required to assist the erector. The erector will also probably need to use a crane or other hoisting apparatus from time to time, and it would not be economic for the sub-contractor to supply this himself for only occasional work.

A lift manufacturer will not normally commence the manufacture of some items until the main framework of the building has been erected. He will then send a representative to site to take exact measurements of the lift well, its verticality, levels of landings and various clearances, and so on. He will not delegate this work to anyone else, since these measurements are of much importance to him, and must be carefully undertaken. Once he has erected the lift, it will have to be inspected and tested by the insurance agency, and cannot be put into use until a certificate of satisfactory test has been issued. This certificate should be passed to the resident engineer, who will pass it on to the employer.

In a similar fashion sub-contractors who have to undertake the supply and erection of chequer plating or handrailing will not normally commence manufacture of their equipment until they have been on site and have taken their own measurements of the structure to be fitted out. Allowance for an inevitable time lag must therefore be made when ordering these sorts of materials.

When machinery has to be installed, such as the lift motor, basement pumps, generators, and electric motors of all kinds, the sub-contractor supplying this machinery will expect to be able to erect the machinery on 'prepared foundations' put in by the main contractor. The main contractor cannot do this unless he has been provided with drawings showing the exact dimensions of the foundations to be put in. If there is not much work to be done the main contractor will usually not start the work until the sub-contractor's erector is on site so that the latter can check the foundation work proposed is correct. Usually the foundation block of concrete will be cast with its top surface about 25 mm low, holes being boxed out for the holding-down bolts. The erector will then place the machinery on the foundation, packing it up to precisely the right level by the use of metal shims and aligning one piece of machinery to another to the required accuracy. Under the supervision of the erector the main contractor's men will then grout in the baseplate or pedestals of the machine and the holding-down bolts to the foundation, the upper 25 mm of foundation being grouted by fixing a small strip of wood round the foundation block. After due time has been allowed for the grout to set, the erector will tighten up the holding-down bolts and check again for the alignment of his plant.

References

Report of Joint Committee on Location of Underground Services. I.C.E.

Form of Sub-Contract Designed for Use in Conjunction with I.C.E. Conditions of Contract. Federation of Civil Engineering Contractors.

CHAPTER 12

Price Increases, Extras, and Claims

Increased prices of materials

In an era of rising prices and wage-rates many civil engineering contracts include a 'rise and fall clause' whereby a contractor is enabled to claim for increased prices and wages he has to pay after submitting his tender. In the contract provision is made for the contractor to list at the back of his tender the basic prices of materials on which his tender is based. He will accordingly be paid extra for any increase of price on those materials, or will have deducted against him any reduction in price of those materials.

The variation will apply only to the materials listed; if none are listed, then no variations will apply. Some contractors cover themselves by stating that the list is to include 'all those materials used in the construction of the works'. This definition is frowned upon by some engineers, who require the materials each to be mentioned by name and the basic price inserted. It was formerly not the practice to allow materials for use in temporary works to be included in the list, but the contractor may now, under most contracts, include all materials, including consumable materials, such as petrol and diesel oil used for running plant, as well as the materials actually used in the structure.

There is a division of opinion as to the advisability of the engineer himself listing certain materials against which a basic price *must* be entered by tenderers; these materials being those which the engineer expects might come down in price and which a contractor might not otherwise include. Yet other engineers do not like to see definite prices quoted, as they feel this is a matter which should be investigated later, if and when the need for payment of an increase arises. An objection to the latter course is that it may be difficult to find what were the prices of materials for some past period independently of investigations made by the contractor in support of his claim.

Complex though the work may be in ascertaining the extras to be paid for increases in price of materials, the method is essentially well defined. The contractor should submit two documents, or sets of documents, when he makes his claim:

(1) a quotation from his supplier stating the price of the materials offered at the date of tender;

157

(2) the actual invoices sent by the same supplier for the goods as actually delivered, together with the official receipt of the supplier for payment made to him by the contractor.

The difference between the prices after any discount has been deducted, is the amount payable to the contractor (or to be deducted from payments if there is a reduction on the original quotation), provided that the quantity so invoiced has actually been used on the works.

Difficulties may arise with these claims where the actual materials delivered are different in quality from those originally quoted and forming the contractor's basic price. If the new materials are better but the *only* ones available, or if the originally quoted materials would not have. met the specified requirements, the contractor cannot claim extra. Only where the contractor is able to offer two or more qualities of materials all meeting specified requirements and the engineer *chooses* a more expensive quality, would the contractor be entitled to extra payment.

More difficulty arises if the supplier who gave the original quotation goes out of business and the contractor is forced to get the same material from some other supplier whose prices are higher. To evaluate the 'extra' payment due under the rise and fall clause this new supplier must be asked to quote the price he would have charged had he been asked to supply his material at the tendering date—the difference between that price and his current price being then payable as an extra, but not any greater difference. It must be remembered that the contractor contracts to undertake 'the supply of all necessary materials, labour, and plant for the construction of the works' and if he has to go farther afield or to other sources to give this service that is his bad luck. His job is to *get* materials— he would not, for instance, be expected to offer to reduce his charges if by chance he should find a cheaper supplier of the same goods.

Claims for wage increases, overtime, etc.

When a rise and fall (or price variation) clause applies to a contract the contractor is normally allowed all increases in standard rates for wages, travelling allowances, subsistence allowances, holidays with pay contributions, national insurance and pension rates, and rates of overtime calculation. These increases must, however, be 'nationally agreed' increases which have the support of and are mutually agreed between representatives of trade unions and employers having the power to make such agreements. If a contractor is already paying more than the standard rates he cannot claim and receive the extra calculated in accordance with the national agreements, unless he actually passes on a like amount to his men. Increases he gives of his own accord to his men cannot be reclaimed, nor can he claim for increases he pays to salaried or other staff who do not come under the national agreements about pay for civil engineering workers.

Sometimes, however, a contractor finds he cannot keep men on the site in sufficient numbers unless he pays them travelling and subsistence payments, or gives them plenty of opportunity to get overtime pay (such as Sunday working), or give them bonuses. If he finds he has not made sufficient allowance for this in his tender he may wish to claim some or all of the extras he is having to pay to keep the men on site. This sort of claim is not valid, even though it may well be true that if he does not pay the extras he will not be able to get sufficient men to construct the works.

As was mentioned in connection with the supply of materials, his contractual obligation is to *get* men and materials in sufficient numbers on the site to construct the works. It is up to him to judge beforehand what the labour market will be and how much he will have to pay; he cannot expect to be reimbursed any additional expense of getting men, simply because he misjudged what he would have to pay men to get them on the site. Of course, the labour market might have so unexpectedly altered that one's sympathies do, in fact, lie with the contractor, so that the claim may be presented to the employer as an ex-contractual claim which the employer might feel he should pay out of a sense of fair play; but there is nothing in the ordinary conditions of contract which obliges the employer to pay this kind of claim if he does not wish to do so. Only if the contractor foresaw the difficulty at his time of tender and included a proviso covering the contingency would the employer become liable to pay. Most contracts, however, distinctly state the contrary. By listing out all the possible extra payments a contractor might have to pay to his workmen and stating that all these extras must be 'included in' the contractor's tendered rates, the contractor is expressly prevented from making a claim on this basis.

Similarly, no claim arises if the contractor has to get workmen from farther afield than he thought he would have to at the time of his tender; although, if he has entered a proviso in his tender to the effect that it is based on being able to obtain a sufficiency of labour through some designated local labour exchange, he may possibly have a valid claim should he find he cannot get enough men through the nominated source. As regards overtime, the cost of it will not therefore be paid to a contractor unless it is overtime expressly ordered by the engineer for some particular purpose. There is an exception to this in the case of extra work paid for at dayworks rates. It would be unreasonable to expect the men on dayworks not to work the same hours as the rest of the men so, in this case, when dayworks are ordered, overtime pay on them will be reimbursed up to the extent of the usual extended hours that are being worked on the job.

Extras

A distinction needs to be made between three types of additional work on a contract, which are as follows:

(i) extras which are *essential* for the completion of the works as portrayed in the contract;

(ii) extras which the engineer or employer *chooses* to adopt;
(iii) extras which arise because *unforeseen conditions* arise.

Confusion often arises between these three different types of extras because, *for accounting purposes*, they are often listed together on contractor's claims, though they are different in their legal implications and they are paid for differently.

Extras which are essential for the completion of the works are not legally extras on the contract at all. They are things which have to be done to get the whole works properly completed, but which may not have been shown on the drawings or billed in the bill of quantities. The practical effect of this definition is of much importance in regard to lump-sum contracts, where extras of this kind can be held not to give rise to any extra payment. Thus, if a lump-sum contract is in general terms for the supply and installation of some equipment 'complete in all respects' the purpose and requirements of that equipment having been specified, then it must be supplied 'complete'. The contractor cannot claim extra payment for something that does not happen to have been mentioned in the specification or in his quotation, if that something is an implied essential for the complete installation. In such a case no 'variation order' for additional work is issued and no extra payment is made.

In the case of bills of quantities civil engineering contracts, however, the work is to be paid for *on measure*. Therefore the position in regard to an essential extra is different. It has to be paid for on measure, and therefore an extra item in the bill of quantities may have to be inserted to cover it, or the quantities under an item may have to be exceeded beyond that stated in the bill. For accounting purposes, though this extra is not a legal extra, any new bill item is usually covered by a variation order, because this keeps the records straight as between the original tender estimate and the actual cost.

Extras which the engineer chooses to adopt can arise in many ways. The engineer may choose to alter the design of the work in some particular because he wishes to effect an improvement upon that shown in the drawings; or the employer may wish to have changes made to the works —he may want a wider door here than is shown on the drawings, or different quality window-frames and so on. He conveys his wishes to the engineer, who, accepting these requests, alters the work the contractor has to do. The great majority of extras on contracts are of this category, and each extra must be covered by the issue of variation order by the engineer authorising extra payment, or altered rates of payment, to the contractor.

Extras arising from unforeseen conditions are not ordered by the engineer at all; they are claimed by the contractor, who must submit all details of the extra expenditure he has been put to in overcoming such unforeseen conditions. The contractor is then reimbursed the extra cost he has been put to. To cover this the engineer need not issue a variation order, but, as in the case of essential extras, a variation order is usually issued for accounting purposes.

Distinctions between payments for extras

It will be noticed that the type of payment for extras may vary as follows:

(i) essential extras	—no payment on lump-sum contracts; —payment on measure in bills-of-quantities contracts, the rates to include profit to the contractor;
(ii) chosen extras	—payment on measure or as may otherwise be agreed, such payments to include profit to the contractor;
(iii) claims for unforeseeable conditions	—payment of the cost of overcoming such unforseeable conditions, plus a reasonable percentage for profit and reasonable costs for any unavoidable delay or disruption of working suffered as a consequence.

It is frequently the case that an extra comprises part of (ii) and part of (iii). Extras often arise in connection with the construction of foundations. When an excavation runs into bad ground, foreseeing that the ground conditions are different from what he expected, the contractor may notify that he will be claiming for 'unforeseen conditions'. The presence of this bad ground may cause the engineer to change his decision regarding the foundations, and he may instruct the contractor to widen or deepen the foundations. In theory, the extra amount to be paid for the added difficulty of getting the excavation down to the original design depth of foundation (as shown on the drawings) is a type (iii) extra. But the extra work involved in widening or deepening the foundation is extra work the engineer has chosen to adopt, and is therefore a type (ii) extra.

In practice, so fine a distinction would not be made, and the rates set for the widening and deepening would take into account the added expense the contractor had been put to in meeting the unforeseen conditions, including a reasonable margin for profit and a reimbursement of the costs of any delay or disruption of working due to the unforeseen conditions as the engineer agrees was unavoidable. Provided the contractor thinks the new rates set are fair, he will not therefore make a claim under (iii). It may generally be taken that if the engineer chooses to adopt an extra on the contract, the rates he fixes for payment of that extra should take into account any unforseeable conditions which are the cause of the order for the extra work. This seems only reasonable, since the extra the engineer chooses to make cannot have been foreseen by the contractor, since it was also not known to the engineer at the time of tender.

Bringing extras into the accounts. Whatever may be the distinction between the various types of extras, it is usual to cover every alteration, addition, or omission from the original bill by the issue of a variation order. This variation order can be issued only under the signature of the engineer. The resident engineer has no power to issue a variation order unless this power has been delegated to him by the engineer, which would be unusual, and would still leave the engineer responsible, since the resident engineer can only act as an *agent* for the engineer and not as the engineer.

The only situation where a variation order is never issued is where altered or additional work has been done by the contractor of his own choice without prior notification that extra payment will be claimed. In that event the engineer is entitled to assume that it is simply the wish of the contractor to do the work in that manner because it is more convenient. Thus, if a contractor finds that class E blinding concrete does not suit him because it will not stand up to the wear and tear caused by the contractor's plant over it he may decide that he will use class D or class C concrete instead, whichever suits him better. This is the contractor's decision, and he has no grounds for claiming extra payment for the better concrete. He does not therefore notify the engineer that he will be claiming extra, and he cannot afterwards do so.

As regards the accounts, all extras should be shown separately in the accounts and should be covered by appropriate variation orders. They will normally include the following:

extra bill items, preferably all set out at the end of the original bill of quantities (not inserted in between original items), including substituted items where rates have been altered;
accounts for work done on dayworks;
accounts for claims made by the contractor for unforeseen conditions;
accounts for increased prices of materials, increase of rates of wages and use of plant, etc.

Thus, every plus or minus to the original tender is covered by the issue of variation order and is represented by a new bill item or an account in the claims submitted by the contractor.

Some miscellaneous points on extras. Several further important points must be remembered. The first is that all extras which are not essential to the construction of the works as originally approved must be reported to the employer through the engineer, and the employer's permission must be obtained for the extra before the work is commenced. Particular care should be taken with the final finishes to the job before ordering special extras—such as special lighting fittings, sun blinds, window-boxes, furniture, special flooring, etc.—because these things are usually of special interest to the employer who would be entitled to refuse to pay for extra things he does not want. He does not usually do this, because he knows the engineer has been acting in good faith to please the employer; but it is discourteous not to take the employer's opinion on such matters first.

Secondly, any sketch given by the resident engineer (or a member of his staff) to the contractor elucidating the details of the work, or suggesting methods of carrying the work out, is not an order for extra work.

Thirdly, care should be taken not to issue an extra-work order which covers or partly covers work which either the contractor would have had to do anyway or which arises because of the need to remedy faulty workmanship or materials. The former error is easy to commit when specifications have become so bulky that both resident engineer and agent may fail to notice a particular sentence in twenty or thirty thousand words. If this happens the situation must be remedied; but no doubt the resident engineer will have a few words to say to the original drafter of the specification, who should have so written it and indexed it that matters can be found in it without difficulty.

Examples of different types of extras

(i) An extra manhole and further lengths of surface-water piping are found necessary. If bill rates are available and the added work merely represents an addition to quantities, no variation order would be issued. If new rates have to be fixed there would be a variation order.

(ii) A contractor advises that the two-coat rendering to walls is not really adequate, though this is all that the specification calls for. He advises that the work should be three-coat for a good job, and quotes a price per square yard for the third coat. The resident engineer should report the matter to his head office, who obtain the employer's approval if necessary, and instructions are then given for the third coat. The extra cost is paid under a new bill item at the rate previously agreed, and a variation order is issued.

(iii) An employer, on being asked his exact requirements for a hot-water supply to a building being erected, appears to require a number of alterations to the original quotation and additions. A fresh quotation is therefore obtained from the plumbing sub-contractors, and the extra cost is mentioned to the employer. If the latter agrees to the extra cost a variation order is issued to the main contractor to cover his altered instructions to his sub-contractor.

(iv) An employer who was to have cleared the site for a building only fells and removes timber, leaving tree stumps and roots behind, some of these being of quite large diameter. The contractor refuses to give a price per tree or per acre for removing these stumps, and says he can only do it on dayworks. Daywork payments are agreed, and an extra-works order is issued. In this case the employer is not given an estimate of the cost of removal, since none was available and he had declined to undertake this part of the work and knew that he must pay for their removal whatever might be reasonable.

(v) A contractor was forced to leave a length of pipe trench excavation open for several months in a public highway. The cause was beyond his control; a valve to be provided by the employer for insertion in this length of pipeline was not delivered at the time expected. The contractor claimed extra payment for (*a*) watching, lighting and fencing the excavation during the delay period, and for (*b*) the extra cost of having to restart the pipeline elsewhere and then to come back and join up the pipeline when the valve arrived. His claim for (*a*) was made up of individual rates per day for providing lamps, fencing, and attendant labour. His claim for (*b*) consisted of a request to be paid for twice the length actually measured.

This is a typical example that is instructive to consider. There are three comments to make: first, the claim is justified, since the employer delayed the contractor; second, the claim for watching, lighting, etc., if based on correct hours and rates is acceptable; third, the claim for restarting elsewhere and then coming back to finish is submitted in the *wrong* form.

It is wrong to meet a contractor's valid claim by 'juggling about' with the quantities. Once started, this practice could so develop that the quantities inserted in the claims bear no relationship to the actual quantities of work undertaken. If the resident engineer is persuaded to do this he is, in fact, certifying extra payments, for which he has no authority. If the contractor thinks that double the rate for the given measurement is what he is entitled to, this is what he should ask for, not 'measurement twice over'. Better still he should quote the extra cost he has been put to on the basis of the hours spent waiting for instructions, moving his equipment, shoring up the excavation, setting up for a start elsewhere, and then reverting back to the work which previously had been stopped. A detailed claim on the latter basis is almost certain to receive authorisation if the hours and rates quoted are correct. This puts the claim on the basis of hard facts. Many contractors make the engineer's task very difficult by asking for round lump-sum extras, refusing to supply a detailed breakdown until repeatedly requested. If they would only give a breakdown in the first instance (even if the facts and figures have to be estimated) many occasions for argument would never arise.

Fixing rates for extras

The *Conditions of Contract* for civil engineering work set out the rates to be paid for altered or extra work. Clause 52 sets out the principles.

Where the extra work 'is of similar character and executed under similar conditions to work priced in the Bill of Quantities' then the Bill prices shall be used. Where the work is not similar or not executed under similar conditions, the Bill prices 'shall be used as the basis for valuation so far as may be reasonable, failing which a fair valuation shall be made.' (Clause 52 (1)).

Provided that 'if the nature or amount of any variation relative to the nature or amount of the whole of the contract work or to any part thereof shall be such that . . . any rate or price . . . for any item of work is . . .

PLATE V

(a) Whenever rain falls on an earth bank this kind of damage is likely to result u n l e s s   p r o p e r thought has been taken how to prevent it.

(b) Floods during construction have a propensity for being bigger and fiercer than anyone expected—especially the contractor.

PLATE VI

Collapse of the side of an excavation should be regarded as a civil engineering sin. It always results in mucky or extra work. It still too often results in loss of life.

PLATE VII

(a) Water ought not to be allowed to get into a column foundation like this. A drainage sump should have been dug at the side before the reinforcing steel was placed.

(b) There is seldom any trench that does not have to be cleaned up by hand labour—as these men are doing.

(c) A properly timbered trench.

Photo (c): W. & C. French Ltd.

PLATE VIII

(a) How not to make a road. The roller is too light; the side ditch too shallow; the 'foundation' is a bog of mud—and the fill material does not look much good either.

(b) Deep ruts like this in an allegedly compacted fill are a sure sign that the moisture content of the fill was too high when placed, or has become too high.

(c) A contractor's temporary road takes a heavy pounding. This road will only last in wet weather so long as the ditch is kept cleaned out and the road surface is kept to a camber.

PLATE IX

(a) A bottom-dump wagon.

(b) A D–8 tracking up a 1 in 2 slope which it takes easily.

(c) A D–8 with a grid roller (for compaction) attached.

(d) A D–6 dozer. It is considerably small and lighter than a D–8.

PLATE X

(a) A motorised scraper being push loaded with a dozer.

(b) Trucks like this are magnificent pieces of machinery—but they are as big as a cottage and have their limitations.

(c) Truck mounted concrete hopper.

(d) The lift-and-place tractor shovel is useful for placing materials up and over.

PLATE XI

(a) Laying the pore water pressure tubing and other cables for the instruments now incorporated in all major earthwork structures. An instructive exercise for the engineers who have to get down on their hands and knees with the workmen.

(b) Testing the *in situ* density of fill by the sand replacement method (on the left) and by the nucleonic density tester (on the right).

PLATE XII

(a) Jetting in a de-watering pipe for ground water lowering. Such pipes, which are set round the perimeter of a proposed excavation site, are connected to a suction pump for removal of the ground water.

(a)

(b) Even in quite reasonable ground a pipe trench is seldom like anything shown on the drawings.

(b)

rendered unreasonable or inapplicable . . . the Engineer shall fix such rate or price as in the circumstances he shall think reasonable.' (Clause 52 (2)).

The engineer may alternatively order that any additional or substituted work is executed on a dayworks basis, in which case priced statements of the labour, plant and materials used on the work have to be submitted by the contractor at the end of each month (Clause 52 (3)).

There is sometimes misunderstanding of the above provisions. Simply stated they are as follows:

(i) contract rates shall apply to altered or added work where such rates are applicable;
(ii) where contract rates are not directly applicable, they can be used as a basis for calculating fair rates; or a fair rate can be set independently;
(iii) provided that the nature or amount of a variation shall not be such that the use of a contract rate is unreasonable.

To take examples, let us consider what would be the likely attitude of the engineer (a) where he orders 10 more items of a certain kind when the original bill already includes 100 of the same items; and alternatively (b) where he orders 100 more items when there are only 10 of such items in the bill. In the former example it is almost certain that bill rates will apply, since to order 10 more when there are already 100 in the bill is scarcely likely to cause any unreasonable addition to the contract; but in the latter, the ordering of 100 more things when there were only 10 in the bill might well cause an addition to the amount of the contract that is unreasonable. In this latter event bill rates need not necessarily apply and the engineer can fix some other rate.

Occasionally engineers confuse the issue by mentioning that some of the prices in the bill may be 'loaded', i.e. some contain a larger amount of profit than others. This is often so. The argument then continues that if such rates are loaded and these same rates are applied to additional work the contractor will receive profit in larger measure than he ought to. But Clause 52 (2) provides against just such a contingency. It agrees that the engineer shall fix a different rate 'if the amount of any variation relative to the whole of the contract' resulting from the application of the bill rate, appears to be unreasonable.

These interpretations are what common sense suggests is right even if Clause 52 of the *Conditions of Contract* did not exist. In general, the engineer will be much better advised to apply common sense and fair dealing to his fixing of rates than to apply what he thinks is a legal interpretation of the wording of the General Conditions. If the contractor receives what he thinks is a fair deal he will not be bothered what the legal interpretation might have been; and if matters are not thereby settled, then the matter inevitably becomes a dispute which must go to arbitration or to the courts for settlement. In that event it is much better for the engineer to argue from the point of view of what is reasonable and fair, rather than on the basis of what he thinks the legal interpretation might be. The law is most often on the side of common sense, but the way it works is often complicated and is best left to lawyers.

What are reasonable rates?   Since bill rates all, or in general, include an element of profit, it must be reasonable to assume that any new rates the engineer fixes must also include an element of profit. In fixing the new rates the engineer does not necessarily have to consider similar types of rates in the bill, unless his judgment tells him this is sensible. Quite often it will be the most reasonable method. Thus, if there are rates for excavation at 1·5 m, 2·0 m and 2·5 m depth, and a new rate is required for excavation to 3·0 m depth, it would be reasonable to fix the new rate in line with the bill rates. This is provided the bill rates appear to the engineer to be reasonable in themselves, and that the work to be done under the new rate represents an extension of like nature and amount to the work in the contract. In most cases, where new work is in line with the work included in the contract, and if the prices inserted in the bill of quantities are reasonable, an extrapolation of these rates is as good a guide as any to the price to be fixed for additional work—but it need not be the *only* guide adopted.

It may be that, when the engineer is about to apply rates for new work which are in line with bill rates, the contractor points out that the bill rates were too low. In this event, if the engineer checks the contractor's information and finds it is correct, he must fix higher rates for the additional work than he might have done from consideration of the bill prices alone. To do otherwise is unreasonable. The engineer must look at the end result—the plus or minus to the 'amount of the whole of the contract work', etc.—and, if this amount becomes unreasonable through applying bill rates or extensions thereof, he must fix another rate which gives a reasonable answer. The intention of Clause 52 (2) is that it should operate fairly to both contractor and the employer; therefore new rates are sometimes higher and sometimes lower than bill rates. The contractor must accept the fact that he has made a loss on certain items in the original bill; the employer must accept that the charge made for certain other items includes a large proportion of profit, but neither should (if they are to receive fair dealing from the engineer) expect their misfortune or fortune to be magnified or multiplied many times over as the result of extra work being undertaken.

If there is no relevant guide in the existing bill rates as to what a new rate should be, the engineer will probably call upon the contractor to suggest the rate he wants. The engineer is then entitled to judge by his own experience, both on this job and on any other jobs, whether the rate asked for is reasonable. He can make his own estimates and computations and compare these with what the contractor is asking. If he does not agree with the contractor's proposed rate he can ask him for a breakdown of the proposed rate showing how it has been calculated. He may agree that the contractor's calculation is valid and therefore accept the rate proposed, or he may adhere to the results of his own calculations and experience. Whatever he chooses, and however he arrives at his final decision, he must give the contractor a full and fair opportunity to place the facts relevant to the extra work before him. He must check such facts and examine the contractor's calculations, and if he can find no fault in them it would be unreasonable of him not to accept the contractor's figure.

On the other hand, the contractor, in putting his case, must adhere to facts and figures. He must not expect the engineer to be influenced by vague statements that 'the job is losing money' or expect the engineer to bargain with him. The engineer has no power to enter into deals with the contractor, nor may he bargain on the basis of 'splitting the difference' between his calculated price and the contractor's. His job is to fix rates which appear to him to be *reasonable*, though this still permits him to come to some compromise between his and the contractor's figures if he feels both figures are approximate.

The contractor must bear in mind that the prices the engineer fixes, if they are to be reasonable, must assume reasonable efficiency on the part of the contractor. Also, if he expects reasonable rates to be applied to him he must be prepared to give the engineer the proper information in good time. It is no use the contractor doggedly adhering to a figure which the engineer cannot accept, when no detailed breakdown is supplied in support of the figure.

Payment for unforeseen difficulties

The payments to be made for unforeseen difficulties are in the nature of claims from the contractor, and therefore the question of fixing suitable bill rates does not apply. The contractor must submit detailed accounts and calculations showing the extra expenditure he has been put to which stems from the unforeseen difficulties. These calculations are often complex, as will be illustrated later.

Claims

Claims by a contractor for extra payment usually arise from:

(i) encountering adverse physical conditions or obstructions which he could not reasonably have foreseen, or

(ii) dissatisfaction with rates fixed by the engineer for altered or additional work, or

(iii) delays caused to him which have affected the progress of his work.

The contractor can put these claims before the engineer at any time after the event and before the termination of the contract, provided that (under the *Conditions of Contract*) if he intends to make a claim which relates to unforeseen conditions he must have given notice, at the time the unforeseen conditions were first revealed, that he intended to make such a claim. There are other, more detailed provisions that must be complied with, as set out in the General Conditions, and the reader is referred to them for further information.

Many contractors' claims for extra payment fail to receive early approval from the engineer because the form in which they are presented is unacceptable. Some unhappy instances of phrases used by contractors in submitting claims, which phrases are of no help to him, are as follows:

(a) '. . . because we have lost a great deal of money on this item';

(b) '. . . because we were put to uneconomic working';

(c) '. . . because our profit margin on this contract (or item) was already cut to a bare minimum', or alternatively '. . . because our prices for these items were already very competitive/keen';

(d) '. . . because the weather was so poor';

(e) '. . . because we encountered a number of unexpected delays and difficulties';

(f) '. . . because we had already included in our prices for doing so-and-so, whereas your Resident Engineer insisted upon what, in our view, was over-strict compliance with the specification against our representation that this was not normal trade practice';

(g) '. . . because our sub-contractors let us down'.

The brief (and brutal) contractual answers to such complaints are:

to (a) and (c) — what the contractor makes or loses on the contract is of no contractual significance;

to (b) and (e) — without facts and proof, no payment;

to (d) — losses caused by weather conditions are the contractor's liability;

to (f) — the resident engineer was within his rights;

to (g) — the contractor is responsible for the misdeeds of his own sub-contractors.

The great objection to submitting such phrases is that they too often invalidate the basis of what might be a justifiable claim.

Need for facts. As with rates, the engineer must have *facts* and *estimates* presented to him in support of any claim. On his side, the contractor should be willing to turn all his records and accounts out for nspection by the resident engineer and the engineer. If he has lost money, or been unfairly paid, or been caused delay—there will certainly be some evidence of this in his accounts and records. The resident engineer has diaries, the inspector's daily returns, and these can also be of assistance, indicating how work has slowed down as difficulties were encountered, or how more men were employed than usual, or how additional plant had to be brought in. In asking for facts, the engineer does not demand calculations that check to the last penny, or records of hours that check to the last half hour. On large claims half a day's error is of no special significance, and estimated prices may have to be worked to for materials wasted, lost time, or standing time. The contractor must, however, beware of putting in claims for losses which really arise from his own inefficiency; for instance, he cannot claim for plant standing idle if the inspector's daily sheets show the plant was broken down and could not have worked.

Claims for delay

Claims are frequently presented by contractors for delay. Apart from simple cases where, for instance, the engineer has had to order a machine to stop working while he considers what altered instructions to give (there being no other work available for that machine), delay claims present many difficulties. In the first instance, it must be stated that there are few precise rules to apply and few clear-cut legal cases to quote. However, some light may be thrown on the general problem by the following points.

A valid delay claim must comply with all three of the following conditions:

(i)   the delay must have been 'real';
(ii) the cause of the delay must be outside the contractor's liabilities and risks;
(iii) the delay must have caused loss or extra expenditure to the contractor which has not been made good to him elsewhere under the contract.

Definitions of delay. A 'real' delay may be defined as a period during which a contractor cannot employ his men or machines or staff at their normal intended output, having regard to the nature and amount of work which is available under the agreed programme of working or under any practicable re-arrangement of that programme.

A delay can affect a portion of the work, or the whole of the work. It can also be complete—such as when the engineer orders a machine to stop working and no other work is available for it; or it can be partial—such as when materials or services to be provided by the employer under other contracts are not forthcoming at sufficient speed to allow the contractor to maintain normal rates of output.

Extension of contract time. An extension of the contract time is not necessarily evidence that a contractor has sustained a delay which would give rise to a valid delay claim. This is a very important point. The extension of the contract period should be considered quite independently of delays. Extension of the contract period may be necessary because the contractor is ordered to undertake additional work. He will be paid bill rates for such work (or rates fixed by the engineer), the rates allowing for any overhead charges which are prolonged. Similarly, if the contractor has made a valid claim for meeting unforeseeable conditions the reimbursement to him of the cost of meeting such unforeseen conditions should have included reimbursement for any delays, standing time, lack of normal output, etc.

Thus, until proved otherwise, any extension of contract time which has been given solely on account of extra works, or because the contractor has had to overcome unforeseen difficulties for which he is claiming independently, should *not* result in a further claim for delay.

Causes of delay. The most frequent causes of valid delay claims are two. The first is where one contractor working for the employer fails to complete his work in time and so delays another contractor. A typical instance of this is where a machinery contractor may fail to deliver his machinery on the due date, and the building contractor is preventing from proceeding with the finishes of the building, the flooring, tiling, plastering, and so on. The second is a change of design which, though it is issued before construction commences on the altered portion of the works, nevertheless causes upset and delay to the contractor's work. The situation must be such that, at the time of notification of the change, no reasonably practicable rearrangement of the contractor's programme can avoid some delay or can be carried out without involving the contractor in some added expense which he is not reimbursed in the rates paid.

An instance of the latter type of delay occurred in the case of the construction of a dam. The upstream surfacing of this dam was to be in riprap. The work commenced, but the riprap proved to be of insufficient size. The design had to be changed, concrete slabbing being substituted for riprap. The rates payable for the slabbing were already set out in the bill. But the necessary re-organisation of the work at this late stage brought about many delays and extra expenses. Delays were caused by having to find and take on more shuttering carpenters, by bringing to the job more machinery for concrete handling, by having to interweave the added concrete work into the existing concreting programme. As a whole, the job progress suffered very badly, because the time when the change was made was October and the concrete slabbing was delayed by frost and snow, and this delayed other work on the dam, so that, as an overall result, completion of the work was at least two months later than it would have been.

Contractors know that delays can be expensive, and the resident engineer and engineer must be prepared to take this into account when they order a change of design, whose effect upon the contract can be widespread and serious.

The resident engineer should particularly note down what are the causes of delays which occur. Those which are due to the employer or the engineer can form the basis of a successful claim by the contractor for standing time for his plant, though before a contractor can successfully claim extra payment on these grounds he must be able to *prove* that it was essential for the employer or the engineer to have made those decisions or carried out those actions the non-execution of which were the supposed cause of the delay.

Claims for misrepresentation can also be made by the contractor, but the obligation is upon the contractor to raise the matter immediately he discovers it. He cannot proceed with the work as if there was no misrepresentation and then make a claim at the end of the contract.

Cost of delay. The example previously mentioned shows how design alteration causing a delay can be very costly. It must, however, be borne in mind that no claim for a delay can be valid unless some actual loss is sustained by the contractor. It is sometimes difficult to prove the amount of the loss when the delay has been piecemeal and has spread, with diminishing effect, through many operations of the contract. The fragmentisation of the delay effect through sundry operations causes the impact of the delay to be diminished, since reasonable counter-measures to offset the delay are available in greater number. The end effect may be that no visible delay to the job as a whole can be pin-pointed, and little or nothing to any particular operation. On the whole, this must be taken as meaning that no provable loss to the contractor was caused by the delay. The employer's thanks may be due to the contractor for overcoming the difficulties, but not the employer's money.

Special aspects of delay claims

Some typical examples of the difficulties that can arise are given below. The opinions given are views advanced by experienced engineers or by lawyers but have not been tested in the courts.

Claim for plant idle. A contractor was delayed because the engineer had to make substantial changes to the design of the works. These were large changes, they involved doing both additional work and work of a greatly changed nature. That delay had been caused to the contractor was not disputed. The engineer had set new rates for the new work and made payments for standing time and loss of output, etc. Nevertheless, the contractor submitted a claim for plant standing idle on the job. When examined in detail the contractor appeared to have claimed for any time any plant was actually standing idle on the job after the initial stoppage and change of design.

Legal advice suggested that:

(i) the deployment and use of plant was the contractor's responsibility— it was not up to the engineer to tell the contractor how he should use his plant, or when it should come on, or go off the site;
(ii) in fixing rates for additional or altered work the engineer should include in those rates for payment for bringing any new plant to site or for substituting one kind of plant for another, or for not using plant, in order to carry out the additional or altered works.

Therefore 'plant idle' was not a claim which could be submitted separately; it related to the rates fixed for the additional work, etc., which should have taken into account the relevance of any plant idle.

The only exception to this would be where the engineer might actually have suspended the operation of any machine.

Claim for loss of profits elsewhere through delay. In this case the contract time had been extended because of additional and altered work, about this extension there was no dispute. The contractor took the view, however, that because the job had taken longer than it should have done, he was prevented from using his organisation (i.e. his staff, machines, etc.) to undertake other contracts elsewhere which would have given him profit.

The legal view advanced was that any alleged loss of profits through not being able to undertake work elsewhere could be recovered only by an action for damages. Remedy could not be sought through the contract itself.

Claim for timber left standing. A contractor was requested to leave timber in an open trench while the engineer considered what alterations of design were necessary. This timber was left in the trench for many months, because of additional work the engineer had to order to be completed first. There was no dispute that a delay had occurred. The contractor, however, presented a claim for this timber at the dayworks rate per cubic metre of the timber, per day, left standing in the trench —i.e. the hire rate for such timber. The money claimed amounted to many thousands of pounds in excess of the buying price of the timber.

The engineer proposed to pay the contractor either the outright purchase price of the timber less a sum deemed to have been included in the original rates for timbering, which could have represented the 'first use' price of the timber; or, alternatively, a figure deemed to reimburse the contractor for having some of his capital locked up in this timber for longer than expected—whichever was the greater. The solution to this problem was not revealed, because the eventual sum agreed upon by both parties in settlement included many other items as well. But the engineer's attitude seems reasonable and the contractor's unreasonable. In deciding what to do in a problem of this type the engineer should remember that, in fixing new rates for additional work, these rates do not have to be the same as laid down by the bill if the result would be unreasonable having regard to the whole or part of the work.

Claim for stopping work. A contractor was building a pumping station, but the pumps were not delivered on time by the pump contractor, who had a separate contract with the employer. At first the contractor waited, hoping the pumps would come along; in the meantime doing what work he could find. During this waiting period certain other troubles arose on matters relating to a third contract, under which a wellboring contractor ran into difficulties, thus further diminishing the amount of work the building contractor could do.

It was agreed with the building contractor that he should stop work completely and withdraw from site until such time as the pumps had arrived and the new well was completed. This stoppage lasted for over a year, during which time labour rates and material prices increased. In view of this the contractor was reimbursed (by complicated calculations) the extra charges and the losses he had sustained up to the date of his departure from site. When invited back to complete the work the outstanding work was rescheduled, and new rates were agreed with him for this work, the rates being such that they covered all the costs of his restart and the increased prices. The advantage offered by the latter method is that it avoids complex calculations and is fair to the contractor.

Arbitration

Most contracts permit disputes to be referred to an arbitrator. Arbitration is unavoidable if the contractor insists upon it. The engineer cannot circumvent this process because he cannot certify for payment anything over and above the amount which he personally considers reasonable, having regard to all the facts. The employer can, however, authorise an *ex contractual* payment if he thinks this is wiser than going to arbitration.

In certain circumstances an arbitration can take place during the currency of the contract for all or only some items in dispute, or over some items to a given date and others to another date. In theory, a second arbitration can take place over the same items previously in dispute but for the period after the given dates to which the first arbitration applied.

If an arbitration takes place during the currency of a contract the situation is complex, and on no account should any moves be made without receiving legal advice. To mention only one of the difficulties, the arbitrator's award may be made in the form of a single lump sum. If a second arbitration occurs on the same contract, then no one (the legal advisers included) will know how the first sum awarded was apportioned over the items in dispute which now appear again as items still disputed for a subsequent period. There are as well many other complications which can arise.

One of the first things to settle when an arbitration seems inevitable is to define the matters in dispute. This may not be easy; it implies that the engineer and contractor must precisely define the magnitude and causes of their disagreement on every single item. Where this has not happened the arbitrator may refuse to proceed with the arbitration.

This is not the place to deal with the detailed aspects of arbitration, but any arbitration experience will emphasise the importance of certain features of the resident engineer's work. His detailed records of delays, outputs, weather, mistakes made, instructions given, agreements verbally entered into will all form vital parts of the engineer's evidence. He will realise the great benefit of having issued clear instructions to the contractor and of having confirmed those instructions in writing. He will realise the importance of keeping all personal or pettifogging complaints out of his correspondence with the agent, because if it is necessary to support the engineer's case by using as evidence copies of correspondence to the agent or contractor, then *all* correspondence may have to be submitted to the arbitrator, not just a selection of it. Personal disputes put in writing may prove acutely embarrassing, and they may seriously weaken the engineer's case by tending to show that a dispute really arose because two men were antipathetic towards each other and were therefore not in a state to act reasonably. In that event the arbitrator might conclude that the dispute need never have arisen had the engineer's staff acted more reasonably.

Some examples of other claims

Deletion of a major item. A contractor had to erect four buildings under a contract. Because of lengthy delays and substantial changes it was thought best to let him build three of the buildings only. He claimed for loss of profit on the deleted work, and he was paid an agreed amount for this. The principle of whether to pay such lost profit or not depends upon the circumstances. One cannot make such a payment just because quantities come different from what the bill of quantities shows, because the whole purpose of a bill-of-quantities contract is to permit such variations within reason. But to delete a whole building may deprive a contractor from getting the rewards he may be deemed reasonably to have expected when he examined the contract documents at the time of his tender.

Prolongation and its effect. Included in a contract were items for:

  (i) bringing drilling equipment to site and setting up ready for use (a lump sum);
 (ii) moving the drilling equipment from hole to hole (per move); and
(iii) drilling (per foot drilled).

The amount of drilling work shown in the bill had to be more than doubled due to a change of design. The engineer certified *pro rata* to the work done under items (ii) and (iii), but refused to certify any extra payment under (i) on the grounds that no other drilling plant had been brought to site, the same plant being used all the time.

In another case, the same kind of claim was made in regard to a lump sum preliminary item in the bill for the supply and maintenance of the resident engineer's offices. Since the office was on site for twice the intended time of the contract, the contractor wanted the lump-sum price for it doubled. The engineer refused to certify anything additional, beyond a sum he judged reasonable to cover the extended period of maintenance of the offices. Perhaps, in this case, he ought to have added an amount representing the loss to the contractor through having capital tied up in these offices longer than expected; for the contractor to claim the cost of the offices and their setting up twice over is, however, unreasonable.

Preliminary items present great difficulty when prolongation of a contract occurs. The situation is much simplified if all 'preliminaries' covering temporary works are deemed to be included and spread over all the items in the bill of quantities which are not provisional. Thus, reimbursement *pro rata* to the prolongation for these preliminary and overhead charges is automatic when bill rates (or similar) are used to cover extra works.

Sub-contractors. The engineer ordered soils investigations to be undertaken on a construction site. The work was let as a separate contract (direct between employer and soils contractor) and not as a sub-contract to the main construction contractor. The latter maintained that the work should have been sub-let under him; he therefore claimed 10 per cent on the sub-contractor's bill. The payment of this claim depends upon the General Conditions of Contract. If these gave sole possession of the site to the contractor his claim might be valid; if they did not he would have no claim.

Location of an operation. A contractor claimed an extra for bringing filling from location B on a site which was rather more distant than location A shown on the contract drawings. The specification, however, stated that he 'must include in his prices for bringing suitable fill from any part of the site'. The 'site' was clearly marked on the contract drawings as 'Land Available to Contractor' and location A had been marked as 'Probable location of fill', but location B was still within the area of the site. The engineer refused to make any payment against the claim on the grounds that both locations were within the site and location A had been qualified as 'probable'. This illustrates the importance of care in putting notes on the drawings and making these notes tally with what is written in the specification.

As an alternative argument in the example above, the contractor maintained that the filling he took from location B was not the same material as the engineer had intended to be taken from location A, as shown by typical grading curves given in the specification for material from location A and when compared with the grading curves of the actual material used from location B. Further, the material intended to be used from A had been described (verbally) as clay for puddle, and the material actually used had been described (verbally on site) as rolled clay. However, within the specification, the material had been described as a sand–silt–clay mixture, a broad enough description to apply to both materials. The engineer had already made an adjustment in the rates to allow for the different placing nature and requirements of the two materials, and he therefore continued to reject the claim for further payment, for the difference of location did not differ from the definition in the specification. The point here is that no altered rate can be fixed by the engineer if the contractor has not had to go beyond the requirements of the specification, irrespective of changes of name or changes within the limiting conditions set by the specification. In winning the rolled clay, instead of puddle clay, the engineer could not agree that the contractor was doing more than required, judging from the specification and drawings.

Typical results of a design change.   Many claims arise when the contractor feels that he has been forced to adopt different methods from those he contemplated in the construction, because of designs being altered as the work proceeds. Such a claim is not valid if the original specification was wide enough to include the altered method of construction. Nevertheless, as a general rule any alteration in design is likely to be the cause of a claim for extra payment. As an example; suppose a retaining wall is to be built in sections between contraction joints which are 20 m apart. These contraction joints are shown on the contract drawings. Later it appears advisable that the contraction joints shall be placed at 10 m intervals, and as a result the contractor puts in a claim for extra payment under a variety of headings. He may claim extra payment for:

(1) making additional construction joints;
(2) additional work on erecting and moving shuttering;
(3) having to alter his barrow runs for concreting more frequently;
(4) being unable to concrete as much in one day as he had originally intended; and
(5) the additional time his men spend cleaning down the concreting plant at the end of each concreting operation.

The total amount claimed as an extra under these headings can be suprisingly large.

It would be the duty of the resident engineer to advise the engineer as to which of the above claims appears valid. It is clear that claim (1) is valid. Claim (2) does not appear to have much substance, since, the total length of wall being the same, the same total amount of shuttering will have to be erected in any case and, on observing the contractor's shuttering methods, it will probably be found that it would take exactly twice the time to shutter a 20 m length of wall than a 10 m length. The contractor has also avoided mentioning that on the 10 m lengths he will only have to provide half the amount of shuttering required for a 20 m length, i.e. his costs should actually be less, since he need not buy or hire so much shuttering. Claim (2) would therefore be rejected.

Claim (3) appears to have just as little substance. Barrow runs are extended as needed, and will usually be along the wall from one central point of access; the contractor's claim appears to be a claim for, say, three hours' work on each of two days instead of six hours' work on one day. As the work is done by general labour, then it is not reasonable to suggest that the contractor had nothing for these men to do for the three hours they would have spent erecting barrow runs.

Claim (4) for concreting in less quantities would again depend on the facts. If a full day's concreting for a proper gang of men was still available on the shorter length of wall and no men were standing idle on account of this shortened length, then the claim is not supported by facts. If, however, the concreting had been cut up into short lengths so retarding progress substantially, then the claim might be allowed to stand, subject to detailed scrutiny.

Claim (5) for cleaning out the mixer more times is clearly valid, providing the mixer was used for this work only, and would not have been producing concrete for other parts of the job.

The example above is typical, and shows the need for the resident engineer to be informed of exactly what is going on every day and the need to note in his diary or to get his assistants to do so.

Claims during maintenance period

Claims may arise during the maintenance period if the contractor is called upon to do remedial work which in his opinion is due to wear and tear of the structure. This problem frequently arises where part of the construction is put into use before the completion or substantial completion certificate is issued. The contractor, of course, is not responsible for wear and tear, and if called upon to renovate part of the work during the maintenance period that is partly due to wear and tear and partly due to faults arising, then an apportionment of the cost will have to be agreed upon; that payable for wear and tear will be an extra. Strictly speaking, this payment is not chargeable to the construction of the works, i.e. capital expenditure, but to renovation, i.e. revenue, and the engineer may refuse to authorise remedial work for wear and tear without first obtaining the authority of the employer, as it has nothing to do with the original construction cost. Reference to the employer on these matters is therefore essential.

References

Hudson's Building & Engineering Contracts, I. N. Duncan Wallace. Sweet & Maxwell. (See reference to this book on page 33.)
Engineering Law and the I.C.E. Contracts, M. W. Abrahamson (1965). C. R. Books Ltd.,
'The Civil Engineer as Arbitrator', E. J. Rimmer. *Journal I.C.E.*, April 1947. (A classic work by an acknowledged authority.)
Rate Fixing in Civil Engineering Contracts. C. K. Haswell. *Proceedings I.C.E.*, February 1963. (But see also the discussion on this paper printed January 1964.)
Schedules of Dayworks Carried out Incidental to Contract Work. Federation of Civil Engineering Contractors.

CHAPTER 13

Earthworks and Machinery

EXCAVATION is often not as simple as the bill of quantities and the specification seem to imply. Only 'necessary excavation' is normally measured and paid for at bill rates, and this is usually defined as the volume vertically above the plan limits of the foundations. The contractor has to make allowance in his rates for any additional excavation for working space, access, or keeping the sides of the excavation stable. Notwithstanding this, some contractors will often claim extra payment for working space on the grounds that this extra excavation 'was inevitable'. Such a claim is invalid and must be dismissed because, if inevitable, then the contractor should have foreseen the need. Sometimes the extra excavation is caused by the contractor's failure to support the sides of the excavation with timbering, but if the specification called for timbering where required (as it normally should) again such a claim is invalid.

The planning of methods of excavation is primarily the agent's job, and the resident engineer will not interfere with the agent's decisions, save where any proposed method is likely to result in harm to the permanent works. The agent must plan to achieve maximum economy of working, and a wide variety of alternatives may exist. Factors which need to be considered are:

(i) means of supporting and draining the proposed excavation;
(ii) excavating output required, and the machinery needed to achieve this;
(iii) choice of machinery in relation to nature of material to be excavated, distance to tip, and output;
(iv) methods of working machinery in and out of the excavation, including provision of access roads;
(v) haulage of excavated material to tip.

Excavating machinery

Bulldozers ('dozers') are used for cutting and grading work and for pushing scrapers to assist in their loading. Dozers are also used for clearance work, for spreading and compacting fill, and for forming and maintaining access roads. The larger sizes are extremely powerful, and are useful for felling trees or for pulling out other vehicles which get bogged down or 'ditched'. Every large site on which earth moving is taking place requires at least one large dozer to complete the necessary complement

178

of equipment, but these large dozers are costly to run and maintain, so that the good agent will never have a 'spare' dozer on his site if he can help it. When used for cutting and grading work, dozers must be used with other earth-lifting and transporting machinery, as they cannot push excavated material very far. Slopes up to 1 in 2 can usually be managed by the dozer, which can also tackle slopes as steep as 1 in 1½ provided the material of the slope gives adequate grip. A dozer cannot climb a 1 in 1½ of loose sand, gravel, or rounded cobbles; but it can do this if the slope is of stiff clay or interlocking angular rock. On these steep slopes of 1 in 1½, or 1 in 2, the dozer must not turn, it must go straight up or down, turning on to flatter ground at top or bottom. Steep sidelong ground is dangerous for a dozer (or any kind of tractor) to work on, particularly if the ground is soft. Whereas the great advantages of dozers are their tractive power, climbing ability, and compactive effort, from these very advantages spring some serious defects. Their worst defect is that they rapidly break up the surface of any road, and they cannot traverse metalled public roads. Thus, in Britain, dozers can only be run about on the site and, even then, only on suitable ground. They can wreck lightly built access roads, they break open the surface of water-bound or tarmac areas, and on soft clays can rapidly ruin what was to have been a finished formation level.

Scrapers can be motorised, or can be drawn by a dozer. The drawn scraper is cheap and long suffering (apart from its operating cables), and is therefore useful for a modest amount of earth moving where the dozer can be used for this work when required, and be on other work later. The haulage distance with the dozer-drawn scraper must not be long, however. For long-distance haulage the motorised scraper, which is very fast, cannot be bettered, but it must often be push-loaded by a dozer, not only because there may not be enough tractive power in the motive wheels when scraping hard ground but also in order to reduce the wear and tear on the balloon tyres, the cost of which may easily be £200 each. The scraper is the machine which gives the cheapest price of any for excavation, subject to limitations of haulage distance and gradient of the haul road. The defects of the scraper are that it requires a large turning circle, it can tackle only relatively gentle slopes on the haulage road, it cannot cut vertical- or near-vertical-sided excavations, and it cannot dig rocky material.

The face shovel (or **digger**) can give very high outputs in all types of materials. It can handle rock if the rock face is broken by drilling and blasting. It is a neat and precise machine and leaves a very clean formation, and its flat tracks do not damage that formation. It loads cleanly and accurately to lorries, it can choose what it digs; if used in the correct size it can do a lot of careful excavation work. Its defects are that it works only above formation level (though this can sometimes be an advantage), and it must therefore work itself 'into the face'. There is a limit to the height of face it can work at, dependent upon the material of that face;

so for deep excavations it is usual to 'bench in' machines at different levels. It also suffers from the defect that it is not very mobile and it must always work on a firm level patch of ground. The agent cannot move a large-sized face shovel around the job daily; even a trip of a hundred yards or so must be taken carefully or, particularly on sidelong or weak ground, the tracks may come off or some other affliction befall the machine.

It is sometimes useful to know the sizes and horsepower of typical excavators. The well-known Ruston Bucyrus excavator sizes run:

Machine	Bucket size m^3	(yd^3)	B.h.p.	Boom length as crane m
10 RB	0·3	$(\frac{3}{8})$	34	9–12
19 RB	0·5	$(\frac{5}{8})$	55	12–21
22 RB	0·6	$(\frac{3}{4}-\frac{7}{8})$	66	12–21
30 RB	0·95	$(1\frac{1}{4})$	98	12–27
38 RB	1·15	$(1\frac{1}{2})$	132	14–30
54 RB	1·9	$(2\frac{1}{2})$	210	18–30

The dragline has a wider range of excavating abilities than any other excavation equipment. Its great advantage is that it can dig below its standing level and off-load at or above its own level. It also has the ability to trench and to cut and grade slopes; it can also place material with a fair degree of accuracy. The most annoying defect of the dragline is that though it 'works itself off' the formation, it is liable to leave that formation well stirred up for 150 mm or more, as the teeth of the bucket rake up the surface rather more than it cleans it. It is also a bit messy in loading vehicles. In trenching work deep trenches can be quickly dug in the right sort of material—the latter being any sort of material into which the teeth of the bucket can get a grip. Sometimes quite a soft rock cannot be excavated by the dragging simply because the bucket rides up any smooth bedding planes in the rock, the teeth of the bucket failing to get a grip.

The hydraulic hoe has now replaced the cable-operated back-acter for digging trenches and pits. Equipped with the appropriate size of bucket and having adequate horsepower, it can excavate trenches in all materials except continuous or massive rock. It can be fitted with a rock breaking point to break up weakly cemented rock. The hydraulic hoe is now universally used for trenching work and it is no longer necessary to distinguish between soft ground (such as clay) and moderately hard ground for the purposes of specifying different classes of excavation so long as the contractor has been informed of the range of material he will encounter.

The tractor shovel or traxcavator has replaced the skimmer bucket for skimming or trimming and area, and is also used for lifting heaps of spoil to lorries etc. It is, in effect, a wide bucket attached to the front of a dozer or tractor. The bucket can be lifted and forward or side-tipped to empty its contents to a higher level. The machine can be used to skim loose material off a formation, but in this case it is best that its tracks are only lightly gripped or have no grips at all so that the formation is not screwed up as the vehicle slews.

The grab is a clamshell bucket either hydraulically or cable operated. The hydraulically operated grab may be fixed to a long rod which is raised or lowered down a frame held vertically (or at an angle) by a crane which can travel sideways on rails, so that trenches up to 30 m deep can be cut with precision for the construction of diaphragm walls. Cable-operated grabs suspended from a crane are sometimes used for excavating pits in loose ground or for handling stockpiles of concrete aggregates, or for excavating soft ground below water. Their output rate is low.

Haulage of excavated material

The haulage distance to tip is an important factor influencing the choice of excavating machinery and method of excavation. The choice lies first between using machinery which can both excavate and transport material (motorised scrapers) and excavating machinery which must off-load to dump trucks, or which can place the excavated material near the excavation. When dump trucks must be used their nature and size is dependent upon the haulage distance and the kind of routes that must be followed. Large dump trucks cannot be used on public roads and, even on site roads, it does not necessarily follow that the largest sizes are the most economical, as they may be very slow on up-grades, slow also on down-grades when fully loaded because of poor braking power, and they may require relatively costly site roads because of imposing high concentrated wheel loadings. In turn, the size of dump truck used determines the size of excavator that most economically goes with it.

Costing of haulage. An important point arises when a contractor sub-lets haulage of material from an excavation, or import of filling at a rate per ton-mile when the excavation or filling is to be paid for per cubic yard in the bill of quantities. Before the contractor can safely quote a rate per cubic yard in his tender he must know the tons of material to be carted per cubic yard of excavation or filling, and he may lose a considerable sum of money if he does not get this factor right.

Consider 300,000 cu. m of excavation to be hauled 5 miles off site. The contractor may have estimated 1·9 tonnes per cu. m, and obtained a quotation of £0·15 per tonne mile for haulage. If he estimates the cost of excavation as 35p. per cubic metre he may possibly make up his tender price as follows:

	£
Excavation	0·35 per cu. m
Haulage 1·9 tonnes by 5 miles at £0·15 tonne-mile	1·43 per cu. m
Overheads and profit	0·27 per cu. m
Tendered price	2·05 per cu. m

If, however, the material he has to excavate turns out to be different from what was expected (a not unusual occurrence) the tonnes per cubic metre could average 10 per cent higher—i.e. 2·09 tonnes per cu. m instead of 1·90. As a result his costs will work out

	£
Excavation	0·35 per cu. m
Haulage 2·09 tonnes by 5 miles	1·57 per cu. m
Total cost	1·92 per cu. m
Balance for overheads and profit	0·13 per cu. m

His expected return of £81 000 for overheads and profit on 300,000 cu. m of excavation will therefore be reduced by half to £39 000. The longer the haulage distance, the more accurately must the contractor know the weight of the material per cubic metre. For suppose, in the above example, the haulage distance is 10 miles, then the 10 per cent increase in weight per cubic metre would change his £81 000 profit and overheads item to a £1 500 loss.

The conversion factor is particularly important in relation to the construction of large earthworks such as dams, where several millions of cubic metres of filling must be dug, hauled, and compacted to give a specified density expressed as a percentage of the optimum density. If the engineer wants the contractor to be interested in achieving a high density of fill he ought to give an incentive for achieving this, and not so word his specification that the higher the optimum density, the less is the profit to the contractor. He should—if he is not prepared to pay per tonne of filling—specify the actual density which his required Proctor percentage compaction implies and should allow an extra-over to be quoted should the actual average density achieved be higher.

To measure the quantities hauled on a tonne-mile basis by sub-contractors can present a problem to the contractor. If he insists on every vehicle being weighed on and off the site the agent will find that a lot of booking work is necessary. A weighbridge will be necessary, or perhaps several weighbridges; these are costly. Also there will be delays to traffic as the weighing is carried out. Usually, therefore, an agent will agree with the contract-haulier what are a suitable number of excavator bucketfuls to make up the appropriate load for a given vehicle. Thus, it may be agreed (after experiment) that 9 bucket-loads from a 0.6 m³ face shovel will fill a 10-tonne lorry with the appropriate weight. Then payment is made simply on the number of lorry loads taken off site. A sharp watch is necessary to prevent under-loading of lorries, and checkers are necessary to count the number of journeys undertaken and to inspect the loads carried. These checkers themselves, and the records they produce, should be subject to independently made checks from time to time, as there are quite a few dodges that can be adopted for increasing the wealth of the contract-haulier (and others) at the expense of the contractor.

Supports to excavations

In the timbering of trenches, cut-off walls, excavations adjacent to existing buildings, roads, rivers, or railways, much care must be exercised. If necessary, the expert advice of a soils engineer must be obtained, even though the work comes under the category of 'temporary works' under the contract. Safety considerations are paramount. The resident engineer must be capable of making the necessary stress calculations to check that the sizes of timber used for support are adequate. At the same time he will give due consideration to the views of the contractor and his foremen and benefit from their long experience on earthworks.

The responsibility for ensuring that an excavation is properly supported so that it is safe for men to work in lies squarely upon the shoulders of the contractor. He is responsible for the safety of his own workpeople, and the liability for any damage which may occur to the work, or extra cost through failure to provide sufficient supports, remains his. Sometimes the resident engineer may think the supports provided by the contractor are inadequate and wonder if he has any powers to insist upon more adequate support being given. Generally speaking the resident engineer may insist upon excavations being properly supported wherever damage, delays, weaknesses, extra work, or difficulty in getting the proper standards of workmanship would follow as a consequence of an earthfall or slip. Where he is otherwise in doubt as to the necessity of further support he should call upon the engineer and his specialist advisers for directions.

Finishing off excavation

Most excavating machinery tends to churn up the material at the bottom of an excavation, and therefore most specifications call upon the contractor to remove the last 150 mm of excavation by hand labour so that a clean undisturbed bottom to the excavation is achieved. The dragline and the bulldozer are the worst offenders in regard to churning up the bottom of the excavation. The teeth of the dragline will rake through the surface of the ground, leaving it as a powdery or muddy mess for some 150 mm depth. The dozer will often screw up the formation as it turns, churning up some 200 mm depth of the formation or even more in soft ground. It is useless trying to get a good undisturbed clean bottom to an excavation with these machines. If machine clearing up must be adopted, then the traxcavator, or hydraulic excavator of appropriate size is to be preferred, according to circumstances. For the laying of water mains, trimming of the bottom of the trench by hand labour is essential.

Rock excavation

The definition of what is 'rock' and what is not, for the purposes of payment, is a frequent point of controversy between contractors and supervising engineers. The new hydraulic excavators will remove soft rock and rock which is reasonably well fissured without any need for the use of compressed air drills for breaking up the material, but the excavation rate (and therefore the cost to the contractor) will depend very much on the hardness of the rock strata as a whole.

Apart from giving as much information as is possible to contractors at the times of tender about the nature of the ground, as revealed in trial pits and borings, the fairest method of dealing with this problem is to relate excavation rates to the size of machine excavator used. This may either be defined in the specification, or tenderers may be asked to state the type of plant they intend to use which is covered by their tendered rates. Extra-over rates may then be called for the use of more powerful machines, and for ripping prior to excavating; and further rates can then be called for excavating with compressed air tools and for blasting. In this manner the contract can be made to give fair payments when ground harder than that expected is encountered.

Special precautions must always be taken when blasting, and a proper warning system adopted so that everyone adjacent to the site of blasting knows when it is to take place. Only experienced men should be allowed to carry out the blasting, and no amateur experiments whatsoever should be allowed. An important point to note is that, even if the site of blasting is an open area and no damage to property may occur, the debris falling over a wide area may create a nuisance. Certainly a farmer who finds his field liberally besprinkled with even small lumps of rock is likely to object, as he may damage his equipment or be prevented from working over the field with his farming machines. Therefore a condition of allowing blasting should be that the contractor must clear up all large lumps over a stated size which have been thrown out by the explosions. The correct use of explosives ought not to result in many lumps of rock being thrown about; all that needs to be done is to loosen the ground *in situ* so that it can be dug out mechanically.

Earth filling and compaction

By far the most important precaution when compacting earth fill is to see that the material is placed and rolled in thin layers. 'End-tipping' should not be allowed; it is often a cause of subsequent trouble. Laying the material in reasonably thin layers, even for the smallest of embankments is vitally necessary, and there is seldom any difficulty in complying with this request.

The specification will usually lay down the maximum depth permitted for any layer and the amount of compaction that must be applied, by number of passes by a given type of machine. Where no such direction lies in the specification, a reasonable thickness to work to, suitable for most soils, would be 300–375 mm loose thickness, i.e. thickness before compaction. Thicker layers can be used with some soils, but there is not much point in permitting thicker layers to be laid if there is any attendant risk of poor compaction, because compliance with the 300–375 mm layering seldom presents real difficulty or extra cost to the contractor. In fact, relatively thin layers offer the advantage that the surface of the work is more frequently covered with new material so that the job is kept in good trim and the haulage vehicles do not repeatedly run over the same routes, so causing excessive rutting of the formation. Thin layers are also useful if watering of the fill is required, so that the material laid down attains a more even moisture content and is more quickly covered over by fresh material before the surface dries out under sun or wind.

A great deal of compaction occurs from ordinary haulage traffic bringing the material in, and from the dozers spreading the material. The wheeled traffic applies concentrated loading, so haulage routes over the formation need to be constantly changed. Dozers do not apply highly concentrated loads, but the larger sizes achieve good compaction by vibration and shaking of the formation as they pass over it. Other machinery is purpose-made for compaction—multi-tyred loaded wagons, vibrating rollers, sheepsfoot or grid rollers, drum rollers of various kinds, and so on. The smooth-surfaced rollers, such as the old steam-roller or the more modern diesel-roller, are seldom very effective in compacting other than the surface of a layer, and their main purpose is for rolling the formation to a flat surface so that rainwater is shed off.

Compacting soils. The standard (Proctor) compaction test is now applied to most soil compaction work, and it will be for the resident engineer to see that the contractor achieves the results required by the designers. There will, no doubt, be an engineer on the resident engineer's staff appointed to watch the compaction of soils if earthwork forms an important part of the contract. The inspectors can also be shown some of the more simple tests, such as gauging the moisture content of the fill, and they may have authority to direct the contractor when to water the fill as necessary. Simple sieve analyses may be undertaken by the inspectors if the material is coarse and precise laboratory work is not required. On earth-dam projects and similar schemes where the control of filling is a vital aspect of the resident engineer's supervision there will be a soils laboratory on site, staffed full time by laboratory assistants. Every engineer should be given a chance of working on this side of the work.

Moisture content. The 'optimum moisture content' of the fill for placing, and the permitted limits of deviation from it, will no doubt be laid down in the specification. The theoretical limits of deviation allowable may have to be varied in practice according to the type of climate experienced, the nature of the material, its grading, the amount of compaction being given, the time of day the soil moisture content is measured, and the position of the sample in the fill. All these factors can have a wide effect on the permitted limits of deviation from the optimum moisture content. It is therefore preferable that these limits are set only after practical experiments have taken place on the site, and not to pre-ordain them in the specification from theoretical or laboratory considerations only.

In a damp cold climate, using a material which does not contain a high-clay percentage but which tends to soak up any showers of rain, placing at optimum moisture content may cause trouble if the wet weather continues. The moisture content of the fill may be increasing all the time, and the result in due course may be an accumulation of moisture in the fill, resulting in typical 'heaving' and rutting under traffic. On many sites also it must be borne in mind that the compaction given may be much more than Proctor, because it consists not only of the purposeful compaction by so many specified passes of the rollers but also of the compaction arising from general traffic over the formation.

Density tests. To find out what compaction has been achieved in the field, *in-situ* density tests are taken for comparison with the standard laboratory optimum Proctor density. Density tests properly taken require time, care, and patience. When the material contains a high gravel portion this applies even more. The gravel percentage must be removed from the sample, because it influences the *in-situ* density according to the percentage of gravel present. Thus, it is no use comparing the *in-situ* density of a sample which contains 60 per cent gravel with the Proctor density done on another sample which contains but 40 per cent gravel—'gravel' being defined in this instance as material over 19 mm size. By complicated weighing and calculation, the *in-situ* density of the material below the 19 mm size will have to be obtained and then compared with the Proctor density on the same material in the laboratory.

In-situ density tests results are necessary for informing the designers that their design assumptions have been complied with in the actual structure; but they are of little use for practical control of the work from hour to hour. The electronic density tester may give quick and accurate results on certain kinds of fill, provided this fill has not been freshly watered on the surface. However, for practical hour-to-hour control judgment 'by eye'—watching the behaviour of the fill as it is compacted, and as it stands up to traffic—is not at all difficult. A heavily laden lorry running over the fill is a kind of *in-situ* density testing machine that can give a clear indication of the compaction achieved. Although figures of compaction cannot be quoted from such observation, the effect is observable, and to the trained eye the effect will convey a reliable message. These observations supplement the routine that will have been laid down for rolling and compacting the fill, and will be confirmed by routine sampling and testing of the fill material.

Choosing materials for fill

It may be necessary to permit only certain materials to be used in the filling. In this event, the resident engineer's inspectors must watch the filling all the time, and must have authority to reject filling which does not comply with the engineer's requirements. The inspector's task will be difficult. Because of the speed of placing, he must judge the quality of the material by sight alone—either in the quarry or as it comes on to site. The distinction between 'good' and 'bad' material must be clearly obvious to the eye, or else the task will be impracticable. It will be helpful if the resident engineer can mark out in the quarry or borrow pit those portions of material which are not suitable for incorporation in the work; but this is not always completely satisfactory, because in the digging process the ground becomes disrupted and mixed together. Sometimes it is more practicable to get the design altered to take into account the changed nature of the material, as revealed by the actual variation in the borrow pit.

The mixing of two or more sorts of different fill materials is seldom liked either by the resident engineer or the agent, because it is difficult to control. It cannot be guaranteed that the loads of the differing materials will always be delivered in the correct ratio or that the materials will be clearly distinguishable from each other. It is not practical to instruct the dozer driver to 'spread them around'. It is better to ask the designers to find some other solution to this problem by zoning of the different materials in different parts of the structure. It is as well to check from time to time that an actual difference does still exist between the supposedly different materials, or money and time will be wasted.

Road-making

The two essential requirements for making a stable road of any kind on soft material are:

(i) in the first instance the road *must* be made thick enough, and
(ii) the base of the road must be drained.

Both these things are much more difficult to do on flat level ground than where the road must be cut out of a hill or placed on an embankment. When a road has to be cut out of a hill not only is the foundation material likely to be stronger than that on the surface but the problem of drainage is obvious, and so it is tackled. When the road is on fill there is usually a choice of fill materials, and soft clay would seldom be used for the purpose, while the problem of drainage is almost self-solving. But on flat ground it is not an attractive idea to dig out more than is absolutely necessary, and the problem of drainage is often difficult. Thus, it happens that what seems simple is difficult, and what looks difficult is easy.

The essential characteristic of the *blinding layer* placed directly on clay is that it must be possible to place it without squeezing it into the clay and loosing it; it must be possible to retain it as a layer. All sorts of materials can do the job, and the only real way to judge the suitability of a material is to watch it being placed. The main course of the road which is next placed must be a material which 'locks together' and which can therefore act as a mattress having resistance against lateral stresses. This can be seen and felt almost by instinct as one sees the material being placed. Shingle, for instance, is almost entirely non-locking. Any rounded aggregate lacks the power to interlock. Flat aggregates, like shales and slates, may also fail to lock properly, and even traditional materials of broken brick, hardcore, and clinker may not always lock together properly to act as a mattress. A well-locking material has a good range of sizes in it, including plenty of big material and not too much small; also it is angular though not necessarily sharp. Given the right material, probably less thickness of it need be placed than some alternative material, partly because it can be placed in a thinner layer without being pushed through the blinding layer below. The surface material need not be watertight, but it is best so. It must, however, be capable of shedding heavy rainfall by being placed to a camber, and by being *kept to a camber*. The drainage to the road is probably the most important item of all, and it must be placed lower than the blinding layer and, even for temporary roads, the drainage *must be kept working*—it must not require continual attention to prevent blockages.

For the construction of permanent roads, the problem is how to construct the road without ruining the foundation material in the act of construction. It may have been calculated that an 450 mm depth of road will suffice on clay whose strength has been tested by taking shear samples, but if a bulldozer is sent straight in to rip out the necessary excavation the engineer may subsequently find that what was reasonably sound clay at 450 mm depth has now been churned up into a 300 mm bog below that depth, and he will have the problem of thickening up the road to perhaps 750 mm.

For road-building on soft clays, therefore, the resident engineer will have to insist that the contractor adopts the right methods. Firstly, the drainage must go ahead of the road-making, and it must be carried out with the least damage possible to the ground. Flat-tracked vehicles should be insisted upon, also small loads, no lorries, and manhandling of drainage pipes if necessary. For the excavation, the skimmer bucket should be used, the machine standing on the hardcore of the road base and slewing round 180 degrees to off-load to vehicles standing behind it on the partially finished road. The concreting of the haunches of the road should proceed slightly ahead of the excavation so that the road material can be placed between good stable edges. All this needs careful planning, because of the need to interleave the various operations, and it may appear to be slow going to an impatient agent. But it will work, and a lot of troubles will be avoided if the road-making is done in this manner. Far better to know that what has been done has been well done, and will never afterwards require attention, then to rush ahead and then have to come back and start all over again as the first attempt begins to show signs of disintegration.

Aspects of the use of contractor's plant

If a contractor hires most of the plant from outside sources for carrying out a contract this does not mean that the contractor is giving poor service. There is an increasing tendency nowadays for contractors to use hire-plant for construction, primarily because it is becoming increasingly recognised that the use and maintenance of plant is, in itself, a skilled occupation. The advantage of hiring outside plant, particularly when the hire rate also includes the provision of a driver, is that the plant is less liable to break down than poorly maintained contractor's plant. It is to the hirer's interest that his plant is kept in good condition and that it is properly and effectively used. From the point of view of the contractor hiring the plant, he has no need to set up his own extensive repair shops on site; he does not have to organise the supply of endless spare parts required for the plant, entailing much clerical work; he does not have to pay when plant breaks down, but merely has to telephone the plant hirer to send a replacement. These are substantial advantages and, in certain circumstances, they are well worth the slightly higher cost to the contractor. Frequently a contractor will use on site some of his own plant and some outside hired plant.

The extent of plant provided by the contractor will depend upon the amount of capital he deems it economic to have 'locked up' in plant. This can amount to several hundreds of thousands of pounds on a large job. The extent will also depend upon the plant repair organisation the contractor feels able to set up and run properly at his headquarters and on his various sites. A contractor who works only in a limited area will naturally tend to own and use a greater proportion of plant than one who undertakes jobs anywhere. The haulage of plant on and off site is costly, and locally hired plant can be more economic to the contractor than hauling his own plant over a long distance. Most contractors, however, will possess a nucleus of their own plant consisting principally of: concrete batching and mixing plant; a suitable range of excavators and dozers, the excavators being also provided with jibs to turn them into mobile cranes where required; compressors; pumps; and diesel generators. The medium-sized contractor will tend to hire the larger sizes of excavators and dozers, and plant which is not in frequent use, or is of a special nature. A wise contractor will always tend to try new designs of plant on hire first, before he purchases any of them, so that he can first see how such plant behaves and the amount of maintenance it requires. Specialist contractors, such as well sinkers and piling specialists, will almost always own most of the plant they use.

Proper use and maintenance of plant is to be encouraged from the engineer's point of view. Ill-used or badly maintained plant will cause a constant series of delays, and there is also a bad psychological effect on the workmen and all concerned with the job if plant is for ever breaking down just when it is needed. Work tends to become skimped if the plant cannot be got going until later than planned, so the resident engineer should encourage the contractor to set up proper maintenance bays, and he should not so force the programme of work that not enough time is allowed for the regular withdrawal and proper maintenance of plant. It is also the contractor's responsibility to say how plant shall be used, and he has a right to refuse to use plant in what he considers is a dangerous manner, or in a manner which will cause excessive wear and tear.

Excavators and cranes should never be worked on sidelong ground; it is dangerous and will cause excessive wear when slewing. Unless mobile cranes are especially designed for the purpose, they should not be used for lifting and transporting loads from one point to another. When these machines have to be moved from one location to another the agent or plant foreman must be permitted to take all necessary precautions. On steep grades an excavator (or digger) should have a dozer following or preceding the excavator on the downhill side, with its blade towards the excavator to catch and hold it, should the driver 'miss the gears', as sometimes happens. Mobile cranes should not be used for lifting heavy loads except with all proper precautions. These mobile cranes often 'bounce' their loads, and this can be dangerous.

References

Earthworks. British Standard Code of Practice CP. 2003. B.S.I. (Contains recommended methods of timbering excavations; describes practical characteristics of soils.)

Foundations. A. L. Little. Edward Arnold Ltd, 1961. (Contains an excellent summary of basic soil mechanics; deals with piling, cofferdams, caissons.)

Cofferdams, S. Packshaw. *Proceedings I.C.E.*, February 1962. (A 'classic' work.)

Builders Plant and Equipment, G. Barber. George Newnes, 1964. (An excellent book.)

'Employment of Contractor's Plant on Civil Engineering Works', R. H. McGibson and J. H. Thomas. *Proceedings I.C.E.*, June 1957. (Well worth reading.)

Soil Mechanics for Road Engineers, Road Research Laboratory, D.S.I.R. H.M.S.O. (A reference book.)

Road Research Laboratory, Road Notes. H.M.S.O.

No. 1. Recommendations for Tar Surface Dressing.

No. 5. Types of Road Surfacing and Maintenance using Tar or Asphaltic.

No. 19. Design Thickness of Concrete Roads.

No. 20. Construction of Housing Estate Roads using Granular Base and Sub-Base Materials.

CHAPTER 14

Concrete Site Work

A great deal of literature abounds on the subject of the design, mixing and placing of concrete and much publicity has been given to the scientific control required for the production of high quality concrete. A young engineer proceeding to site for the first time might therefore expect to see many of these methods adopted in practice. But, on small jobs or on jobs in remote locations or where much use is made of hand labour, he may find no weigh-batching plant, no sieves and weighing machines for testing the aggregates, and no careful control of the mix that he was expecting. Worse still, to his mind, might be the attitude of the contractor who, having taken a few test cubes and finding them satisfactory, intends to go on as he is.

The truth is that good concrete is easy to produce by quite simple methods if care and attention are paid to it. Given a clean bucket and spade, clean water and aggregates, there is no reason why good concrete cannot be produced from even the smallest mixer—and a lot of it is. But the more concrete there is produced on a site, or the more the design assumptions rely upon a guaranteed minimum strength in the concrete, the more important it becomes to have regular control and checking of quality. The degree of control to be exercised therefore depends upon the purpose and design assumptions, and the quality and quantity of concrete required.

How to produce satisfactory concrete

Care and common sense are the two primary requirements for making good concrete. Good concrete for a garden path can be made with a bucket and spade and watering can, or thousands of cubic yards a day can be produced on a civil engineering site using mechanical mixers, silos, vibrators, and the whole paraphernalia of concrete machinery. The principles to be applied in either case are the same and are as follows.

First—choose good aggregates. The best guide is to use well-known local aggregates that are being used satisfactorily on other jobs elsewhere. When prospective suppliers come offering their aggregates on site, ask them who else they supply. Almost certainly a reputable supplier will be able to name dozens of jobs where his aggregate is being used. If so, there should be no worry in using the same aggregate.

But when the aggregates are being delivered on the job (not just the first few loads, but the loads when the supply has really got going) examine random loads as delivered. Take up handfuls of the aggregate and let it drop through the hands so that it can be examined in detail. In so doing watch out for—small balls of clay, soft spongy stones, flaky stones, pieces of brick, soft shale, crumbly bits of sandstone; that is to say, watch out for all stones which are not hard, and watch out for clay and dirt left on the hands.

If the engineer finds more than one or two pieces of weak stone, or more than a single piece of clay from a few handfuls, let him bring this to the notice of the supplier. He need not reject the load out of hand, but it will do no harm to let the supplier know the aggregates are being watched. If a load contains numerous weak stones or more than a few bits of clay it should be rejected.

Second—choose standard cement. There is little difficulty in doing this. The same principal applies as with the choice of aggregates; find the supplier of cement to other jobs and all should be well. Troubles may start when imported cement has to be used, or when special cement has to be used which is not being regularly produced to a recognised standard specification. Avoid the use of such cements for if they are not being produced in bulk to meet a recognised standard specification (British or otherwise) their quality may vary from one batch to the next.

Third—choose reasonably graded aggregates. In this matter, quite a wide variation is permissible, indeed B.S. 882 sets wide limits—but there must be practicable limitations applied notwithstanding. If a '19 mm down' coarse aggregate is ordered, then every load must contain *some* materials of all sizes—19 mm, 13 mm, 10 mm, and 5 mm—loads must not be delivered consisting entirely of 19–13 mm stones, or containing no 19 mm stones. The sand must not contain large amounts of silt and dust. The precise grading that is desirable will be dealt with later; but as a first requirement the demand is for a reasonable amount of the various sizes of coarse aggregate and a sand that does not have an excessive amount of silt, dust, or clay with it.

Fourth—always have washed aggregates. Unwashed aggregates suitable for concreting are rare. They are always dangerous to use. Sometimes a river sand is supplied unwashed—it being assumed that the sand has already been 'washed' by the river. This should not be accepted as a fact. A river carries silt and clay, and more than likely the river sand will have its quota of those materials too. Sea-bed or beach sands and aggregates want washing to remove the salt from them. Hence, always choose washed aggregates, because good concrete cannot be made when clay, organic matter, or salt are present. If there is no economic alternative to using unwashed aggregates, then specialised technical control must be set up immediately; this is a situation to avoid if possible.

Fifth—mix the concrete properly. Modern mechanical mixers are seldom at fault in this respect; the mixing is fast and good. If the mixing is by hand (rare nowadays) common-sense observation is sufficient to show when mixing has been properly achieved. The mixture should be uniform in colour and texture; no 'bare' sand or cement should be visible when the mixture is cut with a spade. It is the water content of a mix that always requires the most vigilant attention. Never let 'slop' be produced. The right sort of mix always looks a bit stiff as it comes out of the mixer or when turned over by hand on mixing boards. It should stand up as a pile of concrete and not spread out as a pool. It should be possible to cut it with a shovel, and the shovel-cuts should remain open for dividing the concrete into separate lumps. Such a concrete will look quite different after it is discharged and worked into some wet concrete already placed. As soon as it is rammed, prodded, or vibrated, it will settle and appear to flow into the existing wet concrete as if it had suddenly become more fluid. It will exhibit the same characteristics when transported by a dumper. The 'heap' of stiff concrete discharged from the mixer to the dumper hopper will appear to flow out to a flat pool of concrete as the dumper bumps its way over the usual site roads. This pool may even sway slightly with the dumper's movements. When the dumper hopper is tipped, however, the concrete should again appear to be stiff. But if, in transport, the concrete slops over the side of the dumper hopper and pours out of it as a semi-fluid instead of as a single lump,—then this shows that too much water has been added.

Sixth—ram the concrete well home. It is no use producing good concrete if it isn't rammed home sufficiently to completely fill the shuttering mould or if it doesn't fully wrap around all reinforcing bars. When hand ramming is used it is practically impossible to over-do the ramming. Keep conscientious men working non-stop on this ramming all the time the concrete is being produced. If mechanical vibrators are used equal vigilance is required. Again the men must see that no portion of the concrete remains unvibrated, and must take special care to vibrate in the corners of the shutters and close to (but not against) the reinforcing bars. Vibrators of the poker immersion type should always be kept moving in, and slowly out of, the concrete. They should not be left suspended vibrating in one position only. They should not be withdrawn suddenly so as to leave an unfilled hole in the concrete. Finally, the concrete should not be subjected to such continuous long vibration in any one spot that water rises to the surface of the concrete and lies on top of it. When this happens, vibration in that area should cease. Where mechanical vibrators are used, always have some suitable hand rammers available as well, in case the vibrators break down.

Seventh—have enough cement in the mix. Everyone knows that cement is the essential item which changes a heap of loose stones and sand into concrete—a man-made rock. Cement is the source of strength in that rock. It is equally obvious that enough cement must be used. There is seldom any trouble in this respect, because most contractors take the sensible view that to err on the side of safety with the cement content entails little extra cost and ensures an up-to-strength concrete. Only if the contractor is too keen on cutting down the cement content to the bare theoretical minimum do troubles start. Once this happens, a stream of special investigations—into the mix, grading, strength, water content, etc.—will have to be undertaken, and these are costly in money and time to both contractor and engineer.

Principal reasons for unsatisfactory concrete. The causes which give rise to unsatisfactory concrete are, basically, failure to comply with one or more of the recommendations given above. In practice, two sorts of failure are most common:

(i) failure to get the required strength, the concrete being otherwise apparently good;

(ii) structural failures, such as honeycombing, sandy patches, crumbly concrete, cracking.

Failure to get the right strength when the concrete appears to be reasonable in all other respects probably lies in the cement itself. Is the cement stale; is it an unusual cement; has the manufacturer tested (in the proper manner) samples of the actual cement being supplied? To get reliable information on this, samples of the cement may have to be sent to an independent laboratory for testing and report. The water supply should also be checked to see if it does not contain some injurious chemicals. A check is necessary to see that the cause is not something too obvious to have been noticed—such as cold weather, or the concrete test cubes produced in the wrong manner, or some error in the cement batching machine.

Where a 'scientific' reason for an apparent failure cannot be found, always look a second time for an obvious reason. The author remembers a classic case of this in regard to paintwork which failed. Upon the failure being observed, the engineer responsible called in the paint manufacturers. They could find nothing wrong with the paint; nor anything wrong with the background. The painter was sure he had not tampered with the paint. The unsatisfactory paint was scraped off, a new coating was put on—and again it failed. The investigations were gone through a second time, and again the results were negative, and repainting a third time was started. The engineer thought he would watch the painter while he was actually painting. To his astonishment he saw the painter add water to the paint; he stopped him. When asked why he was adding water to the paint when previously he had assured everyone he did not tamper with it he replied, 'But it's only water!' In a similar fashion the reason for some concrete turning out poorly may be evidenced by the concretor replying, 'But I thought these were the mixes for *one* bag of cement'—whereas maybe he had been given the aggregate weights for two bags of cement, this being a usual batch size for many cement mixers.

Structural failures of honeycombing, sanding, and similar usually arise from one or the other of two causes—failure to ram and vibrate the concrete in position properly or incorrect grading of aggregates. If the failure is persistent rather than occasional it is almost certainly lack of proper grading. The outstanding causes of the latter are three in number; too many large stones; too much fine or dusty sand; too much water. These structural failures can always be cured or prevented by applying the common-sense rules given above for the production of satisfactory concrete.

Concrete mixes*

The British Standard Code of Practice for Reinforced Concrete (CP. 114) was amended in 1965 and produced in metric units in 1969. Although volume proportioning of concrete is still permitted (Cl. 208), a new Clause, 209, specifies proportioning by weight. This specification by weight is strongly recommended. The actual proportioning of materials on site by weight rather than by volume has, of course, been the practice for many years. The primary change with Cl. 209, however, is a strong recommendation to *specify* a mix by weights instead of nominal proportions, e.g. 1:2:4, etc. expressed as 50 kg cement to ·07 cu. m sand and ·14 cu. m stone.† The new Clause stipulates that either:

(i) the mix should be 'designed' to meet some particular strength requirement, or
(ii) failing this, a 'standard mix' should be used, defined by weight rather than by volume.

In effect, under method (i) experiments are conducted on site to find the correct weights of material to achieve the desired strength values, and by method (ii) a 'standard' type of concrete is selected, the weights of materials to be used being as set out in a table in Clause 209 (reproduced below). In both cases many test cubes must be made, and a statistical analysis of their test results indicates whether the specified requirements are being met.

In regard to the trial mixes under (i), or to the 'standard' mixes under (ii), any predetermination of this kind, whether by volume or weight of coarse to fine aggregate, is bound to be arbitrary to some extent; correct perhaps for the usual gradings, but sometimes incorrect if the aggregates can only be had to certain unusual gradings. Hence, in either case preliminary steps are necessary to find the grading and volume/weight characteristics of the proposed aggregates. This is best illustrated by considering first the production of a nominal mix of concrete described by the 'old-fashioned' method: 1:1:2; 1:2:4 and so on. These 'nominal' mixes are so familiar that they will probably be used for some years yet.

---

* An excellent small but comprehensive booklet that can be referred to is *Report on Concrete Practice*, Part 1, published by the Cement and Concrete Association, 52 Grosvenor Gardens, London, S.W.1. It has the further merit of being free upon request.
† 112 lb cement: 2½ cu. ft sand: 5 cu. ft stone in imperial units.

Nominal mixes by volume

British Standard Code of Practice CP. 114 (Cl. 208 (b)) gives three well-known nominal mixes and the amounts of fine and coarse aggregates usually required per bag (112 lb) of cement to make them up. The data is set out in Table 1 below.

TABLE 1

Nominal Mix Proportions

Nominal mix	Volume of aggregate per 50 kg (112 lb approx)* cement	
	Fine aggregate (sand)	Coarse aggregate
1:1:2	·035 m³ (1¼ cu. ft)	·07 m³ (2½ cu. ft)
1:1½:3	·05 m³ (1⅞ cu. ft)	·10 m³ (3¾ cu. ft)
1:2:4	·07 m³ (2½ cu. ft)	·14 m³ (5 cu. ft)

These are the nominal volumes specified; the ratio of fine to coarse aggregates may need to be altered according to the actual grading of the aggregates available and the actual total grading desired. This the Code permits, provided the sum volume of the aggregates used (each measured separately) equals the sum of the volumes in the above table for the appropriate mix.

For weight batching, which is now usual procedure, it will be necessary to convert the volumes into weights. This is done easily enough for the coarse aggregates by filling a container of known volume with the aggregate and weighing the contents. The filling should be loose, and any excess material above the top edge of the container should be struck off. For the fine aggregate or sand, the procedure can be just the same, but in this case an allowance must be made for the bulking of the sand when damp.

A damp sand will not pack down so tightly as a perfectly dry sand or a completely inundated sand. It may have a 'bulking factor' of up to 30 per cent when at a certain stage of dampness; i.e. a cubic metre of dry sand can, when damp, occupy 1·30 cu. metre of space. It is difficult to get a large sample of sand perfectly dry, and easier to inundate it with water, so it is the latter process which is adopted on site to find the bulking factor of the sand as delivered.

Some damp sand, having a moisture content typical of that being delivered, is put into a parallel-sided water-tight container. Its surface is levelled and the depth of sand h_1 is measured. This sand is then removed temporarily, care being taken not to lose any, and the parallel-sided container is half filled with water. The sand is now put carefully back into the container and rodded so that it is compacted to its least volume. The surface of the sand is kept inundated and is then levelled. The new

* 50 kg of cement (i.e. a new 'metric bag' of cement) represents 110·23 lbs, i.e. 0·984 cwt.

PLATE XIII

(a) Typical honey-combed concrete.

(b) A good concrete mix for vibration, with more than the usual number of vibrators being supplied by the contractor.

(a)

(b)

PLATE XIV

(a) A small weigh-batching plant.

(b) Badly placed reinforcement, badly bent out of position.

*Photos (a) & (b):
J. E. Jones
(Contractors) Ltd.*

PLATE XV

(a) Accurately bent reinforcement of the right size can be set to exact lines.

(b) Well placed wall reinforcement showing correct and even concrete cover to the bars.

(c) The approach to the aggregate stacks should not be a muddy area as this photograph shows; it should be clean so that mud does not get into the aggregates.

(a)

PLATE XVI

Designing works to harness, or withstand, the forces exerted by water plays a great part in the civil engineer's life. Top right (a) is the gated spillway to the Sultan Abur Bakar Dam of the Cameron Highlands Hydro-electric Scheme, Malaysia; below (b) shows flood water passing over the lip of the bell-mouthed spillway to the Tryweryn Dam for Liverpool Corporation Water-works. (*Engineers: Binnie & Partners.*)

height h_2—which will be less than h_1—is measured. The percentage bulking B, at that moisture content, is then

$$B\% = \left(\frac{h_1}{h_2} - 1\right) 100$$

If, therefore, ·07 cu. m of sand with that moisture content is to be used in a mix, then the actual volume of damp sand to be taken from the stockpiles on site must be $(100 + B)\% \times$ ·07 cu. m.

This is simple except that the key question remains: *What is the desirable grading curve of the combined aggregates to achieve a good concrete?* On this matter there is no guidance in British Standards. But some guidance must be obtained before trial mixes can begin. This is dealt with in the following section.

Grading of aggregates and their suitable mixing

British Standard 882 sets out permissible limits of grading for concrete aggregates. These gradings are primarily meant to be a guide for the commercial producers of concrete aggregates. They give wide permissible limits for coarse or all-in aggregates. In regard to the fine aggregate (or sand), four 'Zones' are set up. These are useful indicators of sand grading. In brief, 'Zone 1' sand is coarsest and makes a difficult concrete to work; it is seldom used except for special high-quality concrete and is a sand that is sometimes difficult to procure anyway. Zone 2 sand gives a good concrete mix. Zone 3 gives an easily workable concrete. Zone 4 contains much fine sand, and is not suitable for producing the best concrete.

For type gradings for the total mix, the reader must consult technical publications. Suitable grading curves are given in *How to Make Good Concrete*, by H. N. Walsh, published by Concrete Publications Ltd.; and mix design is also given in *Report on Concrete Practice* Part 1 published by the Cement and Concrete Association. Other gradings are given in Road Note No. 4—*Design of Concrete Mixes*, published by H.M. Stationery Office. The appropriate grading can be chosen from one of these publications or from some other source, and then the engineer can start juggling with the ratio of volumes (or weights) of coarse and fine aggregates at his disposal so that he can get the combination of them which gives a total grading nearest that of his choice.

A reputable aggregate supplier should normally be able to provide typical grading curves for each of his aggregates. If not, the resident engineer must sieve representative samples. Once the separate aggregate gradings are known, the method of proportioning the aggregates is then worked out as shown below.

Example. Suppose the gradings of materials available and the type grading desired for a 19 mm aggregate concrete are as shown in the first three lines of the following table.

A first trial mix of 2 parts coarse aggregate by weight to 1 part sand gives a grading that has too many fines in it (the percentages passing the

10 mm, 5 mm, No. 7 and No. 14 sieves being higher than the type grading). We therefore try another mix of 2·2 parts of coarse aggregate to 0·8 parts sand, and this gives a grading nearer the desired grading. In weighing out the sand, an addition must be made for the weight of moisture in the sand, and perhaps for the weight of moisture in the coarse aggregate also. The former is usually about 8 per cent on the dry weight in Britain; the latter not more than 3 per cent. These moisture content figures can be tested on site by weighing samples of aggregate taken from different parts of the stockpile before and after drying over a stove. There is also a 'speedy' moisture tester for sand which works quite well by a chemical method.

		Percentage, passing (by weight)					
	19 mm	10 mm	5 mm	7	14	52	100
Coarse grading (actual) ...	100	35	15	5	0	0	0
Sand grading (actual) ...			100	98	80	15	10
TYPE GRADING REQUIRED	100	55	35	26	19	6	0

Trial mixes:—

A trial at a ratio of 1 part sand to 2 parts coarse will give:

		19 mm	10 mm	5 mm	7	14	52	100
Coarse (2 parts) ...	...	200	70	30	10	0	0	0
Sand (1 part) ...	...	100	100	100	98	80	15	10
TOTAL (3 parts) ...	...	300	170	130	108	80	15	10
Total %	...	100	57	43	36	26	5	3

There is an excess of fine material, so we try a ratio of 0·8 sand to 2·2 coarse aggregate.

		19 mm	10 mm	5 mm	7	14	52	100
Coarse (2·2 parts)	...	220	77	33	11	0	0	0
Sand (0·8 part) ...	...	80	80	80	78	64	12	8
		300	157	113	89	64	12	8
Total %	...	100	52	38	30	21	4	3

If a nominal volume mix is being followed—such as a '1 : 2 : 4' mix—the total amount of aggregates (in proportion $2\frac{3}{4}$:1) must then be calculated so that it represents the required total volume to be used for 50 kg of cement as given in Table 1 above. When the trial mix is made (probably several different trials will be run one after the other) the concrete will be tested for workability, and test cubes will be cast so that strengths and densities are known.

Designed mixes

Clause 209 of the British Standard Code of Practice 114 recommends that: 'The mix should be designed to have a mean strength that exceeds the specified works cube strength by twice the expected standard deviation.'

If the actual strength of n cubes of concrete are measured as x, x_2, ... x_n, and the average of all these values is $\bar{x}$, then the standard deviation s is given by

$$s = \sqrt{\frac{(x_1 - \bar{x})^2 + (x_2 - \bar{x})^2 + (x_n - \bar{x})^2}{n - 1}}$$

The expression on the right means that the square of the departure of each observation from the mean value is found; these are added together and divided by $n - 1$; and the square root thereof is taken. This represents the 'scatter' of the results—or 'standard deviation'.

Example. Suppose three* test cube results are 19, 24 and 26 N/mm². Mean value 23 N/mm². Number of values 3.

$$\text{Therefore standard deviation } = \sqrt{\frac{(-4)^2 + (1)^2 + (3)^2}{3 - 1}}$$
$$= 3{\cdot}6 \text{ N/mm}^2$$

Thus, taking this example, Clause 209 means that if the designed works cube strength is to be 21 N/mm² at 28 days and the trial mixes give the standard deviation of 3·6 N/mm², then the mean strength of all subsequent test cubes at 28 days must be 21 + 2 × 3·6 = 28·2 N/mm². In no case is the standard deviation to be taken as less than 3·5 N/mm² or that obtained from forty tests on site, whichever is the greater. The Clause contains detailed provisions for evaluating the forty test results and requires that 'a comprehensive statistical check should be made continuously during the progress of the work', with at least one fresh sample of concrete per day being taken when any concrete of a particular strength is being made. Weekly grading analyses of the aggregates are also called for.

The amount of work all this represents, presupposes a large site on which an engineer is available to devote most or all of his time to the work. On a small site the making, and testing after 28 days, of 40 concrete cubes would take a number of weeks—probably five or six, especially if testing must be done off site. The Code permits preliminary judgment to be made on the basis of 7-day strength results provided 7-day required strengths are taken as not less than two-thirds the 28-day required strengths. Clearly, if the initial 7-day test results do not come up to standard a further delay will take place to see what a new set of 7-day and 28-day tests give. To anticipate this possibility it seems that 80 cubes must be cast initially—half, for testing at 7-days, the other half for 28-day testing in case the 7-day tests prove poor. The position is made much worse when several grades of concrete are being produced. At least two grades occur on all sites; three or four grades are quite frequent. These tests are, of course, required to go primarily with specially designed concrete mixes which, in turn, permit higher design stresses to be used. But they are not

* Three are taken to simplify the example. In practice forty are required as a minimum. The unit N/mm² (newton per sq. millimetre) may also be written as MN/m² (meganewtons per sq. metre), to which it is equivalent. Both are equal to 145 lb/sq. in.

necessarily required for the production of good concrete for standard design stresses.

Standard mixes by weight

Clause 209(e) of CP. 114 recommends three 'standard' mixes to be measured by weight which can be used without making trial mixes to meet a specified design strength. These mixes are intended to equate the three nominal volumetric mixes given in Table 1. The salient facts are given in Table 2.

TABLE 2

Standard Mixes by Weight

Equivalent volume mix proportions	Works cube at 28 days	Dry weight of aggregates per 50 kg cement				
		Sand	Coarse Aggregates			
			19 mm max.		38 mm max.	
			Workability		Workability	
			Low	Medium	Low	Medium
	N/mm²	kg	kg	kg	kg	kg
1:1:2	30	65	145	110	165	135
1:1½:3	25·5	80	165	135	200	165
1:2:4	21	90	190	155	225	190
Compaction factor .			·82–·88	·88–·94	·82–·88	·88–·94
Slump (mm) . . .			12–25	25–50	25–50	50–100

Weights in the table above are based on the use of Zone 2 natural sand and aggregates of specific gravity about 2·6. If Zone 3 sand is used the sand weights should be reduced by 10 kg and the coarse aggregate weights increased by 10 kg. If the sand is a crushed stone, the weights of coarse aggregates should be reduced by at least 10 kg without altering the weight of sand.

The above standard mixes only compare on a basis of *alleged* strength with the Table 1 nominal mixes. The volume proportions of fine to coarse aggregate and total aggregate to sand are substantially different from the mixes set out in Table 1. Most Table 2 1:2:4 and 1:1½:3 mixes tend to be substantially richer in cement, and the 1:1:2 standard mix substantially less rich, than the nominal mixes in the 19 mm and 38 mm aggregate sizes. Hence, the standard mixes by weight under Cl. 209 are not comparable with the nominal mixes under Cl. 208. As a result, sometimes more and sometimes less cement will be used per finished cubic metre of concrete (see Table 3 opposite). The same 'comprehensive statistical check' on a running number of 40 cube tests is required. Again it is necessary to mention that desirable though this statistical control is, the engineer need not suppose that without it good concrete cannot be produced. Attention to the seven basic principles set out at the beginning of this chapter, and to some simple site tests, will safeguard the concrete quality.

Simple site checks and tests on concrete quality

Check on cement content. The first check that can be made is to find out how much cement is actually being used per finished cubic yard of concrete. Some specifications require that the contractor is to provide the resident engineer with a weekly return of the number of bags of cement used. If this is in the specification such a return can, of course, be insisted upon; but it is probably equally effective to descend on the contractor from time to time without notice and work out with him the number of bags of cement used on a particular section of the work, or the bags used may be actually counted by the resident engineer or his assistant.

Once having obtained the cement content of the concrete, this can be compared with the specification. Table 3 below gives the advisable

TABLE 3

Minimum Cement Content of Mixes per finished cubic metre of Concrete
(for 19 mm max. aggregate size)

Nominal mixes by volume (as Clause 208)		Standard mixes by weight (as Clause 209)	
Ratio	kg of cement per cubic metre	kg of cement per cubic metre Low workability	Medium workability
1:1:2	485	410	460
1:1½:3	380	365	405
1:2:4	315	330	360
1:2½:5	265		
1:3:6	230		

Figures based on weight of cement at 1440 kg/m³ and on a water/cement ratio of 0·60. For a water/cement ratio of 0·45 add 30 kg cement to figures for 1:1:2 mix and 15 kg for 1:2:4 mix. Intermediate figures pro-rata.

minimum cement content per cubic metre if good concrete is to be produced. In practice, the resident engineer should expect to find test results give figures about 10 kg/m³ higher.

If the cement content is too low immediate steps should be taken to investigate why this is so. If it is unduly high the contractor will no doubt be interested to learn this, and both he and the resident engineer can attempt to achieve a lessening of the cement content to something approaching the given values without reducing test results below permissible value.

Test cube results. Crushing tests on test cubes (procedure as set out in B.S. 1881) are the main strength tests applied to the concrete. As we have seen above, according to the CP. 114 (Cl. 209)—

| Average crushing strength of 40 consecutive test cubes | = | Specified works strength | + | Twice the standard deviation on the 40 tests |

Where several different grades of concrete must be tested, it would be almost hopeless to try to follow the method strictly, on a small site, where the agent is served only by one or two assistant engineers, and the resident engineer likewise. It would also be optimistic to suppose that valid results would come to hand in time to prevent under-strength concrete from being placed in fairly large measure. Cube test results—even when used as a direct indicator of strength—always arrive much too late to be of use in remedying a situation that is gone and past. Every cube failure is of importance to the resident engineer, and he will, if he is wise, take steps to improve the concrete the moment he perceives that even a few cube tests are not up to standard. He cannot afford to go on producing doubtful concrete while awaiting for 40 tests to clock up and a statistical analysis of them to be made.

The strengths stipulated in CP. 114 in relation to both nominal mixes and standard designed mixes are:

TABLE 4

Equivalent nominal mix	Strength at 7 days N/mm²	Strength at 28 days N/mm²
1:1:2	20	30
1:1½:3	17	25·5
1:2:4	14	21

Beam tests. The works beam test has the great advantage that it can be carried out on the site at very small initial cost for manufacturing the apparatus. The size of beam and type of testing apparatus required is set out in B.S. 1881, though other sizes of beam and a simpler testing apparatus may be used on site work for comparative results. It is simple to use, gives very consistent results on the whole, and useful tests can be carried out within three days of casting. This is a great help when wishing to know when it is permissible to strip shuttering. Furthermore, the works beams can be cured in an identical fashion to the actual structure, being placed alongside it and sharing the same weather conditions. And as a final practical advantage the beam test gives a measure of the tensile stress the concrete is capable of withstanding—a matter of considerable importance in the early stages of the work, when loads may be placed on green concrete and it is important to prevent cracking from taking place.

If cube tests are taken from the same concrete samples as beam tests, then a rough ratio may be obtained experimentally, relating the 7-day beam strength with the 28-day cube strength. Strengths at intermediate days may be interpolated using type curves of strength/age ratio as published in Rao's or Faber and Mead's books on reinforced concrete. The author has found beam-test results consistent in themselves. An occasional low test result on a single beam while the others, cast at the same time, give reasonable results is almost certainly due to mishandling of the beam while green. These beams are fragile and must be handled gently.

Density tests. Provided the grading of the coarse and fine aggregate is reasonable, and the water content is not too high, the density of the mixed concrete should be at least 1550 kg/m³ (147 lb/cu. ft) for a 1:2:4 mix and 1585 kg/m³ (149 lb/cu. ft) for a 1:1:2 mix. This is on the assumption that the specific gravity of the stone and sand used is 2·65 (a common value). This density should be obtained by filling a ·015 m³ (½-cu.-ft) container with the freshly mixed concrete, in a similar manner to that used in actual placing and weighing. This test can be easily and quickly done on the spot where concreting is in process. If the density is up to standard, if previous records show that the cement content has been up to standard and there is no reason to suppose conditions have altered, and if the concrete is being satisfactorily placed, then the resident engineer may rest assured that there is nothing much wrong with the concrete. The above weight applies to mixes not less rich in cement than a nominal 1:2:4 mix. For leaner mixes there may be a slight reduction.

The durability and watertightness of a concrete mix depend chiefly on its density. A dense concrete cannot be made with a badly graded aggregate, nor can it be made with an excess of water.

Water content and workability. The water content of a mix should never be higher than that required to make the concrete sufficiently workable in place. It is preferable not to quote a maximum amount of water to be used in any mix; this is dangerous and invites the contractor to put in all that amount of water and perhaps produce a mix a good deal sloppier than it need be.

If the engineer wishes to have an initial guide to the total amount of water in any mix it is best to start from the assumption that, if the mix is workable enough, a water/cement ratio of 0·45 for a 1:1:2 mix and 0·60 for a 1:2:4 mix would be very satisfactory. This means that for a 1-bag-of-cement mix of 1:2:4 the total amount of water in it should be 30 litres (6¾ gallons). This would include the moisture already in the sand (often about 8 per cent) and in the coarse aggregate (not over 3 per cent). Allowing for these in a typical 1:2:4 mix would mean about 16 litres already in the aggregates, and therefore 14 litres to add.

The water/cement ratio should not have to exceed 0·52 for a 1:1:2 mix or 0·67 for a 1:2:4 mix. The higher the ratio, i.e. the more water in the mix, the less is the strength of the concrete. Very roughly increasing the water/cement ratio by one-third from 0·45 will reduce the 28-day strength of the concrete by one-third.

But it is no use tying the contractor down to a very dry mix to achieve a high ultimate strength, only to find that, in intricate reinforced-concrete work, there is serious honeycombing in the concrete around the steel. It is better to sacrifice a little of the strength by adding a little more water to make sure that proper solid placing of the concrete occurs.

The workability (and therefore the water content of a given mix) can always be judged best by watching the concrete as placed. The slump test for workability (now resurrected by the revised CP. 114) is not an adequate test for workability. Its only use is to act as a local 'rule-of-thumb' device for the guidance of inspectors relating to a *specific* mix which has been thoroughly tested in advance. The compacting factor apparatus is preferably to be used for measurement of workability. Values of 0·89 to 0·92 are usually appropriate for reinforced concrete vibrated in place, but in practice, results are sometimes erratic. Both the slump and compacting factor tests are best used to obtain a consistent mix with a given set of aggregates.

When concrete must be placed in the mass a drier mix will be necessary than for concrete placed in small sections and around reinforcement. For mass concrete the mix must never be so wet that excess water comes to the top, or so that the men placing it struggle about in it ankle deep. The amount of water also depends on whether the concrete is vibrated in place or not. Wherever possible the resident engineer will want concrete vibrated into position, in which case considerably less water will be required than if the concrete can only be hand-punned. For high-quality work vibration should always be adopted.

To judge workability (and therefore right water content) one must watch the behaviour of the concrete as placed. What results are seen to have been achieved when the shuttering is struck? How does the concrete appear to 'flow' around the reinforcing bars when pushed into position by rodding, spading, or vibrating? When vibration is used the surface of the wet concrete should shimmer, the concrete sliding about, engulfing bars, wrapping round them without difficulty, and yet at the same time the mix should appear to hang together and no watery scum appear on the surface. Where rodding or spading is used, the workability should be such that it is quite easy to produce a full flush surface against the sides of the forms, which when stripped, shows a clean surface, formed almost entirely of fine aggregate and cement, with only a sprinkling of air holes visible. Wherever concrete starts jamming between reinforcement, or between reinforcement and shuttering, great care should be taken to see that these lumps are dislodged and a more workable and flowing mixture introduced. Special care needs to be taken in the concreting of columns, where the stirrups may easily hang up the concrete, preventing it from flowing under the stirrup and around to the face of the shuttering.

Grading analyses of aggregates. Difficulties over workability or cement content can often be overcome by properly grading the fine and coarse aggregates so as to ensure the right type of mix. If the necessary apparatus is not available the resident engineer can only alter the grading by intelligent guesswork, and though much can be achieved in this way, the more scientific method is quicker. To carry out grading tests a set of sieves is required, two balances and 0·01 m³ and 0·02 m³ cylindrical containers. One balance should read up to 50 kg by 0·5 kg intervals, the other should read up to 5 kg and read in 0·05 kg intervals. Spring balances with a pan on the top are quite suitable.

The engineer must not expect too much accuracy from his sieving experiments. Even if he adopts the quartering method of sampling (a laborious process), he will be lucky if he gets a really representative sample. B.S. 882 lays down that: 'In the case of sampling from stock piles twelve initial samples of about 1 cwt each (50 kg each) shall be taken from different parts of the stockpile, care being taken to avoid sampling a segregated area of coarse or fine material; these initial samples should be well mixed together.' If the resident engineer wants to do this, then he needs to set aside a morning for the job and to find a labourer or two to help.

An alternative is not to aim for scientific accuracy but to try to assess what, if anything, is wrong with the grading. Taking a number of quick sieve gradings, the engineer will soon be able to see into what general grading scheme his aggregates lie, and from this work out the proportions of fine aggregate (also sieved) and coarse aggregate required to obtain the necessary grading within the limits of the specification.

Accuracy of weigh-batcher. The sound of a crowbar or hammer being banged on the base of the hopper to the typical concrete mixing machine is a familiar sound to all who have been on a construction site. Perhaps the agent forbids this practice in order to prevent damage to his machine, but the practice persists. The mixer driver has not much alternative, because the materials tend to stick in the hopper. Likewise they stick in the weigh-batch hopper. Other common troubles are: the glass to the weighing machine gets broken; the pointer develops a zero error; the discharge chute doors stick open; the aggregate bins get over-filled and surplus aggregate falls into the concrete hopper. All these factors tend to upset the accuracy of mix proportions, and the resident engineer will have to make allowance for inevitable errors and arrange fairly frequent checks on the weigh-batching machine.

An actual check of a new weigh-batcher about six months after it had been in use on site revealed the following errors:

Zero error of weigher	0–15 kg

Weight variation of:

Cement (from cement silo)	80–110% of required value
38 mm stone	96–123% of required value
19 mm stone	78–106% of required value
Sand	97–125% of required value

Errors of ± 9 kg for any discharge were so numerous as to indicate that even an experienced operator could not avoid them; errors of ± 18 kg were quite frequent. An inexperienced operator can treble such positive errors.

Construction details

Vibration

Nowadays, nearly all reinforced concrete is placed by using internal or external vibrators. For reinforced-concrete work *in situ*, internal vibrators are best and can be obtained in various sizes, the smallest of which is about 30 mm diameter. The vibrator can be pushed down between the reinforcing bars in quite a thin wall. For flat slabs, although an ordinary poker vibrator can be used, a platform vibrator is more effective as it can vibrate the top surface of the concrete, whereas the poker type is effective only when pushed into the concrete.

Vibration should not continue at one spot longer than is necessary. As the vibrator is plunged in, the freshly placed concrete will slump and spread rapidly, while bursting bubbles of air will appear at the surface. When these have diminished, and mortar appears to be rising to the surface, this is an indication that sufficient vibration has been given. Vibration should not be continued until water appears at the surface, nor, while waiting for further concrete, should the vibrator be left in motion in the previously placed batch. Care must also be taken to lift out the barrel of the vibrator slowly from the concrete so that the hole left by its removal fills up.

Vibrators can be driven by a small petrol engine, by compressed air or electricity, and it is safe to say that once a contractor uses them he will not go back to the laborious business of hand rodding and spading for reinforced-concrete work. A point to remember when considering vibrated concrete work is that the cement content per finished cubic yard will always be higher than for hand-tamped concrete. It is usual in contracts nowadays to stipulate that all main structural concrete shall be vibrated into place.

Placing

Specifications often contain a great variety of clauses dealing with handling of concrete, re-mixing after transportation beyond a certain distance, limiting the height through which concrete is to be dropped, and demanding that no concrete shall be placed when more than a certain time has elapsed since mixing. All these clauses will be found quite easy to comply with in ordinary cases, and even if strict adherence is not enforced, there are usually extenuating circumstances. For instance, if concrete is dropped from a height it may not be necessary to insist on the setting up of a proper chute, or bringing a crane along to handle skips, when in the ordinary course of shovelling, distributing, and vibrating the concrete gets well mixed again. On the question of placing concrete which has been mixed some time ago—say over the dinner break—the usual rule is that no concrete which has reached the state of an initial set (a slight crusty hardening on the outside) is to be placed into position. This is still a safe rule to work to, especially in hot, dry weather, but evidence has been advanced that concrete placed after the initial set has occurred has been found to be stronger than that placed immediately after mixing. Perhaps it would be better for the resident engineer to adhere to accepted methods and leave experimentation to the experts.

Conveyance of concrete. Pumped concrete goes well until a blockage occurs, and then disruption ensues. It is also sometimes difficult to get the process started properly so that the resident engineer may arrive on the job two hours after the theoretical start of an operation, only to find a full-scale dismemberment of the pipeline and the concrete plant in progress. If this happens repeatedly it is not surprising if the agent changes back to the use of concrete skips as being more certain if slower. It is not easy to pump concrete more than about 1000–1200 ft; the mix must be a good rich one, and there are theories that a sharp aggregate is more difficult to pump than a rounded aggregate. One essential operation which must not be forgotten is to send a mortar mix through the pipe first before attempting to push the concrete through. Often it is lack of sufficiency of this first mortar mix (several batches of it may be necessary) which causes trouble. Further troubles can also ensue from using an inter-mixture of old and new pipes, since the older pipes are likely to be worn to a larger diameter internally than the new pipes.

Another snag with pumped concrete is the amount of labour required to reset the pipeline to some different discharge point and the difficulty which sometimes occurs of finding a route for the pipeline which will not interfere with traffic. But when the pumping of concrete does work, then the outputs of concrete per day can be very large, the placing of the concrete is a continuous operation and there is no danger of segregation of the mix; thus it is worth while trying to make the operation work satisfactorily.

Concrete can also be blown through a delivery pipe using a blower. One batch at a time is blown through. This works well unless the concrete blows a shutter down or a bend off the end of the pipeline. Needless to say, care is needed with this method, and proper warnings must accompany each 'shot', or someone may get hurt. The concrete must be directed right into the concreting area (hence the bend required on the end of the pipeline) and must not be directed against shuttering. The method is most frequently used for concreting of tunnel linings, where it is necessary to get the concrete lifted up to the soffit of the tunnel and then turned in horizontally and blown back over the top of the arch shuttering. The shuttering cannot be completely filled with blown concrete, as when the arch is nearly full the new concrete blown in would simply rebound back into the tunnel. The last barrow load or so of concrete must be virtually stuffed in by hand, bit by bit as the stop end shuttering is built up.

The skip method of delivering concrete is, of course, universally used, although it has its dangers and difficulties. Bottom-opening skips sometimes seem to require herculean efforts on the part of workmen to get them opened, then the bucket dances up as the concrete is disgorged. If tip-over skips are used these may swing laterally as the concrete is disgorged, thus needing alert handling by the workmen. This work should always be under the charge of one experienced ganger, who keeps an eye continuously on the safety of the men. He should not be distracted from his responsibilities by being engaged in conversation at times when he should be controlling the lowering of skips. Whenever concrete is being lowered from a height all men working below should wear helmets.

Lifts, bonding, and joints

One of the essential duties of the resident engineer is to work out with the contractor, before concreting of a section is carried out, just how much is to be placed in one lift. It will be obvious that the aim must be to reduce the number of construction joints to a minimum, but in considering the position of these joints, a number of technical and practical points arise. Beams should not be stopped off adjacent to a support where the shear is greatest. Great care should be taken to see that wall concrete is not carried up too far so that there is too little steel projecting to give a proper bond lap to the next lift of steel. The concreting of fillets must receive particular attention so that the necessity of plastering them on afterwards is avoided.

Where water-retaining work is being carried out, every effort must be made to reduce the construction joints to a minimum, and to place as many as possible of these above the water-line. The relationship of the reinforcing steel to the lifts proposed must also receive careful consideration. Whatever is decided upon (and much can be achieved by careful planning), it is most important that a clear decision is arrived at before concreting starts, or the concreting foreman may place too much concrete.

The *bonding* of one concrete layer to the next is a subject about which there are numerous opinions. One very good method, liked by engineers, is that of wire brushing the surface of the concrete when it has reached the appropriate setting stage so that the mortar laitance is removed and the aggregate exposed and washed clean. The drawback to this method is that, as concreting is usually finished in the late afternoon, the time at which the concrete reaches the correct setting stage is any time up till midnight, and the resident engineer is not likely to persuade the contractor to send out men to do this work late at night. In the morning the concrete will usually be found too hard for any wire brushing to be effective, but chiselling can be used to expose the aggregate. The minimum that should be done, judging from a number of opinions, is that the surface should be lightly chiselled or picked, all dust and chippings blown off by compressed air, the surface well saturated with water, and then a layer of at least an inch thick of mortar should be placed on the concrete immediately prior to placing the new concrete. It is important to insist that the cleaning work be done immediately after stripping shuttering.

In water-retaining work it is usually advisable to insert some kind of watertight joint half in the first lift of concrete, projecting into the second lift of concrete. Thin lead d.p.c. can be used if proper rubber waterstop is not to hand. Copper strip may also be used. Whatever is used should be considered as a safeguard, and all the usual precautions as mentioned above should be carried out in addition.

Shrinkage cracking

It is a matter of common experience that concrete cracks due to shrinkage when drying out. Notwithstanding some exceptionally fortunate experiences, it may generally be expected that in concrete work, where no special precautions are taken, any length over 9 m long will show signs of cracks. This applies whether the concrete is mass or reinforced. The shrinkage due to drying has an average value of from 0·2 to 0·5 mm per metre for the first 28 days. The coefficient of temperature expansion or contraction is very much smaller, of the order 0·007 mm per metre per degree centigrade. It is therefore the initial drying-out shrinkage which must be carefully watched. Sometimes cracks may not appear for four to six months after placing of the concrete, and in rich concrete they are usually single, easily observed cracks and not a number of fine hair cracks. The use of large aggregates, low heat (coarsely ground) cement, and keeping both water and cement contents to the minimum allowable, will help reduce cracking. The use of steel shutters instead of wood shutters will also help, as steel releases heat from the concrete more quickly and the temperature rise on setting is therefore reduced.

Such cracks must be carefully chased out and replugged with a very dry mix of sand/cement caulked hard home. The secret of success in these remedial measures is the use of a *dry* mixture for plugging that can be caulked really hard. The chase must first be washed very thoroughly and a sticky grout brushed on and allowed to partially set before plugging. There are various proprietary compounds to add to the plugging mixture, but they will all fail if a wet mix is used or the special fluid or instructions for priming the concrete first are not complied with. One of the chief difficulties in making concrete watertight is to find where the water is getting into the concrete; where it is coming out may be only too obvious. It may therefore happen that more success is obtained by plugging from outside at a definite point than by hopefully plugging at some guessed point or line on the water face of the concrete.

Shuttering

It may take two carpenters and two labourers a fortnight to erect the shuttering for a piece of concrete which can be placed in a day. The value of the shuttering in time and materials may be several times the value of the cement, aggregate, and steel in the concrete. The care and time spent on the shuttering is of great importance, for it is the mould which gives shape, finish, and texture in the building. Every flaw in the formwork will be reflected permanently in the finished structure, hence it is one of the essential duties of the resident engineer to examine the shuttering under three headings:

    (i) Is it true to line and dimension?
    (ii) Is it secure and well strutted to resist all forces on it?
    (iii) Are all joints tight and flush?

The construction of formwork requires skilled attention and a high degree of intelligence on the part of the supervising foreman. He must not only know how to construct and set up the shuttering with absolute accuracy but also how to strut and support it to take the load of the concrete coming on it without any sagging occurring. In addition, an important skill that the foreman must have is that of visualising the work from the drawings and planning out the method of construction. A frequent difficulty which arises is that of removing the shuttering to the inside of tanks, etc., after the concrete has been placed. Quite often a completely confined or an almost confined space is to be built in reinforced concrete, and in cases like these special measures must be taken to deal with the closing area of concrete which may have to use as internal formwork some kind of material which can be left in permanently (such as slate, corrugated iron, or asbestos sheeting). Where there is a small hole available the internal formwork must be erected in pieces small enough for it to come out through the hole provided.

The best method for getting wall and column shuttering vertical is by using a plumb bob. The upper end of this is fixed at a given distance from the face of the shuttering. This same distance is measured back from the base line of the wall or column and the shuttering erected so that the point of the bob lies on the mark, the shuttering being parallel to the string of the bob throughout its length. A point requiring particular attention is the tightness with which boards fit together at the edges, or fit closely to previous concrete lifts. Complete tightness is almost impossible to achieve everywhere unless the boarding used is new, properly seasoned, wrought, and tongued and grooved. Even the use of the latter is not always successful nowadays, due to the greenness of most of the timber available. Where the surface is later to be rendered, great particularity on this matter is not essential, though care must always be exercised. A small gap of up to 5 mm, though causing a 'fin' of concrete to extrude, will not usually cause honeycombing unless the mix is wetter than it should be.

Vertical stop ends in a reinforced-concrete structure are often troublesome items to shutter, and dealing with horizontal bars protruding from the face of a wall is an even more difficult problem. Stop ends can best be dealt with by packing strips of wood between the reinforcement and shuttering and filling the centre portion with further strips, suitably notched to take the horizontal bars. Even if a slight gap is left for the reinforcement, this will not matter too much because, after stripping, the surface can be chiselled and any honeycombed areas broken out to form a clean pocket for the next concrete to bond into.

Bars protruding from the face of a wall are more difficult to deal with, as the contractor is, quite understandably, unwilling to notch or cut holes in his main shuttering timber. If there is no alternative, however, the holes have to be left in the shuttering. The presence of even a few of these difficult bars may preclude the use of steel shuttering for large areas. Steel shutters obviously have the advantage that they may be used many times on a job and a large amount of timber saved. But so often the nature of the work to be concreted is so complicated and diverse, that steel shuttering can only be used in a few cases, despite the ingenuity of a number of different proprietary types available. Even if the contractor is able to use steel forms, he will frequently have to fill up gaps and corners with timber, and the result will show up clearly in the contrasted surface texture of the concrete.

Past papers on shuttering, in various technical journals, strikingly reveal the freedom of engineers in the past to choose the type of shuttering they required to achieve a given surface effect. Given plenty of good, seasoned timber, carpenters and workmen who were prepared to give careful attention to detail, very striking and pleasing effects could be obtained on the surface of concrete. Today, it is not common to find two pieces of tongued-and-grooved wrought boarding which fit together along the whole of their length and are free from knot-holes. In consequence, the resident engineer is sometimes forced to accept inferior workmanship. The best effects nowadays are obtained by the use of steel shuttering, or by lining wood shuttering with carefully designed smooth-faced hardboards. With steel shuttering the designer must study the various ways in which it can be used, and the spacing out of joints must be worked out in advance so that a properly designed architectural effect may be achieved.

Stripping shuttering

One of the first troubles that the resident engineer experiences in concreting work is that of stripping times. Nearly all specifications contain a clause on this subject. Typical instances mentioned are that wall, column, and beam sides are not to be struck until after 3 days, beam soffits (props left under) 7 days, removal of props to beams 14–21 days. These figures are for ordinary Portland cement at normal temperatures.

The effect of applying these rules too rigidly to walls will cause trouble with the contractor. The inexperienced but careful resident engineer will sometimes be amazed at the reactions such applications can cause. He may well wonder why this very definite clause was inserted in the specification initially.

There is a fair way out of this dilemma. The British Standard Code of Practice for Reinforced Concrete suggests that shuttering should not be struck until the concrete reaches a cube strength of at least twice the stress to which the concrete may be subjected at the time of striking.

This is an elastic clause, and since the forces likely to be encountered are usually quite small, it will frequently be found possible to strip wall, column, and beam sides the day after concreting. If the resident engineer puts this solution up to his engineer, and it is approved, he will usually find that the contractor is willing to agree on the matter of stripping by providing a number of test cubes to be tested at 24 hours. If these cubes prove strong enough, the engineer can give permission for the striking to be carried out forthwith, provided the contractor takes responsibility for any damage resulting from the departure from the specification requirements. It must be ensured, however, that no undue loads come on to the concrete immediately, such as the erection of scaffolding, tying of ropes, etc.

It is well to remember that the resident engineer not only has a duty to see that the work is properly carried out in accordance with the terms of the specification but also to see that the work is expeditiously and economically carried out. If he can satisfy himself professionally that stripping shuttering on a 24-hour cycle is a feasible and safe proposition in certain cases, then he will undoubtedly be helping the progress of the work.

Notwithstanding the remarks above, the premature stripping of shuttering from the underside of beams and slabs is very dangerous. Several fatal accidents have been caused by this. Removal of support from these members is a very different matter from removing the cladding to walls.

These few notes, of course, consider only a few basic considerations on the problem of shuttering. There is extensive literature on the subject available to engineers, and a great deal of useful practical information can be obtained by reading up what has been done on previous jobs.

References

A Guide to Specifying Concrete. Part I. Research Report. 1967 I.C.E.

Report on Concrete Practice. Part 1. Cement and Concrete Association.

Design of Concrete Mixes. Road Note No. 4. 2nd Edition 1950. Reprinted 1970. Road Research Laboratory, D.S.I.R. H.M.S.O.

How to Make Good Concrete. H. N. Walsh. Concrete Publications Ltd.

Structural Use of Reinforced Concrete in Buildings. British Standard Code of Practice CP. 114. Part 2 (Metric) 1969. B.S.I.

Design and Construction of Reinforced and Prestressed Concrete Structures for the Storage of Water and Other Aqueous Liquids. British Standard Code of Practice. CP. 2007, Part 2 (metric) 1970. B.S.I.

'Surface Finishing of Concrete Structures', Norman Davey. *Journal I.C.E.*, 1942. (An informative paper.)

'Shuttering', C. Parry. *Journal I.C.E.*, October 1948. (A 'classic' work.)

Building Research Station Digests. H.M.S.O.

No. 5. Materials for Concrete.

No. 13. Concrete Mix Proportioning and Control—1.

No. 14. Concrete Mix Proportioning and Control—2.

No. 16. Aerated Concrete—Manufacture and Properties.

No. 17. Aerated Concrete—Uses.

Properties of Concrete. A. M. Neville. Pitman Publishing. 1970.

CHAPTER 15

Steel Reinforcement in Concrete

Ordinary mild steel reinforcement used in normal concrete work will be supplied by the makers in accordance with B.S. 4449 (metric). This mild steel must have a yield stress* of at least 250 N/mm² (36 000 lb/sq. in.). The maximum tensile stress in bending then allowable in accordance with the British Standard Code of Practice is 140 N/mm² (20 000 lb/in²) for bars up to 40 mm diameter, and 125 N/mm² (18 000 lb/in²) for larger diameter bars.

High yield steel to B.S. 4449, or cold worked to B.S. 4461 (metric), having a minimum yield stress of 410 to 460 N/mm² according to type and diameter of bar, is also used in reinforced concrete. The maximum tensile stress in bending allowable by the Code for this steel is 230 N/mm² for bars not exceeding 20 mm, and 210 N/mm² for larger bars.

Bending Schedules

It is normal practice for the Engineer to supply bar-bending schedules to accompany all reinforcement drawings, and these will form part of the Contract Drawings if not expressly excluded from same. In this case any errors in the schedules will give rise to a claim from the contractor if he finds he must re-bend bars to the correct shape required, or if he cannot use some bars and must order substitute bars. Of course, it is possible to enter a requirement in the Specification to the Contract to the effect that the contractor must check the bending schedules against the reinforcement drawings before he places his order, and is therefore to be responsible for rectifying any errors at no extra charge. This may be a way of passing the legal responsibility to the contractor, but it is not a practical way in terms of economy of human effort. The number of bars may run into several thousands and, human nature being what it is, errors will almost certainly occur here and there. But if the bar schedules have been produced with ordinary care, such errors should be few, should cost little to overcome when found, and can quickly be rectified if some spare lengths of straight bars in the normally used diameters are available and there is a simple hand-operated bar-bending machine on site. It is more of a waste of time

---

* For routine testing the yield stress for B.S. 4449 purposes is taken as the stress corresponding to an increase of 0·5% total strain. (Cl. 15·1 of B.S. 4449.) For cold worked steel to B.S. 4461 the yield strain is 0·43% or 0·41% total strain according to whether the bar is 16 mm diameter and under, or over 16 mm diameter.
Note: 1 N/mm² = 145 lb/in².

and energy to expect the contractor to check all bars since even then, he may not find all errors. Most contractors will not waste their time doing this if, after a trial check or two, it appears that the schedules are reasonably reliable. However, if they appear badly prepared or unreliable, the prudent contractor would no doubt return them to the engineer or take other steps to safeguard his position.

Designing engineers find it useful to produce bar-bending sheets for two reasons. First, they are a check on the accuracy of the contract drawings, and intricate points of intersection of reinforcement will often be revealed where special methods of reinforcing are called for. Second, the bar-bending schedule may often render small detail drawings or further sections unnecessary, and the exact setting-up of the bars in a slab or wall may be made sufficiently clear from the schedule.

Fig. 17 shows a typical drawing of wall and floor reinforcement. Drawn to a small scale and prints taken off, the exact nature of the bars is difficult to ascertain, though their positioning is clear enough. To clarify the draw-

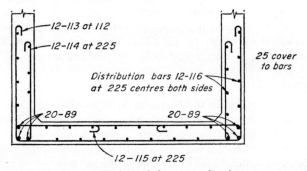

Fig. 17. Typical reinforcement drawing.

ings, either a similar drawing to a much larger scale would be required or two or more sections. But a glance at the bar numbers and reference to the schedule, Fig. 18, immediately shows how the bars are placed.

A sytem of numbering bars must be adopted. Perhaps the most convenient is to quote a bar number as '12–113' or '20–11', etc. where the first figure stands for the diameter of the bar in millimetres, and the second is the bar number, or 'bar mark' as it is otherwise called. Where it is desired to state the number of bars required of a given kind, the notation on the drawing can be put as '3/20–89' meaning 3 No. 20 mm bars, Mark 89.

The method adopted for numbering and the overall collecting together of the bars into the bending schedule requires careful consideration. It may often occur that identical bars are shown in different parts of the same drawing, or even identical bars appear on different drawings. Should these bars all bear the same reference number? This is debatable, but on the whole it seems wiser not to use the same bar number again on another drawing (unless, of course, the second drawing shows a different view of the same bars). There is a conflict of interest here between the needs of the bar fixer and the requirements of the steel-manufacturing firm.

The steel-reinforcement manufacturers proceed by cutting off the lengths of bars required for bending. Thus, they will first deal with all the

MEMBER	BAR MARK	SIZE	No. of Mbrs.	No. in each	TOTAL No.	Length each mm	TOTAL LENGTH m	DIMENSIONS
Conduit WALLS & FLOOR	113	12	-	-	82	4625	379.25	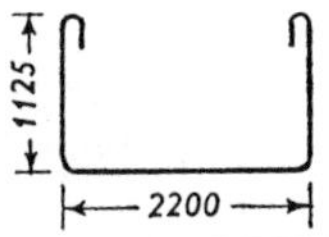
	114	12	-	-	41	5035	206.44	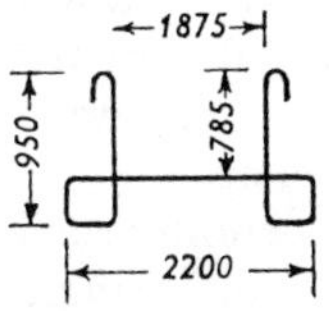
	115	12	-	-	41	4325	177.33	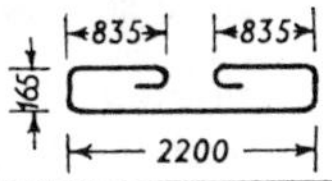
	116	12	-	-	23	9145	210.34	Straight
	89	20	-	-	6	9145	54.87	‖

JOB _____ DRWG. 027 SCHED 03 REV A

JOB No._____

OUTFALL WORKS DATE:_____

Fig. 18. Part of a typical bar bending schedule.

bars on the schedules of one diameter (say 12 mm), cutting off the number required in diminishing or increasing lengths—202 No. at 6175 mm; 186 No. at 6100; 4 at 5650; 102 at 5500 mm, and so on. It may therefore occur that the total number of bars of any given length cut off includes several different shapes (and therefore reference numbers) of bars—the shapes of the bars being different, but the length of steel in each bar being the same. If bars are delivered as straight lengths for bending on site, then the supplier will most likely invoice all bars of the same length under one item, irrespective of their bending schedule reference. As a result, much searching through the bending schedules is necessary to 'tick off' the actual bar numbers received and thus check the delivery.

In theory, of course, each parcel of bars bent off the site should arrive bearing a tag with the reference number. In practice, the easy way out is often taken, and no sign of a reference tag is visible. The bar fixer requires to know mainly two things: (*a*) what drawing shows the bars which have just been delivered to site, and (*b*) whether the bars shown on any particular part of a drawing have been received. It is therefore essential that the bending schedule shows on what drawing a bar number appears. Meanwhile the designer himself is faced with the problem of adopting some kind of system which will enable him to take off the bars from a drawing without errors of omission. Usually he will start with 6 mm bars, working carefully over the drawing, numbering and scheduling at the same time, he will then repeat the process for each larger size of bar. He must be careful not to count bars twice because they happen to be shown on more than one drawing. The minimum requirements for a schedule are:

(1) Bars should be numbered consecutively through the whole job. Where numbers become cancelled this should be stated in the schedule.

(2) Identical bars used in distinctly different parts of the job should bear different reference numbers. The schedule may bear a note showing the similarity, but it is difficult to make such cross references complete.

(3) The bending schedule should be divided into sections which each relate to a single drawing, or a group of drawings covering an appropriate section of the work.

The dimensioning of bent bars should be done in the manner set out in B.S. 4466, and the total length of a bar calculated by the methods set out in that standard. These total lengths should be quoted to the nearest 25 mm above the calculated length.

B.S. 4466 also provides for the use of 'Shape Code' numbers for standard bending shapes (e.g. as for stirrups, etc.) so that only the Shape Code Number need be entered in the bar bending schedule, together with the key dimensions required to go with that Code Number as the Standard lays down. In this case there is no need to give a drawing of the bar. However, the range of standard shapes available is limited. The Standard also lays down a more complicated referencing system for bars which is not really necessary for the medium-sized job, where simple straight numbering up, 1 . . . 999, for bar marks will cover all the different bars on a job.

Setting up the reinforcing steel

A conscientious steel fixer will take charge of the bars himself immediately they are delivered to the site and will supervise their off-loading so that he will know where they have been placed. Actually having seen the bars delivered is often a better fillip to the memory than sitting in an office and ticking off the sheets, though, of course, this must be done as well.

The specification states that all reinforcement shall be 'free from grease, loose scale, and rust', and one of the queries that arises is often: 'Why therefore does the reinforcement often go into the concrete red with rust?' The answer is that, provided there is no loose film of rust over the bars, the bonding between the concrete and the steel is not affected; he would be a fastidious engineer who demanded the cleaning of the steel of rust before it went into the building. To store the steel under cover would necessitate large sheds. In the event, despite the apparently strict requirements of the specification, thousands of buildings have been put up with the steel rusted from weeks of exposure to the weather, with no discernible faults arising therefrom.

The keeping of steel free from grease or oil is of much greater importance. This may at first thought seem a remote possibility; but is a matter on which constant vigilance is required. Wood shuttering for concrete is often treated with oil or grease of some kind on the concrete face to prevent sticking, and if this is not done before the shuttering is erected, inevitably some attempt will be made to brush the oil on the shuttering through the bars. It is extraordinary how frequently this happens; but it is a practice which must be stopped immediately. A further potentially dangerous operation which sometimes receives equally scanty forethought is the painting of surfaces with bitumen to prevent the concrete adhering. This also must not be done through the reinforcement.

Where oiling of shuttering is essential but has been forgotten, there is no alternative but to dismantle the shuttering, oil, and re-erect. Where bitumen painting has been forgotten the problem may be solved by using building paper instead, though care must be taken that the concrete cannot get behind the paper on the wrong side of it.

The specification further states that the crossings of all reinforcement bars shall be wired by not less than two turns of 1·6 mm (16 S.W.G.) soft iron wire, tying the bars rigidly together. A good bar fixer will do this automatically, and it is not too much for the resident engineer to insist that every crossing shall be so treated. The forces produced by placing concrete, especially vibrated concrete, are large, and may easily dislodge bars which are not firmly secured to the main cagework. Also, the advantage of a strong cagework is that, when bars inside the formwork have to be flexed into position to give the right cover, all bars act together and are uniformly positioned.

A minor point here is that the ends of the wires should be clipped off cleanly as near as practicable to the reinforcement so that long strands of wire are not left projecting, becoming visible in the surface of the concrete when shuttering is removed. No steel work at all should be visible anywhere over the face of the finished concrete; it is far better to have too much cover to bars than too little.

It may be suggested that the nearer the steel is to the edge of the concrete, provided it is bonded in well, the more effectively it is used; but the value of the steel becomes greatly diminished if so little cover occurs that moisture and air penetrate, rust and corrosion start, and spalling off of concrete follows. The resident engineer should observe keenly, therefore, that sufficient cover is always provided to the reinforcement. The amount of cover depends on the circumstances, but for normal structures is 13 mm or the maximum size of aggregate, whichever is greater. For water-retaining structures it must not be less than 38 mm.

Footings and foundations. Particular care should be taken with bars to footings and foundations. Frequently the bases of column footings become waterlogged because no pump sump or drainage channel has been provided. Once a column foundation has been dug out, the blinding layer of concrete placed in the base, and the reinforcement erected, it is extremely difficult to get rid of subsequent rain-water collecting in it, and quite impossible to mop up the final 25 mm or so of water below the bars.

Where a resident engineer is faced with the unfortunate occurrence of reinforcement showing on the face of stripped concrete he is confronted with a difficult problem, and one which he should not have allowed to arise. It will be impossible for the bars to be pushed back into deepened chases cut in the concrete, and the only solution will be to apply some form of rendering. This may be a serious and costly matter where other faces may have to be rendered similarly to bring them into line.

The steelwork must therefore be placed (and wired up) as accurately as the formwork. Where grids of reinforcement have to be supported above a flat horizontal surface, allowing sufficient cover underneath, this should be done by wiring a number of pre-cast concrete blocks of the requisite thickness to the underside of the grid. These blocks should be about 25-38 mm square, and their spacing apart will depend on the rigidity of the grid to be supported. Good tie-wiring will help here in making the grid rigid enough to span fair distances without sagging. It should also be noted that the reinforcement should not be raised up on the blocks until just prior to concreting, otherwise the grid will become bent by people walking over it unless the bars are of substantial diameter. The use of pieces of brick or slate as spacers should be forbidden. Spacers must be of concrete only.

Cutting bars. The resident engineer may occasionally be asked for permission to cut bars which may appear too long to manage conveniently and fix in position—especially long vertical bars. This he may agree to do, providing the contractor fits in extra bars to lap the cut, extending on each side for the required bond length for the grade of concrete and steel stresses adopted. Such cuts, if made, should preferably be staggered, and care should be taken not to make them at important points of the structure where high steel stresses may be expected. The number of cuts should be kept to a minimum, and the cutting of bars should only be resorted to in cases of excessive difficulty.

A good job of wired-up reinforcement will look neat at the very first glance; looking along the reinforcement, a satisfactory straight line should be seen. Wall reinforcement should stand up vertically from the footings of its own accord to a height of 2–3 m, depending on the size of the steel used; a glance lengthwise along the wall will show what regularity has been achieved. This can be well nigh perfect, and it should be so. The steel fixer will find it convenient to fit in short bars of the type shown in Fig. 19 to keep his spacing between the two wall grids correct. These bars are left in the concrete.

The reinforcement should be so designed that it can be erected in convenient sections, and so that it becomes unnecessary to bend away steel temporarily to allow placing of concrete. More will be said of this later. The author has walked on jobs where reinforcing bars have been bent and strewn around as if the building had been torn apart by a bomb explosion rather than being in process of erection. Every effort should be made to prevent bars being temporarily bent out of the way, as it is practically impossible to place them back in the intended position without producing kinks in them. Accuracy in placing bars can be obtained, and to be able to see clear straight lines of reinforcement has a good psychological effect on all concerned; the general outline of the work is then much easier to grasp, and a standard of neatness and accuracy is set up which other craftsmen will then be induced to follow. There is an immediate sense of competency and air of a job being well and conscientiously done where neatness and efficiency are clearly apparent to the eye. Fig. 20 shows points to watch for in setting up steel reinforcement.

Practical notes

The theory of reinforced-concrete design is well covered by numerous excellent textbooks. The theory and practice of making good concrete has also been extensively written about. But the practice of building up steel reinforcement and the best shape of bars to adopt for ease in handling and placement has received only a cursory mention. Yet experience on the site in setting-up steel will substantially alter the method of approach of a designer.

Generally speaking, a designer, having obtained the stresses sustained by the various members of his structure, will then proceed to place through these members the steel he requires, cutting off, bending, hooking, and lapping where it appears to him most suitable to do so.

The steel fixer's approach is, however, radically different. Given the steel in his hands, he will with some feeling ask himself, when difficulties arise, how the steel is to be got in. He will previously have received instructions from the general foreman regarding what portion of steel he is to erect, so that access for further concreting and shuttering is not impeded. If, subsequently, he discovers awkward bars which must inevitably go in, even though their ends will wave about, causing difficulty and annoyance, or if he finds bar *a* must be placed before bar *b* can be placed, and that bar *c* can't be placed at all unless the reverse occurs, then he will rightly consider his task impossible. The resident engineer may then expect to be visited with a request to cut some of the bars.

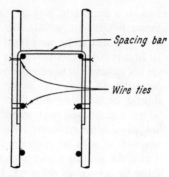

Fig. 19. Short spacing bars used to keep wall reinforcement in correct position.

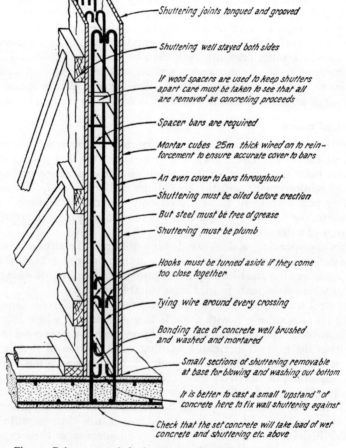

Fig. 20. Points to watch for in erecting shuttering and reinforcement.

The designer with site experience will approach the problem by first asking himself what kind of steel he would expect to see, which would be easy to erect, in the member about to be designed. At first sight this might seem an uneconomical way of designing, but after only a moderate amount of experience the designer himself will usually remark how often the final results seem to conform to a general standard pattern.

Simplicity of steel reinforcement, far from being a sign of simple assumption in design, results from working to a carefully thought-out scheme, throughout the whole of which the final practical result has been constantly borne in mind. The ensuing pattern of reinforcement will be easy to understand, easy to erect, and what is of importance to the designer, easy to draw out in a minimum of well-chosen views. Simplicity, repetition of work, and ease of erection mean lower prices on a job and a greatly enhanced speed of erection. The extra weight of steel to be inserted to achieve uniformity will be fractional, and the cost thereof easily out-weighed by the saving of time and cost on concrete placing items.

The following practical points may be found to be helpful:

(i) Where a choice of reinforcement exists, choose the larger diameter bar for preference (provided allowable bond stresses are not exceeded). The price per tonne of reinforcement, bent to shape and fixed, reduces as the diameter increases. Also the larger sizes of bars (except the very heavy ones above 25 mm diameter) are easier to fix than the small ones, giving a more rigid grid when set up and thereby making it easier to ensure the correct cover of concrete to bars.

(ii) 6 mm-diameter bars should be avoided wherever possible, except where they are used as beam stirrups or column links. This size of bar often finds its way into a design as distribution steel, but it is difficult to handle, being weak and easily bent. It is practically certain that it will get trodden on when placed horizontally in slabs, and the kinks produced can never be eradicated. When placed in walls it will be found too weak to hold up the other reinforcement, and stiffener bars of 12 mm diameter will have to be inserted to brace the framework. Where, therefore, the use of a greater size of bar than 6 mm would be uneconomical, the designer should insert 12 mm bars at appropriate points for stiffening. Alternatively, some form of ready-made steel mesh could be used with advantage.

(iii) As many bars as possible should be of similar bending dimensions. Single bars of one kind should be reduced to the minimum. The steel manufacturers will not usually undertake the bending of single bars, as it is not economic for them to set up their electric bending machines for one bar only. These bars will then have to be bent on site by hand.

(iv) Uniform spacing of bars need not receive such careful consideration as uniform bending. In fact, it is in the spacing of bars that the designer has greatest flexibility. It is just as easy for the steel fixer to place his bars at 140 mm centres as it is at 150 mm centres, and even a few odd bars at uneven spacing present no difficulty.

(v) Bars required for tying other bars on to, for example, top bars in the centre of a beam for hanging the beam stirrups on, should have a diameter of at least 12 mm.

(vi) The designer could well adopt the modern tendency—which makes for ease of placing steel—of eliminating the use of hooks on bars where the hook can be replaced by the corresponding length of straight bar. These hooks, especially in areas of congested steel, have always presented difficulties of erection for the steel fixer and difficulties of placing concrete for the concretor. Of course, the elimination of hooks must not be followed indiscriminately; they are still required in some parts of a structure, e.g. in footings, where bond stresses are usually high, in anchorages to brackets on columns, and in heavily loaded members wherever shear stresses give rise to high local bond stresses. In floor slabs which are continuous over supports and not subjected to strong end-restraints the use of straight bars throughout is usually possible and also of great assistance in placing concrete properly. Right-angle 'half hooks' to bars have no advantage over straight bond lengths or standard hooks, and are not worth adopting.

(vii) Stirrups or links should be used as shear reinforcement in beams rather than using bent-up bars, except in the case of heavy shear stresses, where a combination of both links and bent-up bars is preferable.

(viii) Above about 12 m, an extra charge is made for bars by the steel manufacturer, but the more important factor is the difficulty in transit for long bars, and this should be borne in mind when deciding the maximum length of bar to be used. Vertical bars should not be too long, especially in the upper part of a structure, where it will be most difficult to stay the bars. In general, vertical bars should not extend more than a little over one storey height of the building, while horizontal bars should not be over 12 m long.

(ix) Bars of adequate diameter may be bent to any large radius, e.g. bars horizontally in a large circular tank.

The above notes are meant to act as a guide. It is not possible in all cases to work to a set of rules, and in any job there are bound to be certain points at which special measures must be taken.

Typical reinforcement styles.   Bars in the footing to a wall may take a variety of shapes. Fig. 21 (a) and (b) show two such types. The advantage of (a) is that the bar is all in one piece, and thus spacers will not be required; (b) has the advantage that the distribution steel may be dropped in from above, while (a) requires the distribution bars to be threaded through. The point to note in both cases is that a bar is used which enables the footing to be concreted without hindrance caused by tall vertical steel. Provided the dimension q is adequate for bond, the design is structurally sound. Were the footing steel to be as in Fig. (c), concreting of the footing would have to be carried out from both sides of the wall, often not an easy matter. Column footings should receive a similar treatment in design.

A typical wall and floor reinforcement was shown in Fig. 17. Again the point to note here is that the vertical steel in the walls coming up from the floor should not rise so far that the steel will not stand up of its own accord.

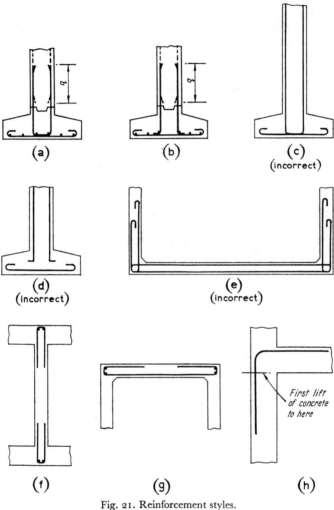

Fig. 21. Reinforcement styles.

Fig. 21 (f) shows a small division wall in plan running across a channel between two main walls. There will be a great temptation on the part of the designer to run the steel in the division wall into the main walls on either side. Bars of the type shown, however, will be found easier to manage by the contractor, who will probably wish to construct the floor and main side walls of the channel first.

Bars in the roof of a conduit may be very conveniently made as shown in Fig. 21 (g). The advantage of this type of reinforcement—which may equally well be used in the sides and bottom of the conduit—is that there is complete access to the inside of the conduit for the concreting of walls up to the level of the underside of the roof.

Negative reinforcement at the ends of beams should be carried well down below the underside of beam level, as shown in Fig. 21 (h), or else it should be kept above the bottom of the beam. This is because the concreting of the column will be carried out in one stage to the underside of beam level, and the negative reinforcement will need some length of insertion in the concrete column to hold it steady.

Enough has been shown of particular instances to indicate the nature of the points which the engineer should bear in mind. The design of reinforcement for concrete is not one of the great arts, but it has this in common with them—that an apparent simplicity and ease of construction often conceals a deal of hard and careful thinking.

References

Bending Dimensions and Scheduling of Bars for the Reinforcement of Concrete. British Standard 4466: 1969 (metric)

Reinforced Concrete Detailer's Manual. B. W. Boughton, Crosby Lockwood & Son 1971.

CHAPTER 16

Pipe-laying

THE art of pipe-laying appears deceptively simple, but it requires care and intelligence to make a good job. One of the basic troubles is that the field conditions are often poor because the whole of the construction takes place below the ground surface; yet, at the same time, the jointing and bedding of pipes must be carried out with strict attention to detail. The two main requirements for success—

    (i) that pipes are not bedded on large stones, and
    (ii) that joints and jointing materials are kept perfectly clean

—are in practice quite difficult to achieve because the pipe trench is so often muddy and stony. Unremitting care is therefore necessary for success, and lack of it will ill repay the contractor, since the cost of locating and remedying leaks can be high.

Excavation and backfill

The excavation should give enough room at the sides of a pipe for a man to stand down in the trench and move along sideways. Joint holes should be excavated before the pipe is lowered into position, and must give enough room for the jointer to reach round to the underside face of the joint. For large-diameter pipes, the joint hole must be large enough for the jointer to crouch down beside the pipe and reach the lower face of the joint. For lead jointing, the hole must give even more room, as the jointer must have sufficient space in which to swing his hammer, and will need to get his shoulders below the swell of the pipe in order to knock up the bottom half of the joint. Knocking up a lead joint on a large pipe is exhausting work, and proper access must be given, or a man cannot be expected to make a joint watertight.

Backfilling must be done in layers and punned, and all large stones liable to damage the coating of the pipe must be removed from contact with it. Only when a 225 mm layer of selected soft material has been punned over the top of a pipe may the backfill be carried out using unselected material.

Handling pipes

The handling of cast-iron pipes should be carried out with much care. A single slip, a single bump of one pipe against another, or lowering too suddenly on to the ground, and upwards of £50 of damage may have been caused. When slung and suspended, a pipe may be tapped sharply to hear if it rings true, or whether it gives a dead sound denoting a crack in it. The test is not infallible, and the pipe should be examined visually as well. Another method is to rub chalk over a suspected area and strike the pipe with a hammer; the crack will show up as a dark line. It is time well spent for the resident engineer, or one of his staff, to supervise the off-loading of pipes, to see that they are not maltreated, and to give a quick but careful examination of the spigot and socket ends while the pipes are on the trailer. Pipes are frequently discovered to be cracked at one end, particularly on the spigot, and to be able to pick out even one of those damaged before delivery will save at least one time-consuming argument between contractor, carrier, and supplier.

Care should be taken not to damage the exterior coating of pipes and, before laying, each pipe should be rolled over, examined, and touched up in the bad spots with bituminous solution. If cast-iron pipes are left out in the open the coating will, in time, frequently crack and flake off. The areas affected should be wire brushed and recoated before laying.

While there is no hard-and-fast rule about which direction pipes should be laid, there is a convenience in laying them with the sockets pointing uphill. It is easier to push a pipe spigot first downhill into a socket, than socket first over a spigot; secondly, the making of a joint is slightly easier when the socket faces uphill. But unless the gradient is very steep (over 1 in 20), it would not be worth while inserting a collar so as to reverse the direction of joints when changing from an up-grade to a down-grade, or vice versa. Pipes can be successfully laid on a downhill grade starting from the top, provided some means of pulling the pipes up tight together is arranged. Concreting in of pipes with substantial concrete blocks keyed into undisturbed ground will be necessary to prevent the joints pulling apart. The frequency of such blocks will vary according to the slope of the pipeline.

Laying pipes

The trench must be prepared and be in good condition *before* the pipe is lowered into it. This means its bottom must be boned level and made free of all sharp stones, an adequate joint hole must have been dug, the trench must be dry, and its sides must be made safe against slips or collapse. Preparation of pipe trenches is a danger spot in civil engineering. The trenches are often quite deep, and because new lengths are continuously being opened, there is always the possibility that changing ground conditions will necessitate proper trench-side support, when none has been required previously. There is sometimes a temptation to try and get through a 'bad spot' as quickly as possible, in the hope that trench support will not be needed. This temptation must be resisted by all concerned, and the resident engineer should never interfere with any precautions the agent or his foreman think are necessary, even if this means a delay in the work. Far too often a man's death is caused because of the collapse of a trench.

If the resident engineer thinks the agent is not taking enough precautions to support the trench he should point out the dangers and offer advice to remedy the matter. He cannot make the contractor take extra precautions unless the specification gives him power to order this work. Usually, the resident engineer should find no difficulty in convincing the agent, but if unreasonable risks persist, the resident engineer should discuss the problem with the engineer.

All pipes must be handled with care to prevent damage to them and their sheathing. Slings or manilla ropes should be used to lift pipes. Chains and wire ropes should be forbidden. Even manilla ropes must be used with care to prevent damage to the sheathing. It is a good precaution for the resident engineer to insist that proper balata slings in sufficient numbers are brought on the job at the very start; they are not all that expensive, and once available on the job they will be used. Wood packing pieces are frequently used to pack ropes off the pipe and prevent the rope from biting into the sheathing. This is not the best practice, but done with care and using adequate pieces of softwood properly placed, it can be tolerated for occasional use.

Large pipes and their fittings, such as bends and tees, are heavy and awkward loads to handle, especially when they have to be set accurately in position one to another. When two or more fittings have to be set together there should be a lifting appliance available for each fitting. This can be dangerous work if not properly supervised. A man waiting down in a pipe trench ready to receive and set in position a heavy fitting being lowered down to him seldom has anywhere he can leap to for safety if a sling slips or the fitting rolls over when it touches the base of the trench. For this reason, packing-off pieces of timber between rope and fitting should be small or not used at all because, the moment the strain is taken off such a rope, the packing may slip and the fitting may be free to turn or fall. Timber props, baulks, and wedges in adequate numbers must be available to wedge the fitting securely into position when lowered. Rather than move this timber and so create a dangerous situation, at least enough concrete to cradle the fitting can be placed, leaving the timber in position for the time being, and as much cut off and removed later, when the concrete has set, as is possible in the circumstances.

It is often difficult to find out the 'centre-line' of a fitting, such as a large 45° or 22½° bend. With pipe fittings for sizes of mains in the 750 mm–2 m size, some time should be spent measuring the fitting so as to find and mark, on the outside and at spigot and socket ends, the diameters that lie truly on the turning axis of the pipe. These positions should be clearly marked with white paint; not with chalk, which will quickly rub off as the pipe is handled. Such marking will save time when assembling awkward bends and the like, especially when a bend is to be set so as to give both a horizontal and vertical throw.

It is also good practice to mark a line round each spigot end, parallel with the end and a distance from it equal to the required depth of insertion of the spigot in the socket. It is a pity manufacturers do not ready-mark their pipes in this way, as the line gives immediate guidance as to whether a spigot has been properly inserted to the correct depth in a socket, and whether two pipes are in line with each other or at an angle. This line can be a chalk mark measured and marked just before insertion of the pipe in a socket.

Cover to pipes.   In Britain all pipes are normally laid below ground, and the standard amount of cover is 900 mm above the top of the pipe. Less than 900 mm is permissible in certain circumstances for short lengths where difficulties have to be overcome; even so, less than 900 mm would not be permitted below a public road, or traffic loading would cause damage to pipes. When pipes have to be laid deep they will need to be partly or wholly surrounded with concrete in order to counteract excessive ground pressures. It depends on the nature and size of the pipe being laid as to when bedding and haunching or fully surrounding with concrete is necessary. A small-diameter 150 mm pipe of spun iron can be laid at a greater depth without concrete support than, say, 600 mm steel main, because it can withstand higher external pressures. In general, it is advisable to consider what concreting is necessary when the cover to a pipe must exceed 2 m; at 3 m cover concreting will almost certainly be necessary.

Choosing a route

One can draw lines on maps and say the pipeline shall go from A to B, thence to C and so on, in straight lines, but even in open country this is not necessarily the best route when examined in detail. Slight departures from the rigid straight lines can

(i)   avoid unnecessary rises and falls;
(ii) bring a dip in the pipeline into a more suitable location for fixing a washout;
(iii) bring a high point to a more convenient location for siting an air valve and its access box;
(iv) put the pipeline in a more convenient position for a landowner by, for instance, making it run along the edge of a field instead of across the centre of a field;
(v)   put the pipeline into land under one ownership, so that negotiations for rights of entry are simplified;
(vi) assist in avoiding very bad patches of ground or known obstacles.

Hence the route needs prospecting in detail in advance and, whatever the plans might show, it is for the resident engineer at the earliest stage in the work to check that the route chosen is the best. It is likely he will find some beneficial changes that can be made, because he and his staff are full time on the job, becoming temporary inhabitants of the area, and so able to discover advice and alternatives that may have escaped the notice of the original survey engineers. In general, it is always best to fix a straight line, or a series of straight lines, for lengths of pipeline across open country. If the pipe is laid otherwise to a series of curves across open country its position may later be difficult to locate unless a large number of marker posts have been erected over the line. Such marker posts should be kept to a minimum, partly because they are always likely to be knocked down and lost, and partly because they are a nuisance and ugly if left standing in open country.

When choosing routes for a water pipeline, strict attention to grades is not as necessary as with a sewer. Sewers must be boned in to a precise, even grade between manholes, and such manholes may have to be provided at every major turn of direction or change of grade. A water pipeline under pressure can be allowed within reason to follow the contours of the ground. Thus, when laying a pipeline in flat ground which nevertheless undulates slightly (say between the 15 m O.D. and 30 m O.D. contours) the pipeline follows the ground contours and is given a standard depth of cover. This main will normally carry water at about 60 m O.D. pressure, so rises and falls will not affect the flow of water provided that air valves are provided at the major high spots.

On the other hand, the ground contours must not be so followed that one pipe rises, the next falls, and the third rises again, and so on. The level changes must be smoothed out so that they are gradual over a number of pipe lengths.

When a pipeline has to traverse hilly ground the amount of variation of cover will be greater, and changes of grade, and dips and peaks, will be more frequent. Air valves will be required at all peaks, washouts at all hollows, and additional air valves will be required whenever there is a fairly sharp reduction of grade in the direction of flow after a lengthy rise, even though the pipeline may continue rising, but less steeply than before. When water follows a rising pipeline its pressure lessens, so that air will be released from solution; this air will tend to collect at the top of a steep rising grade, if the length of pipeline thereafter is flat or rises only gently.

When laying in built-up areas, it is necessary to get trial holes out, ahead of the laying of pipes, to find out the exact location of other pipes and services in the area. Such trial holes need to be kept going at about 15 m, 30 m, and 60 m ahead of the last laid pipe so that there is ample opportunity to start deviating the laying of pipes so as to miss obstacles ahead without resorting to the use of many bends.

In every pipe supply contract there should be a reasonable number of extra bends, so that obstacles met *en route* can be avoided without having to wait for delivery of bends. By far the most useful extra bends to provide are $11\frac{1}{4}$ degree bends (i.e. '$\frac{1}{32}$nd bends'). About half a dozen extra per four or five miles of pipeline should be provided—more if the pipe is being laid in a built-up area, or in difficult country. Such bends would, of course, be provided additional to the bends known to be required from an examination of the intended route of the main.

Inspector's duties and the record book

The pipeline inspector's duties are very important and must be conscientiously carried out. He should himself inspect the trench bed before a pipe is lowered; he must also inspect the joints and the testing of pipes. He should keep a pipe log book in which are entered full details of the laying of the pipeline, pipe by pipe, giving frequent invert levels, details of fittings and connections, and a running total of the chainage laid, together with sketch plans showing other services encountered, and dimensions to locate the position of the pipe from time to time.

Thrust blocks

At every change of direction in the pipeline, at every change of size, at connections and valves, thrust blocks are necessary—usually of mass concrete. It is *not* sufficient to calculate the size of thrust blocks by considering the reaction between pipe and block *only*. Complete or partial failure of a pipe at a bend is almost always due to soil movement behind the block,

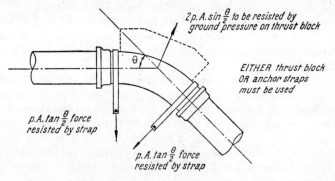

θ = angle of bend
A = internal cross section of pipe – sq. m
p = max. pressure of water – kg. per sq. m

Fig. 22. Thrusts due to pipe bends.

hence it is necessary when calculating the size of blocks required to take particular note of the safe horizontal bearing resistance of the soil. The thrust block must be well keyed into the ground, be concreted right up against undisturbed ground, and, if it is to take horizontal thrusts, have a vertical outer face and not a sloping, irregular one resulting from a poor attempt at taking out a proper vertical-sided pipe trench (see Fig. 22).

The total thrust on a pipe bend is given by the following formula:

$$\text{Thrust} = 2 \cdot p \cdot A \cdot \sin \frac{\theta}{2} \, \text{kg}$$

where p is pressure of water in pipe in kg/m²; A is cross-section area of pipe in m²; θ is the angle of deviation of the pipe in degrees.

There is often confusion on this matter, and the following points may help in clarification:

(i) The thrust given by the above formula is the *total* thrust which acts outwards from the bend along the bisector of the bend.

(ii) The total thrust can therefore be met *either* by a block of concrete on the outside of the bend symmetrically disposed and capable of taking the thrust as given by the above formula, *or* by two straps holding the bend in at each end, each strap taking a force equal to $p \cdot A \cdot \tan \dfrac{\theta}{2}$

Thus for a 90-degree-bend a concrete block will have to be placed on the 45-degree-diagonal on the outside of the bend to take $\sqrt{2} \cdot p \cdot A \cdot$ thrust. If two straps, one at each end anchoring inwards, are used, they will each have to take $p \cdot A \cdot$ pull

(iii) The effect of change of momentum of the water can be ignored.

(iv) The value for p should be the *highest possible*, i.e. the pressure when testing or taking into account water hammer.

(v) The purpose of holding down is to prevent joints pulling apart, but even where flanged joints are used, thrust blocks or holding straps are frequently added to prevent strain on flanges.

(vi) Bends turning down need to be anchored down, as well as being held horizontally.

(vii) Bends turning up need to be supported from below, and require a block for horizontal thrust.

(viii) A suitable factor of safety should be used.

It often happens that, because of the use of machines for excavation, pipe trenches at bends are wider than necessary, and the resulting thrust blocks, when eventually put in after cleaning up the trench corners, are quite a lot larger than the thrust blocks shown on the plan. The contractor will naturally ask for payment for this larger-sized concrete block. He should not normally be entitled to this payment, though he may put forward a number of arguments in support. Since the subject is almost certain to crop up, the resident engineer would be well advised to be explicit on this point before the work commences. He could well ask for hand excavation at bends (though he may not be able to insist upon it), or at least for final hand clearing of the walls of the trench at the point where the thrust is to be taken. He should, in any case, point out that any excess size of block resulting from careless excavation will not be paid for.

Thrust blocks for vertical bends are essential, and those on bends down may have to be reinforced. Other thrust blocks, such as those adjacent to river banks, ditches, or depressions in the ground, must be carefully placed, as the ground may be particularly weak at these points.

Miscellaneous points

The standard classes of cast-iron pipe under B.S. 4622 for spun spigot and socket pipes are for a recommended maximum working water pressure of 100 m for Class 1 pipes and 160 m for Class 3 pipes. These supersede earlier B.S. 1211 Class B, C and D spun iron pipes for 60, 90 and 120 m respectively. Ductile iron pipes and fittings to B.S. 4772 are now increasingly being used as they are tougher than B.S. 4622 'grey iron' pipes and are capable of withstanding higher working pressures.

When using fittings, such as bends, tees, and the like, many engineers dislike connecting up one special fitting to another, but prefer wherever possible to have a length of straight pipe between the specials. The reason for this is that, should a burst on one special pipe occur when it is coupled direct to another special pipe, the work of repair may be complicated and more than one new special may have to be put in. If, however, a straight section of pipe intervenes between two specials this straight pipe can always be cut and a new special with a straight portion of pipe be put in and collared up.

Cutting of cast-iron fittings and pipes in situ is best done by wheel or chisel cutters. Wheel cutters for cutting pipes *in situ* entail much hard work, and the geared rotating-chisel machine is much better. Wheel cutters also involve too much manual labour for pipes over 450 mm diameter. (Four men would be required for about one and a half hours to cut and break out a section of 450 mm pipe with a wheel cutter). Oxy-acetylene flame cutting may be used, but the cut is often irregular, and if there is a small amount of water in the pipe, cutting of the underside may be very difficult. Although the manually worked or machine-driven rotating-chisel cutter is by far the best instrument to use, it is heavy to move about, and must be bought in several different sizes to meet the varying diameters of pipes to be cut.

Laying steel pipes

The most frequently used joint with steel pipes is the Viking Johnson coupling, which is used with plain-ended steel pipes. The spigot and socket steel pipe is not now widely used. Steel pipes may alternatively have welded joints—butt welded, sleeve welded, or spherically welded—and these are more frequently used on large-size pipes where buried underground.

The Johnson coupling normally has a 'central register' which fits just inside the annular space between the pipe ends, keeping them slightly apart. Such couplings can be obtained without the central register, so that in making a final coupling up the joint can be slid back over one pipe, the closing length inserted, and the joint moved over the gap between the two pipes.

Too much trouble cannot be taken over pipe joints; it is useless to let pipe-laying proceed when it is clear that insufficient attention is being paid to jointing. It is equally bad policy to allow pipes to be laid with insufficient care being paid to protecting the surface of the pipe. Leaking joints will be discovered before the contract ends (they will *have* to be); damaged coatings may never be found, yet may be the cause of substantially shortening the life of the pipe.

With steel pipes, protection internally and externally is essential. A bare steel pipe laid in the ground, or carrying corrosive waters, would have virtually no life at all. A steel pipe thus relies entirely on the continuity and durability of its coating. This is by no means easy to achieve. In the Johnson coupling an internal 'backing-up' strip is placed inside the pipe, bridging the gap between the ends of the pipe. A bituminous compound is then poured through a hole in the coupling so as to fill up the whole of the space between the pipe ends and the annular space between the coupling and the outside of the pipe. Great care must be taken to have the bituminous compound heated to exactly the right temperature to pour evenly and in one continuous operation. Air is expelled from a second hole in the coupling.

For the larger-sized pipe, the joint can be inspected from inside and made good where necessary. The backing strip can also be placed by hand. But for pipes of 450 mm diameter and under, direct inspection cannot take place, and the backing strip is placed by a special expanding cone attached to the end of a rod.

It should be noted that where men enter a bitumen-lined pipe they should be wearing rubber shoes. Heavy metal tools or stones and other debris should not be left in the pipe to be kicked about and so damage the internal protective lining.

Moulds are also obtainable for forming a smooth bitumen layer over the outside of the Johnson couplings, thus completing the external protection. If the external mouldings is carried out first the heating of the pipe ends will materially assist in the successful pouring of the bituminous compound inside the coupling where trouble may occasionally occur due to the compound solidifying too quickly.

Asbestos-cement pipes

Asbestos-cement pipes are used largely where above-ground traffic conditions are light. They are extensively used in rural districts. The pipes have the advantage of being extremely resistant to corrosion, and can be laid in all normal circumstances without special precautions against corrosion being taken. They are used in conjunction with cast-iron specials. Care in bottoming up trenches, in backfilling, and giving sufficient protection against vibration and traffic is essential, as the pipes are brittle. Also, unless very carefully handled in transit, and in loading and unloading, a lot of such pipes will be found to be broken before they are laid.

Flanged pipes

Two practical points need mentioning here. When setting up flanged piping care must be taken not to tighten up the flange bolts until it is certain that the exact alignment required has been achieved. If there is lack of alignment between flanges the tightening of the bolts can break the flange. A sledge hammer should not be applied to a spanner for tightening up the bolts, as too great a stress may be placed on them.

The second point is one on which the resident engineer should early satisfy himself. The styles of drilling of flanges for pipes, valves, etc., that have to marry up should be identical. In particular, the type of drilling for the valves should be checked against the type of drilling for the pipes. Where any valves or specials are turned at an angle from the vertical or horizontal, as sometimes happens, it is particularly necessary to check whether the type of drilling specified (i.e. 'off centre' or 'on centre') will work out satisfactorily).

Testing pipelines

Every section of pipeline laid must be tested before it can be accepted by the resident engineer. The personal observation of this test is one of his most important duties. The amount of pipeline to be tested at one time is usually at the discretion of the contractor, but the resident engineer must not let the situation arise that, with so much line to be tested, it would take weeks to find leakages, should they occur.

It is always preferable to test small sections at a time. In some instances the contractor is not allowed to fill back over the joints until after a satisfactory test has been taken. Though it is obviously of great benefit to be able to inspect the exterior of joints under pressure, there are definite disadvantages in not backfilling around the joints. In the first place, if the main is being laid in a road it is almost certain that the necessity of restoring the road fully open to traffic will be of overriding importance. But, even where the main is in open country and joints can be left open, the practice of partly filling over the body of the pipe, and leaving the joint holes open, usually means that proper ramming of material about the body of the pipe cannot be carried out. Bits of timber, bricks, boulders, and sundry oddments are frequently piled up adjacent to the joint hole to prevent the partial backfill spilling into it. There is a risk that, once the test has been satisfactorily passed, and the resident engineer has left, a bulldozer may then push the whole lot into the joint hole in one go. This may not happen, of course, but it is rather likely to.

Before testing, the main should have been most carefully filled, the operation being carried out slowly and all air pockets removed. If lead and yarn joints are being used the water should stand in the main at least 24 hours in order that the yarn may absorb water.

The section of main having been blanked off by various means, e.g. flanges, plugs, and caps leaded in and stayed, or even wooden plugs driven in—and the main filled, it is then pumped up by a small hand-operated ram pump to the required test pressure. The main is left to stand under pressure for a period of between 30 minutes and 24 hours, according to convenience, and at the end of this period the pressure in the main is again noted. If the second reading shows that a fall in pressure has occurred, then the pump is re-actuated, and the amount of water which has to be pumped into the main, to restore its pressure to the initial pressure, is a measure of the leakage from the main. The resident engineer should also call for the pressure in the pipeline under test to be released by the operation of a valve or hydrant some distance away, and he should stay to watch that the pressure as shown on the test gauge does in fact rapidly fall. It used to be an old dodge to have the pressure gauge connected direct to the pump and not the main; it is essential for the resident engineer's prestige that he does not fall victim to this trick.

The pressure should be built up gently, especially if the main has not previously been subjected to pressure. If the first test shows a fault a second test should immediately take place. A permissible factor of leakage has been quoted as '1 gallon of water per inch diameter of main per mile length for 24 hours for every 100 ft head of pressure'. This would give 1¼ gallons leakage in 1 hour on 1 mile of 12-in. pipe tested to 250-ft head. It is a figure suitable for cast-iron pipework.*

If a pipeline fails to pass a test there may be great difficulty in locating the cause of leakage. The truth is that no satisfactory leak detection apparatus has yet been invented. There are a number of pieces of apparatus which are called leak detectors, but no water engineer has yet reported complete success with them; many regard them all as ineffectual. The water engineer usually hopes to detect leakages by the only two methods available to him:

(i) by noticing a damp patch of ground above the pipeline, and
(ii) by 'sounding' the pipe with an iron rod placed on a pipe or fitting.

In the latter method the only leak likely to be 'heard' is one which is so large as to cause a hissing sound of water emerging from the defective pipe or joint. Working on these lines, the first action of a contractor, when trying to locate a leak, should be to keep the water pressure on the pipeline, in the hope that after a day or so a careful inspection of the line will reveal some sodden ground, or water actually emerging from the ground surface. If this does not happen, then the only practical alternative is to open up the ground over the pipe joints, proceeding more or less by instinct as to which joints are most likely to prove defective. Since this is expensive and frustrating work, a wise contractor will put his most

* 4·4 litres per 25 mm diameter of main per mile of length, for 24 hours, for every 30 m head of pressure. This would give 7½ litres leakage in 1 hour on 1 mile of 300 mm pipe under 100 m water head

conscientious men on pipe jointing, and he will try and test the pipeline in as short lengths as possible, with as many joints left exposed to view as is practicable, even if such testing can only be undertaken in the first instance at somewhat less pressure than the final acceptance test. To do this, the contractor will need some easily fixed stop ends for temporary closure of the end of the pipeline. He must remember, however, to give time for all thrust blocks on the line to be properly completed and made secure before the test is started. Air tests, applied every score or so of pipes, are useful where a supply of clean water is not available, or where release of the water after test is a nuisance in the trench and would delay continuation of pipe-laying.

ADDRESSES FROM WHICH CERTAIN PUBLICATIONS MENTIONED MAY BE OBTAINED

H.M. Stationery Office, 49 High Holborn, London W.C.1.
British Standards Institution, 2 Park Street, London W.1.
Institution of Civil Engineers, Great George Street, London S.W.1.
Federation of Civil Engineering Contractors, Romney House, Tufton Street, London S.W.1.
Association of Consulting Engineers, Abbey House, 2 Victoria Street, London S.W.1.
Contractors Plant Association, 28 Eccleston Street, London S.W.1.
Civil Engineering Construction Conciliation Board for Great Britain, Romney House, Tufton Street, London S.W.1.
Cement and Concrete Association, 52 Grosvenor Gardens, London S.W.1.
Concrete Publications Ltd., 14 Dartmouth Street, London S.W.1.

APPENDIX
Conversion Factors

Metric to British units
Length:

1 m = 3·280 84 ft
1 m = 1·093 61 yd
1 km = 0·621 37 mile

Area:

1 m²   = 1·195 99 yd²
1 ha   = 2·471 05 acre
1 km² = 0·386 10 sq. mile
(1 km² = 100 ha)
(1 ha = 10 000 m²)

Volume:
0·01 m³ = 0·353 15 ft³
1 m³   = 1·307 95 yd³
1 litre = 0·219 97 gallon
1 m³   = 219·969 gallon

Weight:
1 kg   = 2·204 62 lb
50 kg   = 0·984 20 cwt
1 Mg   = 19·684 10 cwt
(1 tonne = 0·984 20 ton)

Pressure:
1 kgf/cm² = 14·223 lb/in²
1 N/mm²   = 145·038 lb/in²
(1 N/mm² = 9·807 kgf/cm²)

Density:
1 kg/m³ = 0·062 43 lb/ft³
1 Mg/m³ = 0·752 48 ton/yd³

British to metric units

1 in   = 25·400 00 mm
1 ft   = 304·800 00 mm
1 yd   = 0·914 40 m
1 mile = 1·609 34 km

1 ft²   = 0·092 90 m²
1 yd²   0·836 13 m²
1 acre   = 0·404 69 ha
1 sq. mile = 2·589 99 km²
(1 sq. mile = 640 acre)
(1 acre = 4840 sq. yd.)

1 ft³   0·028 32 m³
1 yd³   = 0·764 56 m³
1 gallon = 4·546 07 litre
1 gallon = 0·004 55 m³

1 lb = 0·453 59 kg
1 cwt = 50·802 kg
1 ton = 1·016 05 Mg

1 lb/in² = 0·070 31 kgf/cm²
1 lb/in² = 0·006 89 N/mm²

1 lb/ft³   = 16·018 5 kg/m³
1 ton/yd³ = 1·328 94 Mg/m³

Index